The Writings of Frithjof Schuon
Series

About This Book

"For well-known reasons, more books than ever before are being published on Islam. Some are good; some are bad. But almost all of them, including scholarly works, tend to deal either with merely outward aspects, or else, on the contrary, with some recondite item of history or theology. Frithjof Schuon's classic defies all categorization. It is a work of fundamental explanation, an exposition both intellectual and spiritual, of a religion which, these days, is an enigma to the majority of people. Frithjof Schuon deals with this incomprehension at its very roots, and defines, with his customary authority, both the nature of religion as such, and the specific and original characteristics of the religion of Islam. It is a unique work, and is highly recommended."
   —**William Stoddart**, author of *Sufism: The Mystical Doctrines and Methods of Islam*

"This is a seminal work which will be accessible to Muslims and non-Muslims alike. With mathematical precision and poetic elegance, Schuon unfolds for us Islam's universal message of the vital connection between God and man, uniquely expressed in the *Shahādah*, its central creed: of the oneness that underlies diversity, and of the primordial norm that lies at its heart and which is the source of all human aspiration. Enhanced by previously unpublished notes and letters from Schuon, this is a book to re-read and to treasure."
   —**M. Ali Lakhani**, editor of *Sacred Web* journal and author of *The Timeless Relevance of Traditional Wisdom*

"Frithjof Schuon's book throws into sharp relief the majesty, simplicity, and profundity of the message of Islam. It presents unsurpassed explications of the Koranic Revelation, the role of the Prophet, the essential doctrines and spiritual methods of Islam, and of Sufism, its mystical heart. At a stroke this radiant and authoritative account dispels the fog of misunderstanding which has surrounded many Western perceptions of this great tradition, and shows how the universal teachings of Islam are of the most urgent relevance in the contemporary world. A veritable jewel of a book!"
   —**Harry Oldmeadow**, La Trobe University, author of *Frithjof Schuon and the Perennial Philosophy*

"Long regarded as a masterpiece, this new edition should be read not only as an original, profound, and beautiful view of the spiritual philosophy, rituals, art, and culture of Islam, but also as a much needed intelligent introduction to Religion in general."
   —**Mateus Soares de Azevedo**, author of *Men of a Single Book: Fundamentalism in Islam, Christianity, and Modern Thought*

"In an age in which the word 'Islam'—both in the West and increasingly even among a younger generation of Muslims estranged from traditional forms of faith—has become almost exclusively identified with a familiar set of highly visible political ideologies, this is a truly providential book. For Frithjof Schuon's works on Islam offer an incomparably clear and articulate introduction to the very heart of the Islamic revelation, in both its spiritual roots and practical manifestations, making this work a clear and insightful 'guide for the perplexed' that is uniquely accessible and enlightening for readers from all backgrounds."
—James W. Morris, Boston College, author of *The Reflective Heart*

"This is a book that grasps Islam in all its fullness, restoring its universalism. It is a work that is strong, essential, dynamic, and engaging, one whose 'verticality' has been in no way diminished by the passage of time."
—Éric Geoffroy, Marc Bloch-Strasbourg II University, author of *Introduction to Sufism: The Inner Path of Islam*

"Frithjof Schuon's *Understanding Islam*—arguably one of his masterpieces—is one of the few works written by a European that achieves a profound insight into the Islamic 'Other'. Schuon's study transcends political history and answers every common misconception by exposing the metaphysical foundations of the Islamic faith, both in its outer and inner manifestations, the Law and the Way. Terse, precise, penetrating, this book offers a deep and true view of Islam unclouded by either prejudice or sentimentality. Unlike other writers who have attempted a definitive study of the subject, Schuon is not concerned with surveying the great wealth of Islamic civilization or with paying lip-service to such things as the Muslim contribution to science. Instead, his interest lies in going to the core of the Islamic revelation; only from there will a full and proper understanding follow. Schuon's starting point is that Islam is an expression of an eternal truth; while its appearance in history is comparatively recent, its message is timeless. To approach Islam from any other premise would be to indulge in a grotesque underestimation. This is a seminal book for anyone who wants to do Islam justice and to know it in its most profound and most important aspects."
—Rodney Blackhirst, La Trobe University, author of *Primordial Alchemy and Modern Religion*

World Wisdom
The Library of Perennial Philosophy

The Library of Perennial Philosophy is dedicated to the exposition of the timeless Truth underlying the diverse religions. This Truth, often referred to as the *Sophia Perennis*—or Perennial Wisdom—finds its expression in the revealed Scriptures as well as the writings of the great sages and the artistic creations of the traditional worlds.

Understanding Islam appears as one of our selections in the Writings of Frithjof Schuon series.

The Writings of Frithjof Schuon

The Writings of Frithjof Schuon form the foundation of our library because he is the pre-eminent exponent of the Perennial Philosophy. His work illuminates this perspective in both an essential and comprehensive manner like none other.

English Language Writings of Frithjof Schuon

Original Books
The Transcendent Unity of Religions
Spiritual Perspectives and Human Facts
Gnosis: Divine Wisdom
Language of the Self
Stations of Wisdom
Understanding Islam
Light on the Ancient Worlds
Treasures of Buddhism (In the Tracks of Buddhism)
Logic and Transcendence
Esoterism as Principle and as Way
Castes and Races
Sufism: Veil and Quintessence
From the Divine to the Human
Christianity/Islam: Perspectives on Esoteric Ecumenism
Survey of Metaphysics and Esoterism
In the Face of the Absolute
The Feathered Sun: Plains Indians in Art and Philosophy
To Have a Center
Roots of the Human Condition
Images of Primordial and Mystic Beauty: Paintings by Frithjof Schuon
Echoes of Perennial Wisdom
The Play of Masks
Road to the Heart: Poems
The Transfiguration of Man
The Eye of the Heart
Form and Substance in the Religions
Adastra & Stella Maris: Poems by Frithjof Schuon (bilingual edition)
Autumn Leaves & The Ring: Poems by Frithjof Schuon (bilingual edition)
Songs without Names, Volumes I-VI: Poems by Frithjof Schuon
Songs without Names, Volumes VII-XII: Poems by Frithjof Schuon
World Wheel, Volumes I-III: Poems by Frithjof Schuon
World Wheel, Volumes IV-VII: Poems by Frithjof Schuon
Primordial Meditation: Contemplating the Real

Edited Writings
The Essential Frithjof Schuon, ed. Seyyed Hossein Nasr
Songs for a Spiritual Traveler: Selected Poems (bilingual edition)
René Guénon: Some Observations, ed. William Stoddart
The Fullness of God: Frithjof Schuon on Christianity,
ed. James S. Cutsinger
Prayer Fashions Man: Frithjof Schuon on the Spiritual Life,
ed. James S. Cutsinger
Art from the Sacred to the Profane: East and West,
ed. Catherine Schuon
Splendor of the True: A Frithjof Schuon Reader,
ed. James S. Cutsinger (forthcoming)

Understanding Islam

A New Translation with Selected Letters

by

Frithjof Schuon

Includes Other Previously
Unpublished Writings

Edited by
Patrick Laude

Foreword by
Annemarie Schimmel

Understanding Islam: A New Translation with Selected Letters
© 2011 World Wisdom, Inc.

Translated by Mark Perry and Jean-Pierre Lafouge

Published in French as
Comprendre l'Islam
Editions du Seuil, 1976

Library of Congress Cataloging-in-Publication Data

Schuon, Frithjof, 1907-1998.
  [Comprendre l'Islam. English]
  Understanding Islam : a new translation with selected letters / by Frithjof
Schuon ; Includes Other Previously Unpublished Writings Edited by Patrick
Laude ; Foreword by Annemarie Schimmel.
    p. cm. -- (The writings of Frithjof Schuon)
  Includes bibliographical references and index.
  ISBN 978-1-935493-90-7 (pbk. : alk. paper) 1. Islam. 2. Sufism. I. Laude,
Patrick, 1958- II. Schimmel, Annemarie. III. Title.
  BP161.2.S313 2011
  297--dc22

                                                              2011012854

Cover: The Kaaba,
Mecca, Saudi Arabia

Printed on acid-free paper in the United States of America.

For information address World Wisdom, Inc.
P.O. Box 2682, Bloomington, Indiana 47402-2682
www.worldwisdom.com

CONTENTS

FOREWORD

People often ask me: "Why do you like Islam?" and my regular answer is: "Because the Muslims take God seriously; they are aware that God the One is near us here and now, and yet cannot be described, either by intellectual or by supra-intellectual means but can be experienced by the pure and loving heart. . .".

It is this aspect of Islam which is lucidly shown in Frithjof Schuon's work: God is *the* Reality, and to be a true Muslim means to believe in the reality of the Absolute and the dependence of all things on the Absolute. Religion, so he holds, ought to be treated as something *sui generis*, something that cannot be described in scholarly technical terms and whose goal is not to tackle social and political problems but rather to guide humankind to a spiritual level on which all problems are seen, and thus eventually solved, through man's faith in and reliance upon the eternal wisdom of the Creator—an idea difficult to understand, let alone to appreciate, for many modern people in whose worldview no room is left for transcendence; and for whom—as the author remarks in passing—religion might "become the handmaid of industry". For the Muslim, however, God the Absolute has destined everything according to His eternal wisdom—"He will not be questioned as to what He does" (Koran 21:23) and "man chooses freely what God wills".

These words remind the reader of the beautiful lines of the Indo-Muslim poet-philosopher Muhammad Iqbal, who in one of his last poems tells a praying person that even though his prayer might not change his destiny, yet it can change his spiritual attitude by bringing him into touch with the Absolute Reality:

> Your prayer is that your destiny be changed.
> My prayer is that you yourself be changed.

This means that you accept willingly and lovingly whatever God has decreed.

As for the Koran, it is, as Schuon says, "a closed book", a book which, being divinely inspired *has* to be difficult and will not disclose the depths of its meaning to the superficial reader; rather, it has to be meditated upon and, as the mystics of yore used to say, has to be understood as if man were listening to God's own words, addressed to him at this very moment. This does not mean simply an intellectual understanding, but an "understanding with one's whole being". The divine threats and promises contained in the Koran are symbols for the equilibrium that exists in the entire universe, as all great religions have taught; this is a kind of "Golden Rule" which is at work throughout the created cosmos, because in God the One and Absolute both *jamāl*—kindness, beauty, relief—and *jalāl*—power, majesty, wrath—are contained (as Rudolf Otto spoke of the *mysterium tremendum* and the *mysterium fascinans*). They manifest themselves in the twofold rhythm of life, be it the heartbeat or the breathing, the two poles in electricity, or simply the contrast of day and night. And yet, as the Islamic tradition states, God's mercy is greater than His wrath.

The Prophet of Islam, so often misunderstood in the West, represents in his "serenity, generosity, and strength . . . the human form oriented toward the Divine Essence", as the author states, and his role is visible in his place in the confession of faith, the twofold *Shahādah*. The *Shahādah* is the center of true Islam; it is the statement that "there is no deity save *Allāh*" (which sacred Name embraces all that is), and that "Muhammad is His messenger". It is this confession of Absolute Divine Unity that makes a human being a Muslim. As for man's response to the Divine Presence, it is prayer; for to exist is to praise God. *Sum ergo oro*, "I am, therefore I pray", as Schuon changes the *cogito ergo sum*. Prayer is the activity of all that is created, and as the Koran asserts so beautifully: the birds with their wings and the flowers with their fragrance, the glaciers and the deserts—everything is created to glorify God, and man's noblest work is to join this chorus of prayer that permeates the Universe, whether we know it or not.

But what is prayer? Prayer is "as if the heart, risen to the surface, came to take the place of the brain which then sleeps with a holy slumber." "My eyes sleep, but my heart is awake", said the Prophet. This constant awareness of and participation in the laud of the universe is the duty and privilege of human beings, as the great leaders of the Muslim worlds have never tired to emphasize.

Schuon's book shows the essence of Islam, compares its worldview with that of Christianity and often brings examples from other religious traditions, all of which his vast erudition comprises. The style of the work reminds the reader sometimes of crystalline pure forms, and yet one often finds passages which touch the heart. I think that everyone, and in particular those who rely solely upon an intellectual approach to the world and ridicule the beautiful ages-old symbols, should study the passage on page 113, in which the author's language soars to poetical heights, and learn that the scientific approach to the universe does not exclude or contradict the religious interpretation of the world: "What most men do not know—and if they could know it, why should they be called on to believe?—is that this blue sky, though illusory as an optical error and belied by the vision of interplanetary space, is nonetheless an adequate reflection of the Heaven of the Angels and the Blessed and that therefore, despite everything, it is this blue mirage, flecked with silver clouds, which is right and will have the final say; to be astonished at this amounts to admitting that it is by chance that we are here on earth and see the sky as we do."

Annemarie Schimmel

EDITOR'S PREFACE

The book presented here by World Wisdom in a revised edition has become something of a classic; among Schuon's works it is probably the one that has most widely contributed to the intellectual reputation of its author, together with his celebrated *The Transcendent Unity of Religions*.

The immediate appeal of *Understanding Islam* is partly a function of its title, which is strongly suggestive of its substantial content. For the unprepared reader, however, this same title can also be misleading, given that there are many ways of understanding the notion of "understanding". Indeed, any attempt at understanding is predicated upon the specific motivations for that understanding, which means that it will be contingent upon—if not informed by—these motivations, at least to some extent. Hence, it is to be feared that potential misapprehensions of this title may have grown in recent years, considering the relatively limited motivations that lie behind most approaches to Islam.

Of late, there has been no shortage of books intent on understanding Islam and on making it understood, but it is no exaggeration to state that the aim and outlook of Schuon's book belongs to a different order; for his understanding is not so much informed by the more or less hasty, peripheral, and perfunctory interrogative, "What do Muslims believe?" as by the more fundamental question, "Why do Muslims believe in Islam?" His interest lies more with the "why" of Muslim faith than with the "what" or the "how" of Islam as a religion. His intention, in other words, is to remain at the level of the fundamental principles and spiritual realities that move believers to believe.

This means that religion is not approached as a set of historical, sociological, and political facts, but as a compelling vision of Reality together with its human consequences. Now, for Schuon, what is most compelling is that which addresses Reality in the most integral manner, and connects us to it in the most profound and all-embracing way; or else that which points to, and allows us to realize, "the nature of things", to use an expression particularly representative of his vocabulary. This perspective allows us to understand why, in the final analysis, Schuon is less interested in reality as it is perceived *from* Islam than in Islam as it stems from and leads back to reality *as it is*, if such a suggestive distinction may be allowed; hence also the unambiguous claim, announced in his preface, concerning Islam's conformity to the *sophia perennis*—the universal wisdom underlying all the major expressions of the sacred. The particularity of Islam is, in that sense, inseparable from the universality of its foundations and goals since, as Schuon himself put it, "to understand a religion in depth, one must understand religion as such".[1]

Most of our contemporaries, however, especially scholars of religion, have denied the reality of "religion as such". Inasmuch as their analytical mode of inquiry and exclusive reliance on external sources of information virtually precludes any other way of envisioning religious phenomena, they have not, in a sense, been unwarranted in doing so. For them "essentialism" is an epistemological delusion, or even an intellectual sin, and religion can only be understood in and through the plurality, both historical and social, of religious phenomena, or phenomena that have been "constructed" as religious. It is evident that such a perspective is irreconcilable with Schuon's own outlook, be it only because they do not, in fact, address the same realities; and even when approaching the same phenomena, they do so in such divergent ways as to end up referring to different things, just as would be the case, figuratively speaking, with one who would understand a text from the point of view of its author's intended meaning, and another whose focus might be on the chemical composition of the ink in which the same text is printed.

For Schuon, understanding Islam cannot merely result from understanding the socio-historical components of its manifestations;[2] it can only stem from a serious consideration of the spiritual end and intention of the message and the related symbolic and operative function of its constituents. This perspective, which transcends the mere literalness of facts while incorporating them in fathoming their ultimate end, presupposes on the part of the reader a degree of spiritual intuition for the nature of the message; and this amounts in fact to a recognition

---

[1] *Gnosis: Divine Wisdom*, "Appendix" (Bloomington, IN: World Wisdom, 2006), p. 135.

[2] Although, obviously, such elements ought not to be discarded or disdained in themselves, provided they are not envisioned in a reductionist way.

of "the truths written in an eternal script in the very substance of the spirit", to quote from Schuon's preface. Thus can be fully grasped the author's central claim that "Islam . . . has given a religious form to that which constitutes the essence of all religions",[3] a statement that echoes the Koranic teaching that Islam is the final reminder and the final form of that which has always been: "Naught is said unto thee (Muhammad) save what was said unto the messengers before thee" (Koran 41:43).

—— ·:· ——

The first edition of *Comprendre l'Islam* was published in France in 1961 by Éditions Gallimard, and reprinted in 1976 by Éditions du Seuil, which has from then onward kept it continuously in print. In the wake of the French original, the book has been translated into English, Italian, Farsi, Arabic, Malay, Turkish, Spanish, German, Portuguese, Romanian, Urdu, and Bosnian. The first English translation by D.M. Matheson was published in 1963 by Allen & Unwin in the United Kingdom and Roy Publishers in the United States. It has since been reprinted numerous times by various publishers, including once by Penguin Books in 1972. World Wisdom's first edition of *Understanding Islam* appeared in 1994, followed by a second edition in 1998; for the latter, the distinguished Islamicist Annemarie Schimmel contributed a very perceptive foreword, which appears also in the present revised and expanded third edition.

As in the recent editions of Schuon's works edited by Dr. James Cutsinger, this one presents a fully revised translation from the original French and includes an appendix, a set of editor's notes, and a glossary. The appendix contains excerpts from Schuon's correspondence and other private writings, which prolong, buttress, or develop some of the major ideas presented by Schuon in this book. Our hope is that these texts, although not initially meant to be disseminated to a broad audience, are of such a general import—given that "mankind is always mankind"—as to be justifiably and not unduly included in a printed

---

[3] *Roots of the Human Condition*, "Outline of the Islamic Message" (Bloomington, IN: World Wisdom Books, 1991), p. 81.

volume of one of his works. The annotations in the editor's notes are intended to facilitate access to the author's references and allusions as well as to suggest certain cross-relations with passages from his other works. In this regard, we have used the Authorized Version throughout for quotations from the Bible. Since the author made his own translations from the Koran, his French for these passages has been rendered directly into English, though the Pickthall interpretation of the Arabic has been given a certain preference when Koranic quotations appear in our editorial notes. The glossary, for its part, provides translations and definitions of the foreign terms and phrases that the author uses in order to express given metaphysical, cosmological, or spiritual realities with conciseness and precision.[4]

Patrick Laude

---

[4] In this connection, it should be added that the relative difficulty of Schuon's works is a function of the nature of Reality and not in the least the effect of a conceptual virtuosity or a form of intellectual "art for art's sake". Furthermore, Schuon has himself noted that his works are no more "difficult of approach than the average works of profane philosophy" (*From the Divine to the Human*, "Preface" [Bloomington, IN: World Wisdom Books, 1981], p. 1).

Frithjof Schuon in Marrakech, 1974

PREFACE

As may be inferred from its title the purpose of this book is not so much to give a description of Islam as to explain why Muslims believe in it, if we may express it thus; in what follows, therefore, the reader is presumed already to have certain basic notions about the religion of Islam such as can be easily found in other books.

What we really have in mind in this as in previous works is the *scientia sacra* or *philosophia perennis*, that universal *gnosis* which always has existed and always will exist. Few topics are so unrewarding as conventional laments about the "researches of the human mind" never being satisfied; in fact everything has been said already, though it is far from being the case that everyone has always understood it. There can therefore be no question of presenting "new truths"; however, what is needed in our time, and indeed in every age as it moves away from the origins of Revelation, is to provide some people with keys fashioned afresh—keys no better than the old ones but merely more elaborated and reflective—in order to help them rediscover the truths written in an eternal script in the very substance of the spirit.

This book is no more restricted to an exclusive program than were our earlier writings. A number of digressions will be found which, though they appear to go beyond the framework indicated by the title, have nonetheless been deemed indispensable in their context. The justification for expressions and forms lies in the truth, and not conversely. Truth is at the same time both single and infinite; hence the perfectly homogeneous diversity of its language.

This book is intended primarily for Western readers, given the language in which it is written and the nature of its dialectic, but there are doubtless some Orientals, of Western formation—men who have perhaps lost sight of the solid grounds for faith in God and Tradition— who equally may be able to profit from it and in any case to understand that Tradition is not a childish and outmoded mythology but a science that is terribly real.

F.S.

God is the Light of the heavens and of the earth.
Koran

The first thing created by God was the Intellect.
The Prophet

God did not distribute to His servants anything
more to be esteemed than Intelligence.
Ali

Islam

Islam is the meeting between God as such and man as such.

God as such: that is to say God envisaged, not as He manifested Himself in a particular way at a particular time, but independently of history and inasmuch as He is what He is and therefore as He creates and reveals by His nature.

Man as such: that is to say man envisaged, not as a fallen being needing a miracle to save him, but as man, a theomorphic being endowed with an intelligence capable of conceiving of the Absolute and with a will capable of choosing what leads to the Absolute.

To say "God" is to say also "being", "creating", "revealing"; in other words it is to say "Reality", "Manifestation", "Reintegration"; to say "man" is to say "theomorphism", "transcendent intelligence", and "free will". These are, according to us, the premises of the Islamic perspective, those which explain its every application and must never be lost sight of by anyone wanting to understand any particular aspect of Islam.

Man thus appears *a priori* as a dual receptacle made for the Absolute, and Islam comes to fill that receptacle, firstly with the truth of the Absolute and secondly with the law of the Absolute. Islam then is in essence a truth and a law—or the Truth and the Law—the former answering to the intelligence and the latter to the will. It is thus that Islam sets out to abolish both uncertainty and hesitation and, *a fortiori*, both error and sin; error in holding that the Absolute is not, or that it is relative, or that there are two Absolutes, or that the relative is absolute; sin places these errors on the level of the will or of action.[1]

The idea of predestination, so strongly marked in Islam, does not eliminate the idea of freedom. Man is subject to predestination because he is not God, but he is free because he is "made in the image of God". God alone is absolute freedom, but human freedom, despite its relativity—in the sense that it is "relatively absolute"—is not some-

---

[1] These two doctrines of the Absolute and of man are to be found respectively in the two Testimonies of the Islamic faith, the first (*lā ilāha illā 'Llāh*) concerning God and the second (*Muhammadun Rasūlu 'Llāh*) concerning the Prophet.

thing other than freedom any more than a feeble light is something other than light. To deny predestination would amount to maintaining that God does not know events "in advance" and so is not omniscient: *quod absit.*

To summarize: Islam confronts what is immutable in God with what is permanent in man. For Christianity, man is *a priori* will, or more exactly, he is will corrupted; clearly the intelligence is not denied, but it is taken into consideration only as an aspect of will; man is will and in man will is intelligent; when the will is corrupted, so also is the intelligence corrupted in the sense that in no way could it redress the will. Therefore a divine intervention is needed: the sacrament. In the case of Islam, where man is considered as intelligence and where intelligence comes "before" will, it is the content or direction of the intelligence which has sacramental efficacy: whoever accepts that the transcendent Absolute alone is absolute and transcendent, and draws from this the consequences for the will, is saved. The Testimony of Faith—the *Shahādah*—determines the intelligence, and the Islamic Law—the *Sharīʿah*—determines the will; in Islamic esoterism—the *Tarīqah*—there are the initiatic graces which have the value of keys and serve to actualize our "supernatural nature". Once again, our salvation, its texture, and its course are prefigured by our theomorphism: since we are transcendent intelligence and free will, it is this intelligence and this will, or it is transcendence and freedom, that will save us; God does no more than fill the receptacles man had emptied but not destroyed; to destroy them is not in man's power.

Again in the same way: only man has the gift of speech, because he alone among earthly creatures is "made in the image of God" in a direct and integral manner; now, if it is this theomorphism which, thanks to a divine impulsion, brings about salvation or deliverance, speech has its part to play as well as intelligence and will. These last are indeed actualized through prayer, which is speech both divine and human, the act[2] relating to the will and its content to intelligence; speech is as it were the immaterial, though sensory, body of our will and of our understanding. In Islam nothing is of greater importance than the

---

[2] But speech is not necessarily exteriorized, for articulated thought also involves language.

canonical prayer (*salāt*) directed toward the Kaaba and the "mentioning of God" (*dhikru 'Llāh*) directed toward the heart; the speech of the Sufi is repeated in the universal prayer of humanity and even in the prayer, often unarticulated, of all beings.

What constitutes the originality of Islam is not the discovery of the salvific function of intelligence, will, and speech—that function is clear enough and is known to every religion—but that it has made of this, within the framework of Semitic monotheism, the point of departure in a perspective of salvation and deliverance. Intelligence is identified with its content which brings salvation; it is nothing other than knowledge of Unity, or of the Absolute, and of the dependence of all things on the One; likewise, the will is *al-islām*, in other words conformity to what is willed by God, or by the Absolute, in respect of our earthly existence and our spiritual possibility on the one hand, and, on the other, in respect both of man as such and of man in a collective sense; speech is communication with God and is essentially prayer and invocation. When seen from this angle, Islam recalls to man not so much what he should know, do, and say, as what intelligence, will, and speech are, by definition. The Revelation does not superadd new elements but unveils the fundamental nature of the receptacle.

We could also express this as follows: if man, being made in the image of God, is distinguished from the other creatures by having transcendent intelligence, free will, and the gift of speech, then Islam is the religion of certainty, equilibrium, and prayer—to take in their order the three deiform faculties. And thus we meet the triad traditional in Islam, that of *al-īmān* (the "Faith"), *al-islām* (the "Law", literally "submission"), and *al-ihsān* (the "Path", literally, "virtue"). Now the essential means of this third element is the "remembrance of God" actualized through speech on the basis of the first two elements. From the metaphysical point of view which matters here, *al-īmān* is certainty of the Absolute and of the attachment of all things to the Absolute; *al-islām*—and the Prophet inasmuch as he personifies Islam—is an equilibrium in terms of the Absolute and in view of the Absolute; and finally *al-ihsān* leads these first two back to their essences by the magic of sacred speech, inasmuch as this speech is the vehicle for both intelligence and will. This role of our aspects of deiformity in what might be called fundamental and pre-theological Islam is all the more remarkable since Islamic doctrine, which emphasizes the transcendence of

3

God and the incommensurability between Him and ourselves, is loath of using analogies made to the advantage of man; thus Islam is far from relying explicitly and generally on man in his quality as a divine image, even though the Koran bears testimony to it in speaking of Adam in these words: "When I shall have formed him according to perfection and breathed into him a portion of My Spirit (*min Rūhī*), fall down before him in prostration" (Koran 15:29 and 38:72) and even though the anthropomorphism of God in the Koran implies the theomorphism of man.

The doctrine of Islam consists of two statements: first "There is no divinity (or reality, or absolute) save the sole Divinity (or Reality, or Absolute)" (*lā ilāha illā 'Llāh*), and "Muhammad (the "Glorified", the Perfect) is the Messenger (the spokesman, the intermediary, the manifestation, the symbol) of the Divinity" (*Muhammadun Rasūlu 'Llāh*); these are the first and the second Testimonies (*Shahādatān*) of the faith.

We are here in the presence of two assertions, two certitudes, two levels of reality: the Absolute and the relative, Cause and effect, God and the world. Islam is the religion of certitude and equilibrium, as Christianity is the religion of love and sacrifice. By this we mean, not that religions have monopolies but that each lays stress on one or other aspect of truth. Islam seeks to implant certitude—its unitary faith stands forth as something manifestly clear without however renouncing mystery[3]—and is based on two axiomatic certainties, one concerning the Principle, which is at once Being and Beyond-Being, and the other concerning manifestation, both formal and supraformal: thus it is a matter on the one hand of "God"—or of the "Godhead" in the Eckhartian sense of this *distinguo*—and on the other of "Earth" and "Heaven". The first of these certainties is that "God alone is" and the second that "all things are attached to God".[4] In other words: "noth-

---

[3] Mystery is as it were the inner infinity of certitude and the latter could not exhaust the former.

[4] These two relationships are also expressed in the following formula in the Koran:

ing is absolutely evident save the Absolute"; then, following from this truth: "All manifestation, and so all that is relative, is attached to the Absolute." The world is linked to God—or the relative to the Absolute—both in respect of its cause and of its end: the word "Messenger" in the second *Shahādah*, therefore enunciates, first a causality and then a finality, the former concerning the world in particular and the second concerning man.[5]

All metaphysical truths are comprised in the first of these Testimonies and all eschatological truths in the second. But it could also be said that the first *Shahādah* is the formula of discernment or "abstraction" (*tanzīh*) while the second is the formula of integration or "analogy" (*tashbīh*): in the first *Shahādah* the word "divinity" (*ilāha*)—taken here in its ordinary current sense—designates the world inasmuch as it is unreal because God alone is real, while the name of the Prophet (*Muhammad*) in the second *Shahādah* designates the world inasmuch as it is real because nothing can be outside God; in certain respects all is He. Realizing the first *Shahādah* means first of all[6] becoming fully conscious that the Principle alone is real and that the world, though on its own level it "exists", "is" not; in one sense it therefore means realizing the universal void. Realizing the second *Shahādah* means first of all[7] becoming fully conscious that the world—or manifestation—is "not other" than God or the Principle, since "to the degree that" it has reality it can only be that which alone "is", or in other words it can only be divine; realizing this *Shahādah* thus means seeing God everywhere

"Verily we are God's (*innā li-Llāhi*) and verily unto Him we return (*wa innā ilayhi rājiʿūn*)." The *Basmalah*, the formula: "In the Name of God the infinitely Good, the ever Merciful" (*Bismi'Llāhi 'r-Rahmāni 'r-Rahīm*) also expresses the attachment of all things to the Principle.

[5] Or again, the cause or origin is in the word *rasūl* (Messenger) and the finality in the name *Muhammad* ("Glorified"). The *risālah* (the "thing sent," the "epistle," the Koran) "came down" in the *laylat al-Qadr* (the "night of the Power that is destiny") and Muhammad "ascended" in the *laylat al-Miʿrāj* (the "night journey") thus prefiguring the finality of man.

[6] We say "first of all" because this *Shahādah* includes the second in an eminent degree.

[7] "First of all" meaning in this case that in the final analysis this *Shahādah*, being like the first a divine Word or "Name", in the end actualizes the same knowledge as the first by virtue of the oneness of essence of the Word or Names of God.

and everything in Him. "He who has seen me", said the Prophet, "has seen God"; now everything is the "Prophet", on the one hand with respect to the perfection of existence and on the other with respect to the perfections of mode or expression.[8]

If Islam merely sought to teach that there is only one God and not two or more, it would have no persuasive force. The persuasive force it possesses comes from the fact that at root it teaches the reality of the Absolute and the dependence of all things on the Absolute. Islam is the religion of the Absolute as Christianity is the religion of love and of the miracle; but love and miracle also pertain to the Absolute and express nothing other than an attitude it assumes in relation to us.

If we go to the very root of things we are obliged to note—setting aside any dogmatic question—that the basic reason for the mutual lack of understanding between Christians and Muslims lies in this: the Christian always sees before him his will—this will that is as it were himself—and so is confronted by an indeterminate vocational space into which he can plunge, deploying his faith and his heroism; by contrast the Islamic system of "outward" and clearly laid down prescriptions seems to him the expression of a mediocrity ready to make all kinds of concessions and incapable of any soaring flight: Muslim virtue seems to him in theory—for he does not know what it actually is—to be something artificial and vain. The outlook of the Muslim is very different: he sees before him—before his intelligence which chooses the One—not a space for the will offering him a temptation for individualistic undertakings, but a system of channels divinely predisposed for the equilibrium of his volitive life, and this equilibrium, far from being an end in itself as is supposed by the Christian, who is accustomed to a more or less exclusive idealism of the will, on the contrary is really

---

[8] In connection with Ibn Arabi a Spanish scholar has spoken of "Islam cristianizado": this is to lose sight of the fact that the doctrine of the *Shaykh al-akbar* was essentially Muhammadan and was in particular even a sort of commentary on *Muhammadun Rasūlu 'Llāh* in the meaning of the Vedantic sayings: "all things are *Ātmā*" and "That art thou".

a basis for escaping from the uncertainties and turbulence of the ego in the peace-giving and liberating contemplation of the Immutable. To summarize: if the attitude of equilibrium which Islam seeks and realizes appears in Christian eyes as a calculating mediocrity unfit for the supernatural, the sacrificial idealism of Christianity is liable to be misinterpreted by the Muslim as an individualism contemptuous of the divine gift of intelligence. If the objection is raised that the average Muslim does not concern himself with contemplation, the answer is that neither is the average Christian preoccupied with sacrifice; every Christian carries in the depths of his soul an urge to sacrifice which will perhaps never be actualized, and in the same way every Muslim has, by reason of his faith, a predisposition to contemplation which will perhaps never actually dawn in his heart. Apart from this, some might also argue that Christian and Muslim mysticism, far from being opposed types, present on the contrary such striking analogies that one feels bound to conclude that there have been either unilateral or reciprocal borrowings; the answer is that, if we suppose the starting point of Sufis to have been the same as that of Christian mystics, the question arises why they should have remained Muslims and how they were able to stand being Muslims; in reality they were saints not "in spite" of their religion but "because of" their religion. Far from having been Christians in disguise, what men like al-Hallaj and Ibn Arabi did was on the contrary to carry the possibilities of Islam to their highest point, as their great predecessors had done. Despite certain appearances, such as the absence of monasticism as a social institution, Islam, which advocates poverty, fasting, solitude, and silence, contains all the premises of a contemplative asceticism.

When a Christian hears the word "truth" he immediately thinks of the fact that "the Word was made flesh", whereas, when a Muslim hears that word he thinks first of all that "there is no divinity apart from the sole Divinity" and will interpret this, according to his level or knowledge, either literally or metaphysically. Christianity is founded on an "event" and Islam on "being", on the "nature of things"; that which appears in Christianity as a unique fact, the Revelation, is seen in Islam as the rhythmic manifestation of a principle.[9] If, for

---

[9] The Fall too—and not only the Incarnation—is a unique "event" deemed capable of determining "being"—that of man—in a total manner. For Islam the fall of Adam is a

Christians, the truth is that Christ allowed himself to be crucified, for Muslims—for whom the truth is that there is only one God—the crucifixion of Christ, by its very nature, cannot be "the Truth", and the Muslim rejection of the cross is a way of expressing this. Muslim "anti-historicism"—which could by analogy be termed "Platonic" or "gnostic"—culminates in this rejection which finally is quite outward and for some[10] even dubious as to its intention.

The attitude of reserve adopted by Islam, not toward miracles, but toward the Judeo-Christian and particularly the Christian, axiomatic assumption of miracles is explained by the predominance of the pole "intelligence" over the pole "existence": the Islamic outlook is based on what is spiritually evident, on the sense of the Absolute, in conformity with the very nature of man which is in this case seen as a theomorphic intelligence and not as a will only waiting to be seduced in either a good or a bad course, that is to say, by miracles or by temptations. If Islam, the last to appear in the series of great Revelations, is not founded on a miracle—though of necessity admitting it, for otherwise it could not be a religion—this is also because the antichrist "will lead many astray by his wonders".[11] Now spiritual certainty which is at the very opposite pole from the "reversing" produced by miracles—and which Islam offers in the form of a penetrating unitary faith, an acute sense of the Absolute—is an element to which the devil has no access; he can imitate a miracle but not what is intellectually evident; he can imitate a phenomenon but not the Holy Spirit, except in the case of those who want to be deceived and anyhow have no sense either of the truth or of the sacred.

---

necessary manifestation of evil but one which does not imply that evil can determine the true nature of man, since man cannot lose his deiformity. In Christianity the divine "action" appears in a way to have priority over the divine "being", in the sense that the "action" reflects on the very definition of God. This way of looking at things may appear cursory, but there is here a very subtle *distinguo* which cannot be neglected when comparing the two theologies in question.

[10] As, for instance, for Abu Hatim, quoted by Louis Massignon in his "Le Christ dans les Evangiles selon al-Ghazzali".

[11] A Catholic writer of the end of the "Belle Époque" could exclaim, "What we need is signs, concrete facts!" It is inconceivable that a Muslim should say such a thing: in Islam it would seem infidelity or even an appeal to the devil or to the antichrist and in any case a most blameworthy extravagance.

Allusion has already been made to the non-historical character of the Islamic perspective. This character explains not only its intention of being simply the reiteration of a timeless reality or a phase in an anonymous rhythm, and so a "reform"—in the strictly orthodox and traditional meaning of the term, and even in a transposed sense, because an authentic Revelation is necessarily spontaneous and comes only from God, whatever the appearances—but it also explains such Islamic ideas as that of continual creation: were God not Creator at every moment, the world would collapse; since God is always Creator it is He who intervenes in every phenomenon and there are no secondary causes, no intermediate principles, no natural laws which can come between God and the cosmic fact, except in the case of man who, being the representative (*imām*) of God on earth, has those miraculous gifts of intelligence and freedom. But in the final analysis not even these gifts escape the divine determination; man freely chooses what God wills; he chooses "freely" because God wills it thus, because God cannot fail to manifest within the contingent order His absolute Freedom. Hence our freedom is real, but with a reality that is illusory like the relativity in which it is produced and in which it is a reflection of That which is.

The fundamental difference between Christianity and Islam may be seen quite clearly in what Christians and Muslims respectively abhor: abhorrent for the Christian is, first, the rejection of the divinity of Christ and of the Church and in the second place morals less ascetic than his own, not to speak of lust. As for the Muslim, he abhors the rejection of *Allāh* and of Islam because the supreme Unity and its absoluteness and transcendence appear to him dazzlingly evident and majestic, and because for him Islam, the Law, is the Divine Will and the logical emanation, in the mode of an equilibrium, of that Unity. Now the Divine Will—and it is here especially that the whole difference appears—does not necessarily coincide with what involves sacrifice, it may even in some cases "combine the useful and the agreeable"; and so the Muslim will say: "That is good which God wants", not: "What is painful is what God wants." Logically the Christian is of the same opinion as the Muslim, but his sensibility and his imagination lead him rather toward the second formulation. In the climate of Islam the Divine Will has in view in the first place, not sacrifice and suffering as pledges of love, but the deployment of the theomorphic intelligence (*min Rūhī*, "of My Spirit"), itself determined by the Immutable and thus including our being, otherwise there is "hypocrisy" (*nifāq*) since to know is to be. In reality the apparent "easiness" of Islam tends toward an equilibrium, as has already been pointed out, whose sufficient reason is in the final analysis "vertical" effort, contemplation, *gnosis*. In one sense what we must do is the opposite of what God does; in another sense we must act like Him: this is because on the one hand we are like God, since we exist, and on the other we are opposed to Him since, in existing, we are separated from Him. For example, God is Love; so we ought to love because we are like Him; yet, He judges and avenges, and this we cannot do because we are other than He. But as these positions are always approximate, morals can and must differ; there is always room in us—at least in principle—for a guilty love and a just vengeance. Here it is all a matter of accent and delimitation; the choice depends on a perspective which is not arbitrary—for then it would not be a perspective—but in conformity with the nature of things or with a particular aspect of that nature.

All the positions described above are founded on the dogmas or, in a deeper sense, on the metaphysical perspectives which they express, that is to say, on a certain "viewpoint" as to the subject and on a certain "aspect" as to the object. Seeing that Christianity is founded on the divinity of an earthly phenomenon—Christ is not earthly in himself but insofar as he moves in space and time—it is obliged therefore to introduce relativity into the Absolute, or rather to consider the Absolute at a still relative level, that of the Trinity;[12] since a particular "relative" is considered as absolute, the Absolute must have something of the relative, and since the Incarnation is a fact of the Divine Mercy

---

[12] To speak of distinction is to speak of relativity. The very term "Trinitarian relationships" proves that the viewpoint adopted—providentially and necessarily—is situated at the metaphysical level specific to all *bhakti. Gnosis* goes beyond this plane in attributing absoluteness to the Godhead in the Eckhartian sense, or to the Father when the Trinity is envisaged "vertically", in which case the Son corresponds to Being—the first relativity "in the Absolute"—and the Holy Spirit to Act.

or Love, God must be envisaged at the outset in this aspect and man in the corresponding aspect of will and affection; and the spiritual path must equally be a reality of love. The Christian emphasis on the will is linked to the Christian conception of the Absolute and this conception in turn is as if determined by the "historicity" of God, if such an expression be permissible.

Analogously, seeing that Islam is founded on the absoluteness of God, it is therefore obliged to exclude terrestrialness from the Absolute—since by its form it is a Semitic dogmatism[13]—and so must deny, at least on the level of words, the divinity of Christ; it is not obliged to deny, in a secondary manner, that there is some relativity in God—for it has to allow for the divine attributes, otherwise it would be denying the totality of God and all possibility of connection between God and the world; but it has to deny any directly divine character outside the sole Principle. The Sufis are the first to recognize that nothing can stand outside the supreme Reality, for to say that Unity excludes everything amounts to saying that from another point of view—that of the reality of the world—it includes everything; but this truth does not lend itself to a dogmatic formulation, though it is logically included in *lā ilāha illā 'Llāh.*

When the Koran affirms that the Messiah is not God it means he is not "a god" other than God, or that he is not God *qua* the earthly Messiah;[14] and when the Koran rejects the dogma of the Trinity it means there is no triad in "God as such", that is, in the Absolute, which is beyond all distinctions. Finally, when the Koran appears to deny the death of Christ, it can be understood to mean that in reality Jesus vanquished death, whereas the Jews believed they had killed the Christ in his very essence;[15] here the truth of the symbol prevails over

---

[13] Dogmatism is characterized by the fact that it attributes an absolute scope and an exclusive sense to a particular "point of view" or "aspect". In pure metaphysics all conceptual antinomies are resolved in the total truth, something which must not be confused with a leveling out of real oppositions by denying them.

[14] In Christian terms: human nature is not divine nature. If Islam insists on this, as it does, in a given way and not in another, that is because of its particular angle of vision.

[15] The Koran says (2:149): "Say not of those that have been slain in the way of God that they are dead; say that they are living, though ye are not aware of it." See also the author's *Gnosis* (World Wisdom, 2006), the chapter "The Sense of the Absolute in Religions", pp. 6-7, note 3.

the truth of the fact in the sense that a spiritual negation takes the form of a material negation;[16] but, from another angle, by this negation, or apparent negation, Islam eliminates the way of Christ insofar as it itself is concerned, and it is logical that it should do so since its own way is different and it has no need to claim those means of grace pertaining to Christianity.

On the plane of total truth, which includes all possible points of view, aspects, and modes, any recourse to reason alone is evidently useless; consequently it is vain to adduce against some dogma of a foreign religion that an error denounced by reason cannot become a truth on another level, for that is to forget that reason works in an indirect way, or by reflections, and that its axioms are inadequate to the extent that it trespasses on the ground of pure Intellect. Reason is formal by its nature and formalistic in its operations; it proceeds by "coagulations", by alternatives, and by exclusions—or, it can be said, by partial truths. It is not, like pure Intellect, formless and "fluid" light; true, it derives its implacability, or its validity in general, from the Intellect, but it touches on essences only through drawing conclusions, not by direct vision; it is indispensable for verbal formulation but it does not involve immediate knowledge.

In Christianity the line of demarcation between the relative and the Absolute passes through Christ; in Islam it separates the world from God, or even—in the case of esoterism—the divine attributes from the Essence, a difference explained by the fact that exoterism

---

[16] The same remark applies to Christianity as when, for instance, the saints of the Old Testament—even Enoch, Abraham, Moses, and Elias—are held to have remained shut out from Heaven until the "descent into hell" of Christ; however, before that descent, Christ appeared between Moses and Elias in the light of the Transfiguration, and in a parable mentioned "the bosom of Abraham"; clearly these facts are capable of various interpretations, but the Christian concepts are nonetheless incompatible with the Jewish tradition. What justifies them is their spiritual symbolism and thus their truth: salvation must of necessity come through the *Logos* which, though manifested in time in a particular form, is beyond the limitations of a temporal condition. Let us also note the seeming contradiction between Saint John the Baptist denying that he was Elias and Christ affirming the contrary: had this contradiction, which is resolved by the difference in the relationship envisaged, been between one religion and another, it would have been exploited to the utmost on the pretext that "God cannot contradict Himself".

must always start from the relative while esoterism starts from the Absolute, to which it gives a more strict, and even the strictest possible meaning. In Sufism it is also said that the divine attributes are predicated as such only in respect of the world and that in themselves they are indistinct and ineffable: thus one cannot say of God that He is in an absolute sense "merciful" or "avenging", leaving aside the fact that He is merciful "before" being avenging. As for the attributes of the Essence such as "holiness" or "wisdom" they are actualized only as distinctions, in relation to our distinctive mind, and they are so without on that account losing anything, in their own being, of their infinite reality, quite the contrary.

To say that the Islamic perspective is possible amounts to saying that it is necessary and therefore cannot not be; it is required by its providential human receptacles. The different perspectives as such have however no absolute quality, Truth being one; in the eyes of God their differences are relative and the values of any one are always to be found in others in some manner. There is not only a Christianity of "warmth", of emotional love, of sacrificial activity, but, framed within this, there is also a Christianity of "light", of *gnosis*, of pure contemplation, of "peace"; and in the same way the Islam that is "dry"—whether legalistically or metaphysically—encloses an Islam that is "moist",[17] an Islam, that is to say, enraptured with beauty, with love, and with sacrifice. This must needs be so because of the unity, not only of the Truth, but also of man, a unity no doubt relative, since differences do exist, but nevertheless sufficiently real to allow of, or to impose, the reciprocity—or the spiritual ubiquity—in question.

A point we would like to mention here is the question of Muslim morality. If we want to understand certain seeming contradictions in that morality we must take into account the fact that Islam distinguishes between man as such and collective man, the latter appearing as a new

---

[17] The terms are used here in an alchemical sense.

creature subject in a certain degree, but no further, to the law of natural selection. This is to say that Islam puts everything in its proper place and treats it according to its own nature; it envisages collective man not through the distorting perspective of a mystical idealism which under the circumstances is inapplicable, but by taking account of the natural laws which regulate each order and are, within the limits of each order, willed by God. Islam is the perspective of certainty and of the nature of things rather than of miracles and idealist improvisation. This is said, not with any underlying intention of indirectly criticizing Christianity which is what it must be, but in order better to bring out the intention and justification of the Islamic perspective.[18]

If there is a clear separation in Islam between man as such[19] and collective man, these two realities are nonetheless profoundly linked together, given that the collectivity is an aspect of man—no man can be born without a family—and that conversely society is a multiplication of individuals. It follows from this interdependence or reciprocity that anything that is done with a view to the collectivity, such as the tithe for the poor or the holy war, has a spiritual value for the individual and conversely; this converse relationship is all the more true because the individual comes before the collectivity, all men being descended from Adam and not Adam from men.

What has just been said explains why the Muslim does not, like the Buddhist and the Hindu, abandon outward rites in following a given spiritual method that can compensate for them, or because he has attained a spiritual degree of a nature to authorize such an abandonment.[20] A particular saint may no longer have need of the canonical

---

[18] If we start with the idea that esoterism by definition considers first of all the being of things and not becoming or our situation in relation to our will, then for the Christian gnostic it is Christ who is the being of things, this "Word from which all things were made and without which nothing was made". The Peace of Christ is from this point of view the repose of the Intellect in "that which is".

[19] We do not say "single man" because it would still have the disadvantage of defining man in terms of the collectivity and not starting from God. The distinction we are making is not between one man and several men but between the human person and society.

[20] The principle of this abandonment of general rites is nonetheless known and is sometimes manifested, otherwise Ibn Hanbal would not have reproached the Sufis

prayers since he finds himself in a state of being steeped in prayer, in a state of "intoxication",[21] but he nonetheless continues to accomplish the prayers in order to pray with and for all and in order that all may pray in him. He incarnates the "mystical Body" which every believing community constitutes, or, from another point of view, he incarnates the Law, the tradition, and prayer as such. Inasmuch as he is a social being he should preach by his example and, inasmuch as he is individual man, permit what is human to be realized and, in some sense, renewed through him.

with developing meditation to the detriment of the prayers and in short with pretentions to freeing themselves from the obligations of the law. In fact a distinction is drawn between dervishes who are "travelers" (toward God: *sālikūn*) and those who are "attracted" (by God: *majādhib*); those in the first category form the vast majority and do obey the Law, whereas those in the second more or less dispense with it and are not much bothered because they are generally held to be half mad and so worthy of pity, sometimes of fear or even of veneration. Among Sufis in Indonesia cases of the abandoning of rites in favor of prayer of the heart alone seem not to be rare; consciousness of Unity is then deemed a universal prayer which gives dispensation from the canonical prayers; the supreme knowledge is held to exclude the "polytheistic" multiplicity (*mushrik*) of the rites, the Absolute being without duality. In Islam in general there always seems to have existed—quite apart from the very special distinction between *sālikūn* and *majādhib*—an external division between those Sufis who were "nomian" and those who were "antinomian", the former being attached to the Law by virtue of its symbolism and its opportuneness and the latter detached from the Law by virtue of the supremacy of the heart (*qalb*) and direct knowledge (*ma'rifah*). Jalal ad-Din Rumi says in his *Mathnawī*: "The lovers of rites form one class and those whose hearts are afire with love form another", a remark addressed to Sufis alone, as is shown by his reference to the "essence of certainty" (*'ayn al-yaqīn*), and clearly not including any suggestion of a systematic alternative, as is proven by the life of Jalal ad-Din himself; no "free-thinking" could draw support from it. Finally let us note that according to al-Junayd, "he who realizes union" (*muwahhid*) should observe "sobriety" (*sahw*) and keep himself from "intoxication" (*sukr*) just as much as from "libertinism" (*ibāhiyah*).

[21] The Koran says: "Do not go to the prayer in a state of drunkenness", which can be understood in a higher and positive sense; the Sufi who enjoys a "station" (*maqām*) of bliss, or even merely the *dhākir* (the man dedicated to *dhikr*, the Islamic equivalent of the Hindu *japa*) could, considering his secret prayer to be like "wine" (*khamr*), in principle abstain from the general prayers; "in principle" for in fact the concern for equilibrium and solidarity, so marked in Islam, tip the scales in the other direction.

The metaphysical transparency of things and the contemplativity corresponding to it mean that sexuality—within the framework of its traditional legitimacy, which is one of psychological and social equilibrium—can take on a meritorious character, as the existence of this framework indeed already shows. In other words it is not only the enjoyment which counts—leaving aside the concern to preserve the species—for sexuality also has its qualitative content, its symbolism which is objective as well as lived. The basis of Muslim morality lies always in biological reality and not in an idealism contrary to collective possibilities and to the undeniable rights of natural laws; but this reality, while forming the basis of our animal and collective life, is not absolute since we are semi-celestial beings; it can always be neutralized on the level of our personal liberty, though never abolished on that of our social existence.[22] What has just been said of sexuality applies by analogy—but only in respect of merit—to food: as in the case of all religions, overeating is a sin, but to eat in due measure and with gratitude to God is, in Islam, not only not a sin but even a positively meritorious action. The analogy is not however total, for in a well-known *hadīth*, the Prophet said he "loved women", not that he loved "food". Here the love of woman is connected with nobility and generosity, not to mention its purely contemplative symbolism which goes far beyond this.

Islam is often reproached with having propagated its faith by the sword. What is overlooked is, firstly, that persuasion played a greater part than war in the expansion of Islam as a whole; secondly, that only polytheists and idolaters could be compelled to embrace the new religion;[23] thirdly, that the God of the Old Testament is no less a war-

---

[22] Many Hindu saints have disregarded caste, but none has dreamt of abolishing the caste system. To the question of whether there are two moralities, one for individuals and the other for the State, our reply is affirmative, subject however to the reservation that the one can always extend to the domain of the other according to outward or inward circumstances. Never in any circumstances is it permissible that the intention "not to resist evil" become complicity, betrayal, or suicide.

[23] This attitude ceased in relation to Hindus, in large measure at any rate, once the Muslims had grasped that Hinduism was not equivalent to the paganism of the Arabs; Hindus were then considered to be the same as the "people of the Book" (*ahl al-Kitāb*), that is to the Monotheists of the Western Semitic traditions.

rior than the God of the Koran, quite the opposite; and fourthly, that Christianity also made use of the sword from the time of Constantine's advent. The question to be put here is simply the following: is it possible for force to be used for asserting and diffusing a vital truth? Beyond doubt the answer must be in the affirmative, for experience proves that we must at times do violence to irresponsible people in their own interest. Now, since this possibility exists it cannot fail to manifest in appropriate conditions,[24] exactly as in the case of the opposite possibility of victory through the force inherent in truth itself; it is the inner or outer nature of things which determines the choice between two possibilities. On the one hand the end sanctifies the means, and on the other hand the means may profane the end, which signifies that the means must be prefigured in the divine nature. Thus the "right of the stronger" is prefigured in the "jungle" to which we unquestionably belong to a certain degree and when regarded as collectivities; but in that "jungle" no example can be found of any right to perfidy and baseness and, even if such characteristics were to be found there, our human dignity would forbid us to participate in them. The harshness of certain biological laws must never be confused with that infamy of which man alone is capable by the fact of his perverted theomorphism.[25]

---

[24] Christ, in using violence against the money changers in the Temple, showed that this attitude could not be excluded.

[25] "We see Muslim and Catholic princes not only become allies when it is a question of breaking the power of a dangerous fellow religionist, but also generously helping one another to conquer disorders and revolts. Not without some shaking of the head will the reader learn that in one of the battles for the Caliphate of Cordova, in A.D. 1010 it was Catalan forces that saved the situation and that on this occasion three bishops gave their lives for the 'Prince of the Faithful'. . . . Al-Mansur had in his company several Counts, who had joined him with their troops, and there was nothing exceptional in the presence of Christian guards at the courts of Andalusia. . . . When an enemy territory was conquered the religious convictions of the population were respected as much as possible; we need only recall here that Al-Mansur—in general a man of few scruples—took pains, at the assault on Santiago, to protect against any profanation of the church containing the tomb of the Apostle, and that in many other cases the Caliphs seized the chance to show their respect for the sacred objects of the enemy; in similar circumstances the Christians adopted a like attitude. For centuries Islam was respected in the reconquered countries, and it was only in the sixteenth century that . . . it came to be systematically persecuted and exterminated at the instigation of a fanatical clergy who had become overpowerful. On the contrary, through the

From a certain point of view it can be said that Islam has two dimensions, the "horizontal" dimension of the will, and the "vertical" dimension of the intelligence: the first we shall term "equilibrium",[26] and the second "union". Islam is in essence equilibrium and union; it does not *a priori* sublimate the will by sacrifice, but neutralizes it by the Law, while at the same time emphasizing contemplation. The dimensions of "equilibrium" and "union"—the "horizontal" and the "vertical"—concern both man as such and the collectivity; there is not identity here assuredly, but there is a solidarity which makes society participate in its own way and according to its own possibilities in the individual's path to Union, and conversely. One of the most important modes of realizing equilibrium is precisely the agreement between the sacred Law relating to man as such and the law relating to society. Empirically, Christianity had by force of circumstances also reached this position, but it allowed certain "fissures" to remain and did not lay stress either on the divergence of the two human planes or, consequently, on the need to harmonize them. Islam, we repeat, is an equilibrium determined by the Absolute and disposed in view of the Absolute; this equilibrium, like the rhythm which in Islam is realized ritually through the canonical prayers following the sun's progress and "mythologically" through the retrospective series of divine "Messengers" and revealed "Books",[27] is the participation of the many in the One or of the conditioned in the Unconditioned; without equilibrium we do not, on the basis of this perspective, find the center, and apart from the center no ascent and no union is possible.

whole of the Middle Ages tolerance of foreign conviction and respect for the feelings of the enemy accompanied the incessant fighting between Moors and Christians and greatly softened the rigors and miseries of the warfare, giving the battles as chivalrous a character as possible. . . . Despite the linguistic gulf between them, this respect for the adversary and the high esteem of his virtues became a common national bond coupled as they were with the understanding shown in the poetry of both sides of the feelings of the other; indeed this poetry eloquently testifies to the love or friendship often uniting Muslims and Christians despite every obstacle" (Ernst Kühnel, *Maurische Kunst* [Berlin, 1924]).

[26] Disequilibrium also includes a positive meaning, but only indirectly; every holy war is a disequilibrium. Certain sayings of Christ can be interpreted as instituting disequilibrium with a view to union, such as "Think not that I am come to send peace on earth"; God alone will then restore the equilibrium.

[27] If equilibrium concerns the "center", rhythm is more particularly related to the "origin" envisaged as the qualitative root of things.

Like all traditional civilizations Islam is a "space", not a "time"; for Islam "time" is only the decomposition of this "space". "No period will come", predicted the Prophet, "which will not be worse than the period before it." This "space", this unvarying tradition—unvarying apart from the unfolding and diversification of forms at the time of the initial elaboration of the tradition—surrounds Muslim humanity as a symbol, like the physical world which unvaryingly and imperceptibly nourishes us with its symbolism; it is normal for humanity to live within a symbol which is a pointer toward Heaven, an opening toward the Infinite. Modern science has pierced the protecting frontiers of this symbol and by so doing destroyed the symbol itself; it has thus abolished this pointer, this opening, even as the modern world in general breaks the space-symbols traditional civilizations represent; what it terms "stagnation" and "sterility" is really the homogeneity and continuity of the symbol.[28] When a still authentic Muslim says to the protagonists of progress: "All that remains for you to do now is to abolish death", or when he asks: "Can you prevent the sun from setting or compel it to rise?" he expresses exactly what lies at the root of Islamic "sterility", namely a marvelous sense of relativity and, what amounts to the same thing, a sense of the Absolute dominating his whole life.

In order to understand traditional civilizations in general and Islam in particular it is also necessary to take account of the fact that the human or psychological norm is for them, not the common man deeply immersed in illusion, but the saint, detached from the world and at-

---

[28] "Neither India nor the Pythagoreans practiced modern science, and to isolate, where they are concerned, the elements of rational technique reminiscent of our science from the metaphysical elements which bear no resemblance to it, is an arbitrary and violent operation contrary to real objectivity. When Plato is sifted in this way he retains no more than an anecdotal interest, whereas his whole doctrine aims at establishing man in the supra-temporal and supra-discursive life of thought of which both mathematics and the sensory world can be symbols. If, then, peoples have been able to do without our autonomous science for thousands of years and in every climate, it is because this science is not necessary; if it has appeared as a phenomenon of civilization suddenly and in a single place, that is to show its essentially contingent nature" (Fernand Brunner, *Science et Réalité* [Paris, 1954]).

tached to God; he alone is entirely "normal" and he alone enjoys on this account a "full right" to exist; it is this outlook which gives them a certain lack of sensitivity in relation to what is purely and simply human. As this human nature is largely insensitive toward the Sovereign Good it should—to the extent that it does not have love—at least have fear.

In the life of a people there are as it were two halves; one constitutes the play of its earthly existence, the other its relationship with the Absolute. Now what determines the value of a people or of a civilization is not the literal form of its earthly dream—for here everything is merely a symbol—but its capacity to "sense" the Absolute and, in the case of specially privileged souls, to reach the Absolute. Thus it is perfectly illusory to set aside this "absolute" dimension and evaluate a human world according to earthly criteria, as by comparing one material civilization with another. The gap of some thousands of years separating the stone age of the American Indians from the material and literary refinements of the White Man counts for nothing compared with the contemplative intelligence and the virtues, which alone make up man's worth and alone make up his permanent reality or that something which enables us to evaluate him in a real manner, namely, in the sight of the Creator. To believe that some men are lagging behind us because their earthly dream takes on modes more "rudimentary" than our own—but often, for that very reason, more sincere—is far more "naive" than to believe the earth is flat or a volcano is a god; the most naive of all attitudes is surely to regard the dream as something absolute and to sacrifice to it all essential values, forgetting that what is "serious" only starts beyond its level, or rather that, if there is anything "serious" in this world, it is so in terms of that which lies beyond it.

One likes to contrast modern civilization as a type of thought or culture with traditional civilizations, but what is overlooked is that modern thought, or the culture it engenders, is only an indeterminate flux, which in a sense cannot be defined positively since it lacks any principle that is real, hence pertaining to the Immutable. Modern thought is not in any definitive sense one doctrine among others; it is the result of a particular phase determined by its own unfolding and will become what materialistic and experimental science or machines make it; no longer is it human Intellect but machines—or physics, or chemistry, or biology—that decide what man is, what intelligence is, what truth is. Under these conditions man's mind depends more and more on the "atmosphere" produced by its own creations: man no longer knows how to judge in human terms, that is to say, with respect to an absolute which is the very substance of intelligence; going astray in a relativism that leads nowhere he lets himself be judged, determined, and classified by the contingencies of science and technology; no longer able to escape from the dizzy fatality they impose on him and unwilling to admit his mistake,[29] the only course left to him is to abdicate his human dignity and freedom. It is then science and machines which in their turn create man and it is they also which "create God", if one may so express it;[30] for the void thus left by dethroning God cannot remain empty, the reality of God and His imprint in human nature require a substitute of divinity, a false absolute which can fill the nothingness of an intelligence deprived of its substance. There is a great deal of talk these days about "humanism", talk which forgets that once man abandons his prerogatives to matter, to machines, to quantitative knowledge, he ceases to be truly "human".[31]

When people talk about "civilization" they generally attribute a qualitative meaning to the term; now civilization only represents a value provided it is supra-human in origin and when it entails for the "civilized" man a sense of the sacred: only a people who really have this sense and draw their life from it are truly civilized. If it is objected that this reservation does not take account of the whole meaning of the term and that it is possible to conceive of a world that is "civilized" though having no religion, the answer is that in this case the "civilization" becomes irrelevant, or rather—since there is no legitimate choice between the sacred and other things—that it is the most fallacious of aberrations. The sense of the sacred is fundamental for

---

[29] There is here a kind of perversion of the instinct of self-preservation, a need to consolidate error in order to have one's conscience at peace.

[30] The speculations of Teilhard de Chardin provide a striking example of a theology that has succumbed to microscopes and telescopes, to machines and to their philosophical and social consequences, a "fall" that would have been unthinkable had there been here the slightest direct intellective knowledge of immaterial realities. The inhuman aspect of the doctrine in question is very telling.

[31] What is most integrally human is what gives man the best chances for the hereafter, and this is what also corresponds most deeply to his nature.

every civilization because fundamental for man; the sacred—that which is immutable, inviolable, and thus infinitely majestic—is in the very substance of our spirit and of our existence. The world is miserable because men live beneath themselves; the error of modern man is that he wants to reform the world without having either the will or the power to reform man, and this flagrant contradiction, this attempt to make a better world on the basis of a worsened humanity, can only end in the very abolition of what is human, and therefore the abolition of happiness too. Reforming man means binding him again to Heaven, reestablishing the broken link; it means tearing him away from the reign of the passions, from the cult of matter, quantity, and cunning, and reintegrating him into the world of the spirit and serenity, we would even say: into the world of sufficient reason.

In this vein of thought, and because there are so-called Muslims who do not hesitate to describe Islam as "pre-civilization", a distinction must be drawn here between a "fall", a "decadence", a "degeneration", and a "deviation". The whole of humanity is "fallen" through the loss of Eden and also, more particularly, because it is involved in the "iron age"; some civilizations, such as most traditional worlds of the East at the time of the expansion of the West, can be called "decadent";[32] a great many savage tribes are "degenerate" according to the degree of their barbarism; as for modern civilization it is "deviated" and this deviation is itself more and more combined with a real decadence that is especially palpable in literature and art. In answer to the qualification used above, we would readily speak of "post-civilization".

Here a question arises, perhaps outside of our main subject, but nonetheless connected with it since in speaking of Islam it is necessary to speak of tradition and in dealing with tradition it must be explained what it is not. The question is this: what is the practical significance of the requirement, so often formulated today, that religion ought to be oriented toward social problems? Quite simply, it means that reli-

---

[32] It was not, however, this decadence which rendered them open to colonization, but on the contrary their normal character, which excluded "technical progress"; Japan, which was hardly decadent, was no more successful in resisting the first assault of Western arms than other countries. We hasten to add that in these days the old opposition between West and East is hardly valid anywhere in the political field or is valid only within nations; outwardly there are only variants of the modern spirit which oppose one another.

gion ought to be oriented toward machines, or, to put it bluntly, that theology ought to become the handmaid of industry. No doubt there have always been social problems resulting from abuses due on the one hand to the fall of humanity and on the other to the existence of very large collectivities containing uneven groupings. But in the Middle Ages—which by its own standard was far from being an ideal epoch—and even much later, the craftsman drew a large measure of happiness from his work, which was still human, and from surroundings which were still in conformity with an ethnic and spiritual genius. Whatever the situation may have been at that time, the modern worker exists and the truth does concern him: he should understand, first of all, that there is no question of attributing to the wholly artificial quality of "worker" a character belonging to an intrinsically human category, since the men who are in fact workers may belong to any natural category whatsoever; secondly, he should understand that every outward situation is only relative, man always remaining man; that truth and spiritual life can adapt themselves, thanks to their universality and imperative character, to any situation whatever, so that the so-called "problem of the industrial worker" is at root quite simply the problem of man placed in those particular circumstances, and so still the problem of man as such; finally, that truth does not require that we allow ourselves to be oppressed, possibly by forces which, themselves also, only serve machines, any more than the truth allows man to base his demands on envy, which in any case could never be the measure of man's needs. It must be added that, if all men obeyed the profound law inscribed in the human condition, there would no longer be either social or general human problems. Leaving aside the question of whether mankind can be reformed—which in fact is impossible—one should in any case reform oneself and never believe that inward realities are of no importance for the equilibrium of the world. It is just as important to beware of a chimerical optimism as of despair, because the former is contrary to the ephemeral reality of the world we live in and the latter to the eternal reality we already bear within ourselves, which alone makes our human and earthly condition intelligible.

According to an Arab proverb which reflects the Muslim's attitude to life, "slowness comes from God and haste from Satan",[33] and

---

[33] *Festina lente*, the Ancients would say.

this leads to the following reflection: as machines devour time, modern man is always in a hurry, and as this perpetual lack of time creates in him reflexes of haste and superficiality, modern man mistakes these reflexes—which compensate all kinds of disequilibrium—for proofs of superiority and scorns the men of old with their "idyllic" habits, and especially the old-style Oriental with his slow gait and his turban, which takes so long to wind on. Having no experience of it, people today cannot imagine what the qualitative content of traditional "slowness" consisted of nor the manner of "dreaming" of men of olden days; instead they content themselves with caricature, which is much simpler and is moreover demanded by an illusory instinct of self-preservation. If the outlook of today is so largely determined by social preoccupations—clearly materialistic in their basis—it is not merely because of the social consequences of mechanization and the human condition this engenders, but also because of the absence of any contemplative atmosphere such as is essential to the welfare of man whatever his "standard of living", to use this expression as barbarous as it is common.[34]

We referred to the turban when speaking of the slowness of traditional rhythms,[35] and on this point we wish to pause somewhat. The association of ideas between the turban and Islam is far from fortuitous: "The turban", said the Prophet, "is a frontier between faith and unbelief"; and he also said: "My community shall not decline so long as they wear

---

[34] Any contemplative attitude is today labeled "escapism"—in German *Weltflucht*—hence any refusal to situate total truth and the meaning of life in external agitation. A hypocritically utilitarian attachment to the world is dignified as "responsibilities" and people hasten to ignore the fact that flight—supposing it is only a question of that—is not always a wrong attitude.

[35] This slowness does not exclude speed when speed follows from the natural properties of things or results naturally from the circumstances, showing it then to be in accord with the corresponding symbolisms and spiritual attitudes. It is in the nature of a horse to be able to gallop and an Arab *fantasia* is executed at high speed; a sword stroke must be of lightning speed; so must life and death decisions. The ablution before prayer must be made quickly.

the turban." The following *ahādīth* are also quoted in this context: "At the Day of Judgment a man shall receive a light for each turn of turban (*kawrah*) round his head"; "Wear turbans, for thus you will gain in generosity." The point we wish to make is that the turban is deemed to give the believer a sort of gravity, a consecration, and a majestic humility;[36] it sets him apart from chaotic and dissipated creatures—the *dāllūn*, the "strayers", of the *Fātihah*—fixing him on a divine axis—*as-sirāt al-mustaqīm*, the "straight path" of the same prayer—and thus destines him for contemplation; in brief the turban is like a celestial counterpoise to all that is profane and empty. Since it is the head, the brain, which is for us the plane of our choice between true and false, the lasting and the ephemeral, the real and the illusory, or between what is grave and what is futile, it is the head which should also bear the mark of this choice; the material symbol is meant to reinforce the spiritual consciousness, and this is, moreover, true of every religious headdress and even of every liturgical vestment or merely traditional dress. The turban so to speak "envelops" man's thinking, ever prone to dissipation, forgetfulness, and infidelity; it recalls the sacred imprisoning of his passional nature prone to flee from God.[37] It is the function of the Koranic Law to re-establish a primordial equilibrium that was lost; hence the *hadīth*: "Wear turbans and thus distinguish yourselves from the peoples ('lacking in equilibrium') who came before you."[38]

At this point something must be said about the Muslim woman's veil. Islam makes a sharp separation between the world of man and that of woman, between the collectivity as a whole and the family

---

[36] In Islam the angels and all the prophets are represented as wearing turbans, sometimes of different colors according to the symbolism.

[37] When Saint Vincent de Paul designed the headdress of the Sisters of Charity, he intended to impose on their gaze a kind of reminiscence of monastic isolation.

[38] Hatred of the turban, like hatred of the "romantic" or the "picturesque" or what belongs to folklore, is explained by the fact that the "romantic" worlds are precisely those in which God is still plausible. When people want to abolish Heaven, it is logical to start by creating an atmosphere which makes spiritual things appear out of place; in order to be able to declare successfully that God is unreal they have to construct around man a false reality, one that is inevitably inhuman because only the inhuman can exclude God. The objective is to falsify the imagination and thus to kill it; the modern mentality is the most prodigious lack of imagination possible.

which is its kernel, or between the street and the home, just as it sharply separates society and the individual or exoterism and esoterism. The home—and woman who is its incarnation—is regarded as having an inviolable and hence a sacred character. Woman even in a certain manner incarnates esoterism by reason of certain aspects of her nature and function; "esoteric truth", the *Haqīqah*, is "felt" as a feminine reality, and the same is true of *barakah*. Moreover the veil and the seclusion of woman are connected with the final cyclic phase in which we live—where passions and malice are increasingly dominant—and they present a certain analogy with the forbidding of wine and the veiling of the mysteries.

— ⁘ —

The differences between traditional worlds are not limited to differences of perspective and of dogma, there are also differences of temperament and of taste: thus the European temperament does not readily tolerate exaggeration as a mode of expression, whereas for the Easterner hyperbole is a way of highlighting an idea or an intention, of emphasizing the sublime or of expressing what cannot be described, such as the apparition of an angel or the radiance of a saint. A Westerner attaches importance to factual exactitude, but his lack of intuition regarding the "immutable essences" (*aʿyān thābitah*) offsets this, greatly diminishing the range of his critical insight; an Easterner on the contrary has a sense of the metaphysical transparency of things but is apt to neglect—rightly or wrongly depending on the case—the accuracy of earthly facts; for him the symbol is more important than the experience.

Symbolical hyperbole is in part explained by the following principle: between a form and its content there is not only analogy, but also opposition; if the form, or the expression, must normally reflect what it transmits, it can also be "neglected" in favor of the pure content owing to the distance separating the "outward" from the "inward", or it may be as it were "shattered" by the superabundance of the content. The man who is attached only to the "inward" may have no awareness of outer forms, or conversely; one man will appear sublime because he is a saint and another pitiful for the same reason; and what is true of men is true also of their speech and writings. Sometimes the price of profundity or sublimity is a lack of critical sense regarding appearances; but this certainly does not have to be the case, for we are dealing here only with a paradoxical possibility. In other words, to take the example of an artist, when pious exaggeration arises from an overflowing of evidence and of sincerity, it has the "right" not to notice the fact that its draftsmanship is poor and it would be ungrateful and disproportionate to reproach it for this. Piety as well as truthfulness requires us to see the excellence of the intention and not the weakness of the formal expression wherever such an alternative presents itself.

The pillars (*arkān*) of Islam are these: the double testimony of faith (the *shahādatān*), the canonical prayer repeated five times a day (the *salāt*), the fast of Ramadan (*siyām*, *sawm*), the tithe (*zakāt*), the pilgrimage (the *hajj*); to these is sometimes added the holy war (the *jihād*), which has a more or less accidental character since it depends on circumstances;[39] as for the ablution (the *wudhū* or the *ghusl* according to circumstances), it is not mentioned separately for it is a condition of the prayer. As we have already seen, the *Shahādah* indicates in the final analysis—and it is the most universal meaning which interests us here—discernment between the Real and the unreal and then, in the second part, the attaching of the world to God in respect both of its origin and of its end, for to look on things separately from God is already unbelief (*nifāq*, *shirk*, or *kufr*, as the case may be). The prayer integrates man into the rhythm of universal worship and—through the ritual orientation toward the Kaaba—into its centripetal order; the ablution preceding the prayer brings man back virtually to the primordial state and in a certain manner to pure Being. The fast cuts man off from the continual and devouring flux of carnal life, introducing into our flesh a kind of death and purification;[40] the alms vanquish egoism

---

[39] The same applies on the plane of the human microcosm both to the intelligence and to the will: neither desire nor discernment is exercised in the absence of an object.

[40] Ramadan in the Muslim year is what Sunday is in the Christian week or the Sabbath in the Jewish week.

and avarice and actualize the solidarity of all creatures, for alms are a fasting of the soul, even as the fast proper is an almsgiving of the body. The pilgrimage is a prefiguration of the inward journey toward the kaaba of the heart and purifies the community, just as the circulation of the blood, passing through the heart, purifies the body; finally the holy war is—always from the point of view adopted here—an external and collective manifestation of discernment between truth and error; it is like the centrifugal and negative complement of the pilgrimage—complement, not opposite, because it remains attached to the center and is positive through its religious content.

Let us recapitulate once again the essential characteristics of Islam as seen from the viewpoint that matters to us. What is striking about Islam, under normal conditions, is the unshakable character of its conviction and also the combative nature of its faith; these two complementary aspects, the one inward and static and the other outward and dynamic, derive essentially from a consciousness of the Absolute, which on the one hand renders one immune to doubt and on the other repels error with violence;[41] the Absolute—or consciousness of the Absolute—thus engenders in the soul the qualities of rock and of lightning, the former being represented by the Kaaba, which is the center, and the latter by the sword of the holy war, which marks the periphery. On the spiritual plane Islam lays stress on knowledge, since it is knowledge which realizes the maximum of unity in the sense that it pierces the illusion of plurality and goes beyond the duality of subject and object; love is a form and a criterion of unitive knowledge or, from another point of view, a stage on the way to it. On the earthly plane Islam seeks equilibrium and puts each thing in its place; moreover it makes a clear distinction between the individual and the collectivity while also taking account of their reciprocal solidarity. *Al-Islām* is the human condition brought into equilibrium on the basis of the Absolute, both in man's soul and in society.

---

[41] In this perspective error is the denial of the Absolute or attributing an absolute character to the relative or the contingent, or the admitting of more than one Absolute. This metaphysical intention must not, however, be confused with the associations of ideas to which it can give rise in the consciousness of Muslims, associations that can have a merely symbolic meaning.

The foundation of spiritual ascent is that God is pure Spirit and that man resembles Him fundamentally through the intelligence; man goes toward God by means of that which is, in him, most conformable to God—namely the Intellect—which is at once both penetration and contemplation and has as its "supernaturally natural" content the Absolute which enlightens and delivers. The character of a path depends on a given preliminary definition of man: if man is defined as passion, as the general perspective of Christianity would have it,[42] then the path is suffering; if as desire, then the path is renunciation; if as will, then the path is effort; if as intelligence, then the path is discernment, concentration, contemplation. This could also be expressed as follows: the path is such and such "to the extent that"—not "because"—man has such and such a nature; this enables us to understand why Muslim spirituality, though founded on the mystery of knowledge, nonetheless also includes both renunciation and love.

The Prophet said: "God has created nothing more noble than intelligence, and His wrath is on him who scorns it", and he also said: "God is beautiful and He loves beauty." These two sayings are characteristic of Islam: for it the world is an immense book filled with "signs" (*āyāt*), or symbols—elements of beauty—which speak to our understanding and are addressed to "those who understand". The world is made up of forms, and they are as it were the fragments of a celestial music that has become frozen; knowledge or sanctity dissolves our frozen state and liberates the inner melody.[43] Here we must recall the verse in the Koran which speaks of the "stones from which streams spring forth", whereas there are hearts which are "harder than stones", a passage reminiscent of the "living water" of Christ and of the "rivers

---

[42] Though there is here no principial restriction.

[43] The dervish songs and dances are symbolical, and thus spiritually efficacious, anticipations of the rhythms of immortality, and also—what amounts to the same thing—of the divine nectar which secretly flows in the arteries of all created things. Herein, moreover, lies an example of a certain opposition between the esoteric and exoteric orders which cannot fail to arise incidentally: both music and dance are proscribed by the common Law, but esoterism makes use of them as it does of the symbolism of wine, which is a forbidden beverage. In this there is nothing absurd, for in one respect the world too is opposed to God, though "made in His image". Exoterism follows the "letter" and esoterism the "divine intention".

of living water" which according to the Gospel, "flow from the hearts of saints".[44]

These "streams" or "living waters" are beyond all formal and separating crystallizations; they belong to that domain of "essential truth" (*Haqīqah*) toward which the path (*Tarīqah*) leads—starting out from the "collective road" (*Sharī ah*) formed by the general Law—and at this level truth is no longer a system of concepts—although intrinsically adequate and indispensable—but an "element", like fire or water. And this leads us to a further consideration: if there are different religions—each of them by definition speaking an absolute and hence an exclusive language—this is because the difference between the religions corresponds exactly, by analogy, to the difference between human individuals. In other words, if the religions are true it is because each time it is God who has spoken, and if they are different, it is because God has spoken in different languages according to the diversity of the receptacles. Finally, if they are absolute and exclusive, it is because in each of them God has said "I". We know all too well, and it is moreover in the natural order of things, that this thesis is not acceptable on the level of exoteric orthodoxies,[45] but is so on the level of universal orthodoxy, that to which Muhyi ad-Din Ibn Arabi, the great enunciator of *gnosis* in Islam, bore witness in these terms: "My heart is open to every form: it is a pasture for gazelles,[46] and a cloister for Christian monks, a temple for idols, the Kaaba of the pilgrim, the tables of the Torah, and the book of the Koran. I practice the religion of Love;[47]

---

[44] Jalal ad-Din Rumi said: "The ocean that I am is drowned in its own waves. Strange limitless ocean that I am!"

[45] This word indicates a limitation, but *a priori* contains no reproach, the human bases being what they are.

[46] The "gazelles" signify spiritual states.

[47] Here it is not a question of *mahabbah* in the psychological or methodological sense but of truth that is lived and of "divine attraction". Here "love" is opposed to "forms" which are envisaged as "cold" and as "dead". Saint Paul also says that "the letter killeth, but the spirit maketh alive". "Spirit" and "love" are here synonymous.

in whatsoever direction His caravans advance,[48] the religion of Love shall be my religion and my faith" (*Tarjumān al-ashwāq*).[49]

---

[48] Literally: "His camels". "Camels", like the "gazelles" above, here indicate realities of the spirit; they represent the inward and outward consequences—or the dynamic modes—of "love" or in other words of "essential consciousness".

[49] Similarly, Jalal ad-Din Rumi says in his quatrains: "If the image of our Beloved is in the temple of idols, it is an absolute error to circumambulate the Kaaba. If the Kaaba is deprived of His perfume, it is a synagogue. And, if in the synagogue we feel the perfume of union with Him, the synagogue is our Kaaba." In the Koran this universalism is, among others, formulated in these two verses: "To God belongeth the East and the West; whithersoever ye turn, there is the Countenance of God" (2:115)—"Say: Call '*Allāh*' or call '*ar-Rahmān*'; whatever the Name ye call, to Him belong the most beautiful Names" (17:110). In this second verse the Divine Names can signify spiritual perspectives and so the religions. The various religions are like the beads of the rosary; the cord is *gnosis*, their single essence passing through them all.

The Koran and the *Sunnah*

The great theophany of Islam is the Koran; it presents itself as being a "discernment" (*furqān*) between truth and error.[1] In a sense the whole of the Koran—one of the names of which is indeed *al-Furqān* ("the Discernment")—is a sort of multiple paraphrase of the fundamental discernment expressed by the *Shahādah*; its whole content is summed up in the words: "Truth hath come and error [*al-bātil*, the empty, or the inconsistent] hath vanished away; lo! error is ever bound to vanish" (Koran 17:81).[2]

Before considering the message of the Koran, we wish to speak about its form and the principles determining that form. An Arab poet once claimed that he could write a book superior to the Koran, disputing its excellence even from the mere standpoint of style. Such a judgment, which is clearly contrary to the traditional thesis of Islam, is understandable in the case of a man who does not know that the excellence of a sacred book is not *a priori* of a literary order; many indeed are the texts conveying a spiritual meaning in which logical clarity is joined to powerful language or grace of expression without their having on this account a sacred character. That is to say, the sacred Scriptures are not such because of the subject they deal with or the manner in which they deal with it but by reason of their degree of inspiration, or what amounts to the same thing, by virtue of their divine origin; it is this which determines the content of the book, not the converse. Like the Bible, the Koran may speak of a multitude of things other than God; for example, it speaks of the devil, of the holy war, of the laws of succession, and so on and so forth without being on that account less sacred, whereas other books may treat of God and of sublime matters without being on that account the Divine Word.

For Muslim orthodoxy the Koran is not only the uncreated Word of God—uncreated though expressing itself through created elements

---

[1] In this context it is significant that in Islam God Himself is often called *al-Haqq*, the Truth. The Sufi al-Hallaj exclaimed: *Anā'l-Haqq*, "I am the Truth", not "I am Love".

[2] Or, in another passage: "... We (*Allāh*) strike error with Truth that it may be crushed, and lo! error vanisheth away" (21:18).

such as words, sounds, and letters—but also the model *par excellence* of the perfection of language. Seen from outside, however, this book appears, except for approximately the last quarter, the form of which is highly poetic—though it is not poetry—to be a collection of sayings and stories that is more or less incoherent and sometimes incomprehensible at first approach. The reader who is not forewarned, whether he reads the text in translation or in Arabic, runs up against obscurities, repetitions, tautologies, and, in most of the long *sūrah*s, against a certain dryness, unless he has at least the "sensory consolation" of that beauty of sound which emerges from ritual and correctly intoned reading. But such difficulties are to be met with in one degree or another in most sacred Scriptures.[3] The seeming incoherence of these texts[4]—for instance the Song of Songs or certain passages of the Pauline Epistles—always has the same cause, namely the incommensurable disproportion between the Spirit on the one hand and the limited resources of human language on the other: it is as though the poor and coagulated language of mortal man would break under the formidable pressure of the Heavenly Word into a thousand fragments, or as if God, in order to express a thousand truths, had but a dozen words at his disposal and so was compelled to make use of allusions heavy with meaning, of ellipses, abridgements, and symbolical syntheses. A sacred Scripture—and let us not forget that for Christianity Scripture includes not only the Gospels but the whole Bible with all its enigmas and seeming scan-

---

[3] There are two principal modes or degrees of inspiration—one direct and the other indirect—represented in the case of the New Testament by the sayings of Christ and by the Apocalypse for the direct mode, and by the stories in the Gospels and by the Epistles for the indirect. In Judaism this difference is expressed by comparing the inspiration of Moses to a luminous mirror and that of the other prophets to a darkened mirror. Among Hindu sacred books the texts of secondary inspiration (*smriti*) are in general more easily accessible and seem more homogeneous than the *Veda*, which is directly inspired (*shruti*), and this shows that the immediate intelligibility and readily perceived beauty of a text are in no way criteria of inspiration or of the degree of inspiration.

[4] It is this "incoherent" surface of the language of the Koran—not the grammar or the syntax—with which the poet mentioned above considered he should find fault. The style of the revealed Books is always normative. Goethe characterized very well the style of sacred texts in his *Westöstlicher Diwan*: "Thy song turns like the vault of heaven; the origin and the end are ever identical."

dals—is a totality, a diversified image of Being, diversified and trans-figured for the sake of the human receptacle; it is a light that wishes to make itself visible to clay, or wants to take the form of that clay; or still in other words, it is a truth which since it must address itself to beings made of clay or of ignorance, has no means of expression other than the very substance of the natural error of which our soul is made.[5]

"God speaks tersely", say the Rabbis and this also explains both the bold ellipses, at first sight incomprehensible, and the superimposed levels of meaning found in the Revelations.[6] Moreover—and herein lies a crucial principle—for God the truth lies in the spiritual or social efficacy of the words or the symbol, not in the factual accuracy when this is psychologically inoperative or even harmful; God first wants to save, rather than to inform, and His concern is with wisdom and im-mortality, not with outward knowledge, still less with curiosity. Christ called his body "the Temple", which may seem astonishing when one thinks that this term primarily, and apparently more logically, des-ignated a stone building; but the stone Temple was much less than Christ the receptacle of the living God—since Christ had come—and in reality the term "Temple" applied with far more reason to Christ than to the building made by the hands of men; it can even be said that the Temple, whether that of Solomon or that of Herod, was the image of the body of Christ, temporal succession not entering into question for God; in this manner sacred Scriptures at times displace words and

[5] In his *Kitāb fīhi mā fīhi*, Jalal ad-Din Rumi wrote: "The Koran is like a young married woman: even if you try to remove her veil she will not show herself to you. If you discuss the Koran you will discover nothing and no joy will come to you. Because you have tried to pull off the veil, the Koran refuses itself to you; by employing cunning and making itself ugly in your sight and undesirable, it is saying to you: 'I am not the one you love.' Thus it can in this manner show itself under any kind of light." See also *Discourses of Rumi* (Murray, 1961), p. 236. According to the teaching of Saint Augus-tine and other Fathers, and repeated by Pius XII in his encyclical *Divino Afflante*: "God has purposely strewn difficulties throughout the Holy Books He has Himself inspired in order that we may be stimulated to read and study them with greater attention and in order to exercise us in humility by the salutary recognition of the limited capacity of our intelligence."

[6] For instance, it is said that the *Bhagavad Gītā* can be read according to seven different threads of meaning. We have mentioned this principle several times in our previous works.

even facts for the sake of a higher truth which eludes men. But it is not merely intrinsic difficulties that are found in the revealed Books, there is also the matter of their distance in time and the differences in mentality in different periods, or rather the qualitative inequality of the phases of the human cycle; at the origin of a tradition—whether we are speaking of the age of the *Rishi*s or of that of Muhammad—the language was different from what it is today; the words were not outworn, they then contained infinitely more than we can divine; many things which were evident for the reader of earlier times could be passed over in silence but needed to be rendered explicit—not added to—at a later stage.[7]

A sacred text with its seeming contradictions and obscurities is in some ways like a mosaic, or even an anagram; but it suffices to consult the orthodox—thus divinely guided—commentaries in order to find out with what intention a particular affirmation was made and in what respects it is valid, or what the underlying implications are that enable one to connect elements which at first sight appear incongruous. These commentaries sprang from the oral tradition which from the beginning accompanied the Revelation, or else they sprang by inspiration from the same supernatural source; thus their role is not only to insert missing, though implicit, parts of the text and to specify in what relationship or in what sense a given thing should be understood, but also to explain the diverse symbolisms, often simultaneous and superimposed one on another. In short, the commentaries providentially form part of the tradition; they are as it were the sap of its continuity, even if their committal to writing or in certain cases their remanifestation after some interruption occurred only at a relatively late date in order to meet the requirements of a particular historical period. "The ink of the learned (in the Law or in the Spirit) is like the blood of the martyrs", said the Prophet, and this indicates the capital part played in every traditional cosmos by orthodox commentaries.[8]

---

[7] We have no wish to devote space here to the deployment of unintelligence in modern "textual criticism", whether "psychological" or of some other kind. Suffice it to point out that in our times the devil has not only laid hold on charity, which he seeks to reduce to an atheistic and materialistic altruism, but has also taken hold of the exegesis of Holy Writ.

[8] Jalal ad-Din Rumi, in the work quoted above, wrote: "God Most High does not

According to the Jewish tradition it is not the literal form of the holy Scriptures which has the force of law, but solely their orthodox commentaries. The *Torah* is a "closed" book and does not yield its meaning; it is the sages who "open" it, for it is in the very nature of the *Torah* to require from the beginning the commentary of the *Mishnah*. It is said that the *Mishnah* was given out in the Tabernacle, when Joshua transmitted it to the Sanhedrin; by this the Sanhedrin was consecrated and thus instituted by God like the *Torah* and at the same time. And this is important: the oral commentary, which Moses had received on Sinai and transmitted to Joshua, was in part lost and had to be reconstituted by the sages on the basis of the *Torah*: this shows very clearly that *gnosis* includes both a "horizontal" and a "vertical" continuity, or rather that it accompanies the written Law in a manner that is both "horizontal" and continuous and also "vertical" and discontinuous; the secrets are passed from hand to hand, but the spark may at any time leap forth on mere contact with the revealed Text depending on a particular human receptacle and on the imponderables of the Holy Spirit. It is also said that God gave the *Torah* during the daytime and the *Mishnah* by night;[9] and again, that the *Torah* is infinite in itself whereas the *Mishnah* is inexhaustible through its movement in time. We would add that the *Torah* is like the ocean which is static and inexhaustible, and the *Mishnah* like a river which is always in motion. *Mutatis mutandis* all this applies to every Revelation and particularly to Islam.

In the case of Islam, or rather as regards its esoterism, the following argument has been made in its favor: if there must be authorities for the Faith (*īmān*) and the Law (*islām*), there must also be authorities for the Path (*ihsān*), and these are none other than the Sufis and their duly qualified representatives. The logical necessity for authorities in

---

speak to just any man; like the kings of this world He does not speak with any cobbler; He has chosen ministers and deputies. Man accedes to God by going through the intermediaries He has appointed. God Most High has made an election among his creatures in order that a man may come to Him by going through him whom He has chosen." This passage, which refers to the Prophets, is also applicable to the authorized interpreters of the tradition.

[9] The reader will recall here that Nicodemus came to find Christ by night, and this implies a reference to esoterism or to *gnosis*.

this third domain—which the theologians of "the outward" (*ulamā azh-zhāhir*) are forced to admit, though they cannot explain it—is one of the proofs of the legitimacy of Sufism, therefore also of its doctrines and methods as well as of its organizations and masters.

These considerations concerning the sacred Books call for some sort of definition of the epithet "sacred" itself: that is sacred which in the first place is attached to the transcendent order, secondly, possesses the character of absolute certainty and, thirdly, eludes the comprehension and control of the ordinary human mind. Imagine a tree the leaves of which, having no kind of direct knowledge about the root, hold a discussion about whether or not a root exists and what its form is if it does; if a voice then came from the root telling them that the root does exist and what its form is, that message would be sacred. The sacred is the presence of the center in the periphery, of the immutable in the moving; dignity is essentially an expression of it, for in dignity too the center manifests outwardly; the heart is revealed in gestures. The sacred introduces a quality of the absolute into relative things and confers on perishable things a texture of eternity.

In order to understand the full scope of the Koran we must take into consideration three things: its doctrinal content, which we find made explicit in the great canonical treatises of Islam such as those of Abu Hanifah and at-Tahawi; its narrative content, which depicts all the vicissitudes of the soul; and its divine magic or its mysterious and in a sense miraculous power.[10] These sources of metaphysical and eschatological doctrine, of mystical psychology and theurgic power lie hidden under a veil of breathless utterances, often clashing in shock, of crystal-

---

[10] Only this power can explain the importance of the recitation of the Koran. In his *Risālat al-Quds*, Ibn Arabi quotes the case of Sufis who spent their whole life in reading or in ceaselessly reciting the Koran, and this would be inconceivable and even impossible to realize were there not, behind the husk of the literal text, a concrete and active spiritual presence which goes beyond the words and the mind. Moreover it is by virtue of this power of the Koran that certain verses can chase away demons and heal illnesses, at least in certain circumstances.

line and fiery images, but also of passages majestic in rhythm, woven of every fiber of the human condition.

But the supernatural character of this Book lies not only in its doctrinal content, its psychological and mystical truth, and its transmuting magic, it also appears in its most outward efficacy, in the miracle of its expansion; the effects of the Koran in space and time bear no relation to the literary impression which the written words may give to a profane reader. Like every sacred Scripture, the Koran is also *a priori* a "closed" book, though "open" in another respect, that of the elementary truths of salvation.

It is necessary to distinguish in the Koran between the general excellence of the Divine Word and the particular excellence of a given content which may be superimposed as, for example, when it is a question of God or of His qualities; it is like the distinction between the excellence of gold and that of some masterpiece made from gold. The masterpiece directly manifests the nobility of gold; similarly the nobility of the content of one or another sacred verse expresses the nobility of the Koranic substance, of the Divine Word, which in itself is undifferentiated; it cannot, however, add to the infinite value of that Word. This is also related to the "divine magic", the transforming and sometimes theurgic virtue of the divine discourse referred to above.

This magic is closely linked with the actual language of the Revelation, which is Arabic, and so translations are canonically illegitimate and ritually ineffectual. A language is sacred when God has spoken in it;[11] and in order that God should speak in it, it must have certain characteristics such as are not found in any modern language; finally, it is essential to understand that after a certain cyclical period and the hardening of the terrestrial ambience which it comprises, God no longer

---

[11] From this the reader might conclude that Aramaic is a sacred language since Christ spoke it, but here three reservations must be made: firstly, in Christianity, as in Buddhism, it is the *Avatāra* himself who is the Revelation so that, apart from their doctrine, the Scriptures have not the central and plenary function which they have in other traditions; secondly, the precise Aramaic words used by Christ have not been preserved, which corroborates what has just been said; thirdly, for Christ himself Hebrew was the sacred language. Though the *Talmud* affirms that "the Angels do not understand Aramaic", this language has nonetheless a particularly high liturgical value; long before Christ it was "made sacred" by Daniel and Esdras.

speaks, at least not as Revealer. In other words, after a certain period, whatever is put forward as new religion is inevitably false;[12] the Middle Ages mark roughly the final limit.[13]

Like the world, the Koran is at the same time one and multiple. The world is a multiplicity which disperses and divides; the Koran is a multiplicity which draws together and leads to Unity. The multiplicity of the holy Book—the diversity of its words, aphorisms, images, and stories—fills the soul and then absorbs it and imperceptibly transposes it into the climate of serenity and immutability by a sort of "divine ruse".[14] The soul, which is accustomed to the flux of phenomena, yields to this flux without resistance; it lives in phenomena and is by them divided and dispersed—even more than that, it actually becomes what it thinks and does. The revealed Discourse has the virtue of accepting this tendency while reversing its motion thanks to the celestial nature of the content and the language, so that the fishes of the soul swim without distrust and following their habitual rhythm into the divine net.[15] The mind, to the degree that it can bear it, must be infused with a consciousness of the metaphysical contrast between "substance" and "accidents"; a mind thus regenerated keeps its thoughts first of all on God and thinks all things in Him. In other words, through the mosaic

[12] The same can be said of initiatic orders. One can—or rather God can—create a new branch of an ancient lineage or found a congregation around a pre-existing initiation, if there is an imperative reason for doing so and if this type of congregation forms part of the practices of the tradition in question, but in no circumstance has anyone a right to found a "society" having "Self-Realization" as its aim, for the simple reason that such a realization is exclusively the province of the traditional organizations. Even if someone sought to incorporate a genuine initiation into the framework of a "society" or of some kind of "spiritualist" fellowship—thus a profane association—one can be certain that this very framework would wholly paralyze its efficacy and inevitably bring about deviations. Spiritual treasures do not fit into just any sort of framework.

[13] In fact Islam is the last world religion. As for the Sikh brotherhood, this is an esoterism analogous to that of Kabir, the special position of which is explained by the quite exceptional conditions arising from the contiguity of Hinduism and Sufism; but here too it is a case of a final possibility.

[14] In the sense of the Sanskrit term *upāya*.

[15] This is true of every sacred Scripture and is notably true of Bible history: the vicissitudes of Israel are those of the soul seeking its Lord. In Christianity this function of "transforming magic" appertains especially to the Psalms.

of passages, phrases, and words, God extinguishes the agitation of the mind by Himself taking on the appearance of mental agitation. The Koran is like an image of everything the human brain can think and feel, and it is by this means that God exhausts human disquiet, infusing into the believer silence, serenity, and peace.

In Islam, as also in Judaism, the Revelation relates essentially to the symbolism of the book: the whole Universe is a book whose letters are the cosmic elements—the *dharma*s as Buddhists would say—which, by their innumerable combinations and under the influence of the divine Ideas, produce worlds, beings, and things. The words and sentences of the book are the manifestations of the creative possibilities, the words as content, the sentences as container; the sentence is, in effect, like a space—or a duration—comprising a predestined series of different combinations of possibilities and constituting what may be called a "divine plan". This symbolism of the book is distinguished from that of speech by its static character: speech is situated in time and implies repetition, whereas a book contains affirmations in a simultaneous mode; in a book there is a certain leveling out, all the letters being similar, and this is moreover highly characteristic of the Islamic perspective. But this perspective, like that of the *Torah*, also includes the symbolism of speech, which is then identified with the origin; God speaks and His Speech is crystallized in the form of a Book. Clearly this crystallization has its prototype in God, and indeed it can be affirmed that the "Speech" and the "Book" are two sides of pure Being, which is the Principle that both creates and reveals; however, it is said that the Koran is the Word of God, not that the Word proceeds from the Koran or from the Book.

First of all the "Word" is Being as the eternal Act of Beyond-Being, of the Divine Essence;[16] but, taken as the sum of the possibilities of manifestation, Being is the "Book". Then, on the level of Being itself,

---

[16] The *Gottheit* or *Urgrund* of Meister Eckhart's doctrine.

the Word—or according to another image the Pen[17]—is the creative Act, while the Book is the creative Substance;[18] there is here a connection with *Natura naturans* and *Natura naturata* in the highest sense attributable to these concepts. Finally, on the plane of Existence—or, it could be said, of Manifestation—the Word is the "Divine Spirit", the central and universal Intellect which brings about and perpetuates the miracle of creation, as it were "by delegation"; in which case the Book is the sum of the "crystallized" possibilities, the world of innumerable creatures. The "Word" is then the aspect of "dynamic" simplicity or of simple "act", while the "Book" is the aspect of "static" complexity or differentiated "being".[19]

Or again: it can be said that God created the world like a Book and His Revelation came down into the world in the form of a Book; but man has to hear the Divine Word in Creation and by that Word ascend toward God; God became Book for man and man has to become Word for God; man is a "book" through his microcosmic multiplicity and his state of existential coagulation, whereas God, when envisaged in this context,[20] is pure Word through His metacosmic Unity and His pure principial activity.

The most obvious content of the Koran consists not of doctrinal expositions, but of historical and symbolical narratives and eschatological

---

[17] See also the chapter "*An-Nūr*" in the author's book *L'Oeil du coeur.*

[18] According to Hindu doctrine this is the Divine *Prakriti.*

[19] In Christianity the place of the "Book" is taken by the "Body" with its two complements of "flesh" and "blood" or "bread" and "wine"; *in divinis* the "Body" is, first, the primary self-determination of Divinity, and thus the first "crystallization" of the Infinite; next it is Universal Substance, the true "mystical Body" of Christ; and finally it is the world of creatures, the "crystallized" manifestation of this Body.

[20] For we have seen that God-as-Being is the Book *par excellence*, and that, on the plane of Being, the pole Substance is the first reflection of this Book; the Word, which is its dynamic complement, then becomes the Pen, the vertical axis of creation. However, man too has an aspect of Word represented by his name; God created man in naming him; the soul is a Word of the Creator when considered in its simplicity or its unity.

imagery; the pure doctrine emerges from these two sorts of pictures in which it is set. Leaving aside the majesty of the Arabic text and its quasi-magical resonances, a reader could well become wearied of the content did he not know that it concerns ourselves in a quite concrete and direct way, for the "disbelievers" (the *kāfirūn*), and "associaters" of false divinities with God (the *mushrikūn*), and the hypocrites (the *munāfiqūn*) are within ourselves; likewise that the Prophets represent our Intellect and our consciousness, that all the tales in the Koran are enacted almost daily in our souls, that Mecca is our heart and that almsgiving, the fast, the pilgrimage, and the holy war are so many virtues, whether secret or manifest, or so many contemplative attitudes.

Alongside this interpretation there is another which concerns the phenomena of the world around us. The Koran is the world, both outside and within us, and always connected to God both through the origin and the end; but this world, or these two worlds, show fissures harbingers of death or destruction or, to be more precise, transformation, and this is what the apocalyptic and eschatological *sūrahs* teach us; everything that concerns the world also concerns us, and conversely. These *sūrahs* transmit to us a multiple and striking image of the fragility both of our earthly condition and of matter, then of the ineluctable reabsorption of space and of the elements into the invisible substance of the causal "protocosm"; this is the collapse of the visible world into the immaterial—a collapse, to paraphrase Saint Augustine, "inwards" or "upwards"; it is also when creatures, torn away from the earth, confront the dazzling reality of the Infinite.

In its "surfaces" the Koran presents a cosmology which deals with phenomena and their final end, and in its "edges", a metaphysic of the Real and the unreal.

Not surprisingly, the imagery of the Koran is inspired above all by conflict; Islam was born in an atmosphere of conflict and the soul in search of God must fight. Islam did not invent strife; the world is a constant disequilibrium, for to live means to struggle. But this struggle is only one aspect of the world and it vanishes with the level to which it belongs; hence the whole of the Koran is suffused with a tone of powerful serenity. In psychological terms it could be said that the combative aspect of the Muslim is counterbalanced by his fatalism; in the spiritual life the "holy war" of the spirit against the seducing soul (*an-nafs al-ammārah*) is transcended and transfigured by peace in God, by consciousness of the Absolute; it is as if in the last analysis it were no longer we who are fighting, and this brings us back to the symbiosis of "combat and knowledge" in the *Bhagavad Gītā* and also to certain aspects of the knightly arts in Zen. The practice of Islam, at whatever level, is to repose in effort; Islam is the way of equilibrium and of light which comes to rest upon that equilibrium.

Equilibrium is the link between disequilibrium and union, just as union is the link between equilibrium and unity, which is the "vertical" dimension. Disequilibrium and equilibrium, lack of rhythm and rhythm, separation and union, division and unity: such are the great themes of the Koran and of Islam. Everything in being and in becoming is envisaged in terms of Unity and its gradations, or the mystery of its negation.

For the Christian, what is necessary for coming to God is "unreservedly to renounce oneself", as Saint John of the Cross put it; thus the Christian is astonished to hear from the Muslim that the key to salvation is to believe that God is One; what he cannot know straightaway is that everything depends on the quality—on the "sincerity" (*ikhlās*)—of this belief; what saves is the purity or the totality of the belief, and that totality clearly implies the loss of self, whatever the form in which this is expressed.

As for the negation of the Christian Trinity in the Koran—and this negation is extrinsic and conditional—we must take account of certain shades of meaning. The Trinity can be envisaged according to a "vertical" perspective and according to either of two "horizontal" perspectives, one of them being supreme and the other not: the "vertical" perspective—Beyond-Being, Being, and Existence—envisages the *hypostases* as "descending" from Unity or from the Absolute, or from the Essence it could be said, in other words it envisages the degrees of Reality; the supreme "horizontal" perspective corresponds to the Vedantic triad *Sat* (supra-ontological Reality), *Chit* (absolute Consciousness), and *Ānanda* (infinite Beatitude), which means that it envisages the Trinity inasmuch as it is hidden in Unity;[21] the non-supreme "horizontal" perspective on the contrary situates Unity as an essence hidden within the Trinity, which is then ontological and represents the three fundamental aspects or modes of Pure Being, whence the triad: Being-Wisdom-Will (Father-Son-Spirit). Now the concept of a Trinity seen as an unfolding (*tajallī*) of Unity or of the Absolute is in no way opposed to the unitary doctrine of Islam; what is opposed to it is solely the attribution of absoluteness to the Trinity alone, or even to the ontological Trinity alone, as it is considered in exoterism. This last point of view does not, strictly speaking, attain to the Absolute and this is as much as to say that it attributes an absolute character to what is relative and ignores *Māyā* and the degrees of reality or of illusion; it does not conceive of the metaphysical—but not "pantheistic"[22]—identity between manifestation and the Principle; still less, therefore, does it conceive of the consequence this identity implies from the point of view of the Intellect and the knowledge which delivers.

Here a comment is called for about the "disbelievers", the *kāfirūn*, namely those who according to the Koran do not belong, as do Jews and Christians, to the category of "people of the Book" (*ahl al-Kitāb*). If the religion of these "disbelievers" is false—or if disbelievers are such because their religion is false—why have Sufis declared that God can be present, not only in churches and synagogues, but also in the temples of idolaters? It is because in the "classical" and "traditional" cases of paganism the loss of the full truth and of salvific efficacy results essentially from a profound modification in the mentality of the worshipers and not from the possible falseness of the symbols; in all the religions which surrounded each of the three Semitic forms of monotheism, as also in those forms of "fetishism"[23] still alive today, a mentality once contemplative and hence in possession of a sense of the metaphysical transparency of forms had ended by becoming passional,

---

[21] The Absolute is not the Absolute inasmuch as it contains aspects, but inasmuch as it transcends them; inasmuch as it is Trinity it is therefore not Absolute.

[22] Not pantheistic since it is in no sense "material", nor even "substantial" in the cosmological sense of that term.

[23] This word is here used only as a conventional sign to designate decadent traditions; in using it, we have no intention of judging the value of any particular African or Melanesian tradition.

worldly,[24] and strictly speaking superstitious.[25] The symbol through which the reality symbolized was originally clearly perceived—a reality of which it is rigorously speaking an aspect—became in fact an opaque image that was no longer understood, thus an idol, and this decadence of the general mentality could not fail in turn to react on the tradition itself, weakening and falsifying it in various ways; most of the ancient paganisms were characterized by an intoxicating love of power and sensuality. There is, assuredly, a personal paganism to be met with even within those religions which are objectively living, just as conversely truth and piety may be actualized in a religion which is objectively decadent, but this presupposes in this case the integrity of its symbolism. However, it would be completely mistaken to believe that any of the great world religions alive today could in its turn become pagan; they have not the time to become so, and their sufficient reason for being is, in a sense, that they should endure till the end of the world. That is why they are formally guaranteed by their founders, which is not the case with the great paganisms that have disappeared; these had no human founders and their perennial subsistence was conditional. The primordial perspectives are "spatial" and not "temporal"; Hinduism alone of all the great traditions of the primordial type has had the possibility of being renewed through the ages thanks to its *Avatāra*s.[26] In any case our intention here is not to enter into details

---

[24] According to the Koran, the *kāfir* is in effect characterized by his "worldliness", that is, by his preference for the things of this world and his inadvertence (*ghaflah*) regarding the goods of the next world.

[25] According to the Gospels, the pagans imagine they will be answered "for their much speaking". At root, "superstition" consists in the illusion of taking the means for the end or of worshiping forms for their own sake and not for their transcendent content.

[26] Moreover nothing prevents the possibility of other branches of the primordial tradition—of "hyperborean" or "Atlantean" affiliation—from having also survived on the fringes of history, though this could not be so in the case of the great traditions of urbanized peoples. Apart from this, when speaking of paganism—and we are adopting this conventional term without regard either to its etymology or its unpleasant associations, which chiefly arise from abuses—there is doubtless always need to make a reservation as regards a sapiential esoterism inaccessible to the majority and in fact incapable of acting upon that majority.

but simply to make it clear why, from the point of view of some Sufi, it is not Apollo who is false but the way of regarding him.[27]

But to return to the "people of the Book". If the Koran contains elements of polemic concerning Christianity and all the more concerning Judaism, it is because Islam came after these religions, and this means that it was obliged—and there is always a point of view allowing of doing so—to present itself as an improvement on what preceded it. In other words the Koran enunciates a perspective which makes it possible to go beyond certain formal aspects of the two more ancient monotheisms. The situation is analogous, not only in the position of Christianity in relation to Judaism—where the point is self-evident by reason of the messianic idea and because the former is like a "bhaktic" esoterism of the latter—but also in the attitude of Buddhism toward Brahmanism; here too the later appearance in time coincides with a perspective that is symbolically, though not intrinsically, superior. The tradition that is apparently being superseded clearly has no need to take account of this fact, since each perspective is a universe unto itself—thus a center and a standard—and since in its own way it contains all valid points of view. By the logic of things the later tradition is "condemned" to the symbolic attitude of superiority,[28] on pain of non-existence one might almost say. But there is also a positive symbolism of anteriority and in this respect the new tradition, which is from its own point of view the final one, must incarnate "what came before", or "what has always existed"; its novelty—or glory—is consequently its absolute "anteriority".

Pure Intellect is the "immanent Koran"; the uncreated Koran—the *Logos*—is the Divine Intellect, which crystallizes in the form of the

---

[27] Thus also how he was represented, as is proven by "classical" art.

[28] This attitude is necessarily legitimate from a certain angle and at a certain level and is explained, in the field of Monotheism, by the fact that the Jewish, Christian, and Islamic religions correspond respectively to the paths of "action", "love", and "knowledge" to the extent that they can, as exoterisms, do so and without prejudice to their most profound content.

earthly Koran and corresponds "objectively" to that other immanent and "subjective" revelation which is the human Intellect.[29] In Christian terms it could be said that Christ is like the "objectification" of the Intellect and the Intellect is like the "subjective" and permanent revelation of Christ. Thus there are two poles for the manifestation of Divine Wisdom and they are: firstly, the Revelation "above us" and, secondly, the Intellect "within us"; the Revelation provides the symbols while the Intellect deciphers them and "recollects" their content, thereby again becoming "conscious" of its own substance. Revelation is an unfolding and Intellect a concentration; the descent coincides with the ascent.

But there is another *haqīqah* on which we would like to touch upon at this point, and it is this: in the sensory order the Divine Presence has two symbols or vehicles—or two natural "manifestations"—of primary importance: the heart within us, which is our center, and the air around us, which we breathe. Air is the manifestation of ether, the weaver of forms, and it is at the same time the vehicle of light, which also makes manifest the element ether.[30] When we breathe, the air penetrates us, and symbolically it is as though it introduced into us the creative ether together with light; we breathe in the Universal Presence of God. There is also a connection between light and coolness, for the sensation of both is liberating; what is light outwardly is coolness inwardly. We inhale luminous, cool air and our respiration is a prayer, as is the beating of our heart; the luminosity relates to the Intellect and the freshness to pure Being.[31]

The world is a fabric woven of threads of ether; we and all other creatures are woven into it. All sensory things come forth from ether, which contains all; everything is ether crystallized. The world is an

---

[29] It is "subjective" because empirically it is within us. The term "subjective", when applied to the Intellect, is as improper as the epithet "human"; in both cases, the terms are used simply in order to define the way of approach.

[30] The Greeks left the element ether unmentioned, no doubt because they conceived it as being hidden in the air, which is also invisible. In Hebrew the word *avir* designates both air and ether: the word *aor* has the same root and means "light".

[31] In Islam it is taught that at the end of time light will become separated from heat, and heat will be hell whereas light will be Paradise; the light of heaven is cool and the heat of hell dark.

immense carpet; we possess the whole world in each breath because we breathe the ether from which all things are made,[32] and we "are" ether. Just as the world is an immeasurable carpet in which everything is repeated within the rhythm of continual change, or again, in which everything remains similar within the framework of the law of differentiation, so too the Koran—and with it the whole of Islam—is a carpet or fabric in which the center is everywhere repeated in an infinitely varied way and in which the diversity is but a development of the unity. The universal "ether", of which the physical element is only a distant and grosser reflection, is none other than the Divine Word which is everywhere "being" and "consciousness" and everywhere "creative" and "liberating" or "revealing" and "enlightening".

The nature which surrounds us—sun, moon, stars, day and night, the seasons, the waters, mountains, forests, and flowers— is a kind of Revelation; now these three things—nature, light, and breath—are profoundly linked with one another. Breathing should be linked with the remembrance of God; we should breathe with reverence, with the heart so to speak. It is said that the Spirit of God—the divine Breath— was "over the waters" and that it was by breathing into it that God created the soul, as it is also said that man, who is "born of the Spirit", is like the wind; "thou hearest the sound thereof, but canst not tell whence it cometh, and whither it goeth."

It is significant that Islam is defined in the Koran as an "expansion (*inshirāh*) of the breast", that it is said, for example, that God "hath expanded our breast for Islam"; the connection between the Islamic perspective and the initiatory meaning of breathing and also of the heart is a key of the first importance for understanding the Sufic arcanum. It is true that, by the very force of things, the same path also opens out onto universal *gnosis*.

The "remembrance of God" is like breathing deeply in the solitude of high mountains: here the morning air, filled with the purity of the eternal snows, dilates the breast; it becomes space and heaven enters our heart.

But this image includes yet a more differentiated symbolism, that of the "universal breath": here expiration relates to cosmic manifesta-

---

[32] This is a symbolic manner of speech, for ether being perfect plenitude is motionless and could not move.

tion or the creative phase and inspiration to reintegration, to the phase of salvation or the return to God.

One reason why Westerners have difficulty in appreciating the Koran and have even many times questioned whether this book contains the premises of a spiritual life[33] lies in the fact that they look in a text for a meaning that is fully expressed and immediately intelligible, whereas Semites, and Eastern peoples in general, are lovers of verbal symbolism and read "in depth". The revealed phrase is for them an array of symbols from which more and more flashes of light shoot forth the further the reader penetrates into the spiritual geometry of the words: the words are reference points for a doctrine that is inexhaustible; the implicit meaning is everything, and the obscurities of the literal meaning are so many veils highlighting the majesty of the content.[34] But, even without taking into consideration the sibylline structure of many sacred sentences, we can say that the Easterner draws much from a few words: when, for example, the Koran recalls that "the next world is better for you than the here below" or that "earthly life is but a play" or affirms: "In your wives and your children ye have an enemy" or: "Say: *Allāh*! then leave them to their vain talk"—or finally when it promises Paradise to "him who has feared the station of his Lord and refused desire to his soul"—when the Koran speaks thus, there emerges for the Muslim[35] a whole ascetic and mystical doctrine, as penetrating and as complete as any other form of spirituality worthy of the name.

Man alone has the gift of speech, for he alone among all the creatures of this earth is "made in the image of God" in a direct and total

[33] Louis Massignon answers this question in the affirmative.

[34] This is the way the Bible was read in the Middle Ages, following in the footsteps of Antiquity. The denial of the hermeneutical interpretation, which was the bulwark of traditional and integral intellectuality, inevitably led in the end to the "criticism"—and destruction—of the sacred Texts; for instance there is nothing left of the Song of Songs once only the literal meaning is accepted.

[35] Note that we say "for the Muslim", not "for every Muslim".

manner. And since it is by virtue of this likeness—provided it is actualized by appropriate means—that man is saved, thus by virtue of the objective intelligence[36] associated with free will and truthful speech, whether articulated or not, it is easy to understand the capital part played in the life of the Muslim by those sublime words which are the verses of the Koran; they are not merely sentences which transmit thoughts, but are in a way beings, powers, or talismans. The soul of the Muslim is as it were woven of sacred formulas; in these he works, in these he rests, in these he lives, and in these he dies.

At the beginning of this book we saw that the intention of the formula *lā ilāha illā 'Llāh* becomes clear if by the term *ilāh*—the literal meaning of which is "divinity"—one understands reality, the level or nature of which remains to be determined. The first proposition of the sentence, which is negative in form ("There is no divinity. . ."), relates to the world and reduces it to nothingness by taking away from it any positive character; the second proposition, which is affirmative (". . . save the Divinity, *Allāh*"), is related to Absolute Reality or to Being. The word "divinity" (*ilāh*) can be replaced by any word expressing a positive idea; in the first part of the formula this word would then remain indefinite, but in the second proposition it would become defined absolutely and exclusively as Principle,[37] as in the case of the Name *Allāh* (The Divinity) with regard to the word *ilāh* (divinity).[38] In the *Shahādah* there is metaphysical discernment between the unreal and the Real, and then combative virtue; this formula is both the sword of knowledge and the sword of the soul, while also marking the peace that Truth brings, serenity in God.

---

[36] It was the objectivity of human intelligence which enabled Adam to "name" all things and all creatures; in other words it is this objectivity which enables man to know objects, plants, and animals, whereas they do not know him. But the highest content of this intelligence is the Absolute; to be able to compass the greater is to be able to compass the lesser, and it is because man can know God that he knows the world. Human intelligence is a proof of God after its own fashion.

[37] One of the works of the Shaykh al-Alawi contains indeed a whole litany drawn from the *Shahādah: lā quddūsa illā 'Llāh* ("there is no saint save *Allāh*"); *lā 'alīma illā 'Llāh* ("there is no sage save *Allāh*"); and so on through all the divine attributes.

[38] We have already seen that the first Testimony is directly followed by the second—that of the Prophet—which it includes implicitly and which issues from it as if by polarization.

Another fundamental tenet of Islam—and no doubt the most important after the double Testimony of faith—is the formula of consecration, the *Basmalah*: "In the Name of God, the infinitely Good,[39] the ever Merciful" (*Bismi 'Llāhi 'r-Rahmāni 'r-Rahīm*).[40] This is the formula of the Revelation, found at the head of every *sūrah* of the Koran except one which is considered as a continuation of its predecessor; this consecration is the first phrase of the revealed Book, for with it begins "That which opens" (*Sūrat al-Fātihah*), the introductory *sūrah*. It is said that the *Fātihah* contains in essence the whole of the Koran, that the *Basmalah* in turn contains the whole of the *Fātihah*, that the *Basmalah* is itself contained in the letter *bā*, and that this is contained in its diacritical point.[41]

The *Basmalah* forms a kind of complement to the *Shahādah*: the *Shahādah* is an intellectual "ascent" and the *Basmalah* an ontological "descent"; in Hindu terms the former could be called Shivaite and the latter Vaishnavite. If we may be permitted to return once again to two Vedantic formulas of the highest importance, we shall say that the *Shahādah* destroys the world because "the world is false, *Brahma* is true", whereas the *Basmalah* on the contrary consecrates and sanctifies the world because "all is *Ātmā*"; but the *Basmalah* is already contained in the *Shahādah*, namely in the word *illā* (a contracted form of *in lā*, "if not") which is the "isthmus" (*barzakh*) between the negative and positive propositions of the formula, the first half of this word itself being positive (*in*, "if") and the second negative (*lā*, "no" or "none"). In other words the *Shahādah* is the juxtaposition of the negation *lā ilāha* (no divinity) and the Name *Allāh* (the Divinity), this confron-

---

[39] Here we give the fundamental meaning of this Name. No objection can be raised to the translating of the Name *Rahmān* as "Compassionate", for compassion is as it were the essence of mercy.

[40] From this is derived the word *basmalah*, which means the act of saying: *Bismi 'Llāh* .... The Arabic spelling is *Bismi Allāhi ar-Rahmāni ar-Rahīm*.

[41] The letter *bā*, the second letter in the Arabic alphabet—the first being the *alif*, a plain vertical line with an axial symbolism—is formed by a horizontal line slightly curved like a bowl and is distinguished by a point beneath it. Ali, the Prophet's son-in-law, and at a later date the Sufi ash-Shibli both compared themselves to this point under the *bā* in order to express their state of "supreme Identity". This diacritical point corresponds to the first drop of the divine Ink (*Midād*) to fall from the Pen; it is the Divine Spirit (*ar-Rūh*), or the Prototype of the world.

tation being linked by a word the first half of which, being positive, indirectly refers to *Allāh* and the second half, being negative, indirectly refers to "unreality"; thus in the center of the *Shahādah* there is a kind of inverse image of the relationship which it expresses, and this inversion represents the truth according to which the world possesses the degree of reality proper to its level, since nothing can be cut off from the Divine Cause.

And it is from this mysterious heart of the *Shahādah* that the second *Shahādah* springs, like Eve drawn from the side of Adam. The Divine Truth, having said "no" to the world which would be God, says "yes" within the very framework of this "no" because the world cannot in itself be cut off from God: *Allāh* cannot not be there in a certain fashion or in conformity with certain principles resulting both from His nature and from that of the world.

From a somewhat different point of view it can also be said that the *Basmalah* is the divine and revelatory ray which brings into the world the truth of the double *Shahādah*:[42] the *Basmalah* is the "descending" ray and the *Shahādah* is its content, the horizontal image which, in the world, reflects the Truth of God; in the second *Shahādah* (*Muhammadun Rasūlu'Llāh*) this vertical ray is itself reflected and the projection of the Message becomes a part of the Message. The *Basmalah* consecrates everything including especially the vital functions with their inevitable and legitimate pleasures. Through this consecration something of the Divine Beatitude enters into their enjoyment; it is as though God entered into the enjoyment and participated in it, or as though man entered a little, but with full right, into the Beatitude of God. Like the *Basmalah*, the second *Shahādah* "neutralizes" the denial enunciated by the first *Shahādah*, which symbolically speaking already bears within itself its "compensatory dimension" or its "corrective" in the word *illā* from which springs forth the *Muhammadun Rasūlu'Llāh*.

---

[42] In the same way that Christ is the Word brought into the world by the Holy Spirit. In this case, the *Shahādah* is the Message made manifest; on the other hand, when it was said above that the *Basmalah* is contained in the first *Shahādah*—like the second *Shahādah* in the word *illā*—this referred to the *Shahādah in divinis*, envisaged, that is to say, as the unmanifest Truth.

This question could also be approached from a rather different angle: the consecration "In the Name of God, the infinitely Merciful, the ever-acting Merciful" presupposes something in relation to which the idea of Unity, enunciated by the *Shahādah*, has to be realized, and this relationship is indicated in the *Basmalah* itself in the sense that, being divine utterance, it creates that which should then be brought back to the Uncreated. The Names *Rahmān* and *Rahīm*, both deriving from the word *Rahmah* ("Mercy"), mean respectively the intrinsic Mercy of God and His extrinsic Mercy; thus the former indicates an infinite quality and the latter a limitless manifestation of that quality. The words could also be respectively translated as "Creator through Love" and "Savior through Mercy", or drawing inspiration from a *hadīth*, we could comment on them thus: *ar-Rahmān* is the Creator of the world inasmuch as He has furnished *a priori* and once and for all the elements of well-being of this lower world, while *ar-Rahīm* is the Savior of men inasmuch as He confers on them the beatitude of the beyond, or inasmuch as He gives them here below the seeds of the next world or dispenses its benefits.

In the Names *Rahmān* and *Rahīm* the Divine Mercy confronts human incapacity in the sense that consciousness of our incapacity is, when coupled with trust, the moral receptacle of Mercy. The Name *Rahmān* is like the luminous sky; the Name *Rahīm* is like a warm ray coming from the sky and giving life to man.

In the Name *Allāh* there are the aspects of awe-inspiring Transcendence and enveloping Totality; were there only the aspect of Transcendence it would be difficult, if not impossible, to contemplate this Name. From a different point of view it can be said that the Name *Allāh* breathes forth at one and the same time serenity, majesty, and mystery: the first of these qualities relates to the indifferentiation of the Substance, the second to the loftiness of the Principle, and the third to the Ipseity, which is both secret and lightning-like. In the written form of the Name *Allāh* in Arabic, we distinguish a horizontal line, that of the very motion of writing, then the upright strokes of the *alif* and the *lam*, and then finally a more or less circular line, symbolically reducible to a circle; these three elements are like indications of three "dimensions": serenity, which is "horizontal" and undifferentiated like the desert or a blanket of snow;[43] majesty, which is "vertical" and im-

---

[43] This is what is expressed by the verse already quoted: "Say: *Allāh!* Then leave them

movable like a mountain;[44] and mystery, which extends "in depth" and relates to ipseity and to *gnosis.* The mystery of ipseity implies that of identity, for the divine nature, which is totality as well as transcendence, includes all possible divine aspects including the world with its countless individualized refractions of the Self.

The *Fātihah,* "That which opens" (the Koran), has, as we have already mentioned, a capital importance, for it constitutes the unanimous prayer of Islam. It is composed of seven affirmations or verses: 1. "Praise be to God, Lord of the worlds; 2. The Infinitely Good, the Ever Merciful; 3. King of the Last Judgment; 4. It is Thee we worship, and it is in Thee we seek refuge; 5. Lead us on the straight path; 6. The path of those on whom is Thy Grace; 7. Not of those on whom is Thy Wrath, nor of those who go astray."

"Praise be to God, Lord of the worlds": the starting point of this formula is our state of existential enjoyment; to exist is to enjoy, for breathing, eating, living, seeing beauty, carrying out some work—all this is enjoyment. Now, it is important to know that every perfection or satisfaction, every quality, whether inward or outward, is but the effect of a transcendent and unique cause, and that this cause, the only cause there is, produces and determines countless worlds of perfection.

"The Infinitely Good, the Ever Merciful": the Good signifies that God has in advance given us existence and all the qualities and conditions this implies, and since we exist and are also endowed with intelligence, we ought not to forget these gifts nor attribute them to ourselves; we did not create ourselves, nor did we invent either the eye or light. The Merciful: God gives us our daily bread, and not that alone: He gives us our eternal life, our participation in Unity and thus in what is our true nature.

to their vain talk" (6:92), or by this other verse: "Is it not in the remembrance of *Allāh* that hearts rest in security?" (Koran 13:28).

[44] "*Allāh!* There is no divinity save He, the Living (*al-Hayy*), the Self-Subsistent (*al-Qayyūm*)" (Koran 2:255 and 3:2).

"King of the Last Judgment": God is not only the Lord of the worlds, He is also the Lord of their end; He deploys them, then destroys them. We, who are in existence, cannot be unaware that all existence is bound to end, that both microcosms and macrocosms terminate in a sort of divine naught. To know that the relative comes from the Absolute and depends on it is to know that the relative is not the Absolute and disappears in face of it.[45]

"It is Thee we worship and it is in Thee we seek refuge": worship is the recognition of God outside us and above us—and thus submission to the infinitely distant God—whereas refuge is the return to the God within us, at the deepest level of our heart; it is trust in a God who is infinitely near. The "outward" God is like the infinity of the sky; the "inward" God is like the intimacy of the heart.

"Lead us on the straight path": this is the path of ascent, the way which leads to liberating Unity; it is the union of will, love, and knowledge.

"The path of those on whom is Thy Grace": the straight path is that whereby Grace draws us upwards; it is through Grace alone that we can follow this path; but we must open ourselves to that Grace and conform to its requirements.

"Not of those on whom is Thy Wrath, nor of those who go astray": not of those who oppose Grace and by that fact place themselves in the ray of Justice or of Rigor, or who sever the bond linking them to pre-existing Grace; through wanting to be independent of their Cause, or wanting to be themselves the cause, they fall like stones, deaf and blind; the Cause abandons them. "Nor of those who go astray": these are they who, without directly opposing the One, are nonetheless, through weakness, lost in multiplicity; these do not deny the One, nor do they want to usurp its rank, but they remain what they are, following their multiple nature as though not endowed with intelligence; they live finally beneath themselves and give themselves up to cosmic powers, though without being lost if they submit to God.[46]

---

[45] The reader will have noticed that the "Last Judgment" comprises a temporal symbolism in contrast to the spatial symbolism of "Lord of the worlds".

[46] According to the Islamic interpretation, these three categories of Grace, Wrath, and straying concern respectively the Muslims, who follow the middle way, the Jews, who rejected Jesus, and the Christians, who made a God of him; the choice of the symbols

——— ·|· ———

Formulas run through the life of the Muslim like weft through warp. The *Basmalah*, as we mentioned, inaugurates and sanctifies every undertaking, it ritualizes the regular actions of life such as the ablutions and meals; the formula *al-hamdu li 'Llāh* (praise be to God) brings them to a close in relating their positive quality to the sole Cause of all quality and thus "sublimating" all enjoyment so that everything can be undertaken according to grace, earthly effect of the Divine Beatitude; in this sense all things are done as symbols of that Beatitude.[47] These two formulas mark the two phases of sacralization and completion, the *coagula* and the *solve*; the *Basmalah* evokes the Divine Cause— and therefore the presence of God—in transitory things and the *Hamdalah*—the praise—in a sense dissolves these things by reducing them to their Cause.

The formulas "glory be to God" (*subhāna 'Llāh*) and "God is greater" (*Allāhu akbar*) are often associated with the *Hamdalah*, in accordance with a *hadīth*, and recited with it. "Glory be to God" is said to nullify a heresy that is contrary to the Divine Majesty; thus this formula more especially concerns God in Himself; it separates Him from created things whereas the *Hamd* on the contrary connects things to God in a certain manner. The formula "God is greater"—the *Takbīr*— opens the canonical prayer and marks the change during prayer from one ritual position to another; it expresses by the comparative of the word "great" (*kabīr*)—often taken, moreover, in the sense of a superlative—that God will always be "greater", or the "greatest" (*akbar*), and so shows itself to be a kind of paraphrase of the *Shahādah*.[48]

---

is plausible from an exoteric point of view, but the meaning is universal and refers to the three fundamental tendencies in man.

[47] Cf. the *Bhagavad Gītā* (9:27-28): "Whatever thy work, thine eating, thy sacrifice, thy gift, thine austerities, make of it an offering to Me, O son of Kunti. Thus thou shalt be released from the bonds of action, whether their fruit be good or bad; with a soul firmly set on renunciation thou shalt be delivered and attain to Me." According to an idea current among Muslims, a meal taken without the *Basmalah* is eaten in the company of Satan, and the same applies to any important action.

[48] According to tradition, all these formulas, when recited a certain number of times,

Another formula of quasi-organic importance in the life of a Muslim is the following: "if God wills it" (*in shā'a 'Llāh*); in saying this the Muslim recognizes his dependence, his weakness, and his ignorance in the face of God and at the same time abdicates all passional pretention; this is essentially the formula of serenity. It is also an affirmation that the end of all things is God, that it is He alone who is the absolutely certain outcome of our existence; there is no future outside Him.

If the formula "if God wills it" concerns the future insofar as we project into it the present—represented by our desire which we actively affirm—the formula "it was written" (*kāna maktūb*) concerns the present insofar as in it we meet the past—represented by the destiny we passively undergo. Similarly the formula *mā shā'a 'Llāh* (what God has willed—"has come" being implied) places the idea of "if God wills it" (*in shā'a 'Llāh*) in the past and the present; the event, or the beginning of the event, is past, but its unfolding, or our ascertaining of the past or continuing event, is in the present. Muslim "fatalism", the soundness of which is corroborated by the fact that it is perfectly consistent with activity—history is there to prove it—is the logical consequence of the fundamental conception of Islam according to which everything depends on God and returns to Him.

The Muslim—and especially he who observes the *Sunnah* right down to its minutest ramifications[49]—lives in a fabric of symbols, participating in their weaving, since he lives them, and thus benefits from all these means of remembering God and the next world, even if only indirectly. For the Christian, living morally in the empty space of vocational possibilities and so of the unforeseeable, this situation of the Muslim appears to be a superficial formalism or even Pharisaism, but such an impression fails to take account of the fact that for Islam the

---

miraculously wipe out sins, be they as numberless of the drops of water in the sea. Here there is an analogy with the "indulgences" attached in Catholicism to certain formulas or prayers.

[49] As al-Ghazzali in particular recommended. The opposite opinion also exists, namely that the legal minimum suffices for going to Paradise provided there is either great purity of soul, or great virtue, or profound inner knowledge. In this context let us recall that Muslims divide actions into five categories: 1. what is indispensable (*fardh* or *wājib*); 2. what is recommended (*sunnah, mustahabb*); 3. what is indifferent (*mubāh*); 4. what is inadvisable (*makrūh*); 5. what is forbidden (*harām*).

will is not a matter of "improvisation";[50] the will is determined or channeled for the contemplative peace of the mind;[51] the outward is only an outline, because the whole spiritual rhythm unfolds inwardly. To pronounce formulas for each and every occasion may amount to nothing, and seems like nothing to one who conceives only of moral heroism, but from another point of view—that of virtual union with God through the constant "remembrance" of things divine—this verbal way of introducing into life spiritual "points of reference" is on the contrary a means of purification and of grace about which no doubt can be entertained. That which is spiritually possible is by the same token legitimate and even necessary in an appropriate context.

One of the most prominent doctrines in the Koran is that of the Divine Omnipotence; this doctrine of the utter dependence of all things on God is enunciated in the Koran with a strictness that is exceptional in the climate of monotheism. At the beginning of this book the problem of predestination was touched on in showing that, if man is subject to fate, it is because—or insofar as—he is not God, not inasmuch as he participates ontologically in the Divine Liberty. To deny predestination, we said, would amount to maintaining that God does not know future events "beforehand" and is therefore not omniscient; which would be an absurd conclusion, for time is merely one mode of extension of existence and the empirical succession of its contents is only illusory.

This question of predestination also raises that of the Divine Omnipotence: if God is all-powerful, why can He not abolish the ills from which creatures suffer? If it is inadmissible to suppose that He wants to do so but cannot, it is equally inconceivable that He could do so but does not want to, at any rate insofar as we trust our human sensibility. The answer must be as follows: Omnipotence, being something definite, cannot pertain to the Absolute in the strictly metaphysical sense of that term; it is one quality among others, which is as much as

---

[50] On this point, as on others, there is nothing absolute about the divergence in perspective, but the differences of emphasis are nonetheless real and profound.

[51] This is why the required attitude is called an *islām*, an abandonment to a pre-existing frame for the will; the root of this word is the same as that of the word *salām*, "peace", and this indicates the idea of a "supernatural release", an idea also contained in the word *inshirāh*, meaning the enlarging of the breast by the Islamic faith.

to say that, like Being to which it appertains, it belongs already to the domain of relativity, though not on that account falling outside the principial domain; in short it relates to the personal God, the ontological Principle, which creates and is personified in relation to creatures, not to the supra-personal Divinity, which is the absolute and ineffable Essence. Omnipotence, like every attribute relating to an attitude or an activity, has its sufficient reason in the world and exerts an effect on it; it is dependent on Being and could not be exerted beyond that. God, "in creating" and "having created", is all-powerful in relation to what His work includes, but not so in relation to that which, in the divine nature itself, is the cause of both creation and of the inner laws of creation; He does not govern that which makes the metaphysical necessity of the world and of evil. He governs neither relativity—of which He is, as ontological Principle, the first affirmation—nor the principial consequences of relativity; He can abolish a specific evil, but not evil as such; but that is what He would abolish were He to abolish all ills. To speak of the "world" is to speak of "relativity", of the "unfolding of relativities", of "differentiation", and of the "presence of evil"; since the world is not God it must include imperfection, otherwise it would be reduced to God and thus cease to exist (*ex-sistere*).

The great contradiction in man is that he wants the multiple but without wishing to pay the ransom of this sundering; he wants relativity with its savor of absoluteness or infinity, but without the suffering arising from its sharp edges; he desires extension but not limitation, as if the former could exist apart from the latter and as if pure extension could be found on the plane of measurable things.[52]

Perhaps all this could be more precisely expressed if the problem is formulated as follows: the Divine Essence—Beyond-Being—contains in its indistinction, and as a potentiality comprised within its very infinity, a principle of relativity; Being, which generates the world, is the first of the relativities, that from which all the others flow; the function of Being is to deploy in the direction of "nothingness", or in an "illusory" mode, the infinity of Beyond-Being, which thus becomes trans-

---

[52] The whole of modern civilization is built upon this error, which has become for it an article of faith and a program.

muted into ontological and existential possibilities.[53] Since Being is the first relativity it cannot abolish relativity; as we have seen, if it could do so it would abolish itself and *a fortiori* bring creation to naught; what we call "evil" is only the extreme repercussion of limitation, and so of relativity; the Omnipotent can no more abolish relativity than He can prevent two and two from making four, for relativity, like truth, proceeds from His nature, and this amounts to saying that God has not the power not to be God. Relativity is the "shadow" or "outline" which allows the Absolute to affirm itself as such, first before itself and then in an innumerable[54] gushing forth of differentiations.

The whole of this doctrine can be found expressed in the Koranic formula: "And He has power over all things" (*wa Huwa 'alā kulli shay'in qadīr*). In Sufi terms it is said that God, inasmuch as He is Powerful, and thus Creator, is envisaged on the plane of the "attributes" (*sifāt*) and quite clearly these could not govern the "Essence" or "Quiddity" (*Dhāt*); the "Power" (*qadr*) relates to "all things", to the existential totality. If we say that the Omnipotent has not the power not to be all-powerful, creator, merciful, and just, and that He also cannot prevent Himself from creating and deploying His attributes in creation, it will no doubt be objected that God created the world "in full freedom" and that He manifests Himself freely in it; but this is to confuse the principial determination of the divine perfection with freedom as regards facts or contents; the perfection of necessity, a reflection of the Absolute, is confused with the imperfection of constraint, a consequence of relativity. That God creates in perfect freedom means that He cannot be subject to any constraint, since nothing is situated outside Him, and things appearing to be outside Him cannot affect Him, the levels of reality being incommensurably unequal. The metaphysical cause of creation or of manifestation is in God, and therefore it does not prevent Him from being Himself, hence from being free; it cannot be denied that this cause is comprised in the divine nature unless freedom is confused with caprice, as it too often is by

---

[53] The former concern Being itself—and these are the divine attributes such as Omnipotence and Mercy—and the latter concern Existence, the world, things.

[54] This expression is purely symbolic, for on the plane of the macrocosm as a whole we are already beyond the realm of earthly number.

theologians—at least in fact and by implication—without recognizing the logical consequences of their sentimental and anti-metaphysical anthropomorphism. Like "Omnipotence", the "Freedom" of God has no meaning except in relation to the relative; none of these terms—we must insist—applies to the ultimate Aseity; this means, not that the intrinsic perfections crystallized in these attributes are absent beyond relativity—*quod absit*—but on the contrary that they have their infinite plenitude only in the Absolute and the Ineffable.[55]

The question of divine punishment is often associated with that of Omnipotence and also with that of Wisdom and Goodness, and arguments such as the following are brought forward: what interest can an infinitely wise and good God have in keeping a record of our sins, of the manifestations of our wretchedness? To ask oneself such a question is to overlook the central element of the problem and to turn on the one hand immanent Justice and the Law of equilibrium into a psychological contingency and on the other—since sin is minimized—human mediocrity into the measuring rod of the Universe. First of all, to speak of God "punishing" is only a way of expressing a certain causal relationship; no one would dream of accusing nature of meanness because the relationship of cause and effect takes place in it according to the inherent logic of things: because for example, nettle seeds do not produce azaleas, or because, when a swing is pushed, a pendular and not an upward movement results. The good reason for the sanctions beyond death is apparent once we are aware of human imperfection; being a disequilibrium, that imperfection ineluctably calls forth

---

[55] Mazdeism formulated the problem of Omnipotence and of evil in a way which avoids the appearance of contradiction in the Divine Principle, by opposing to Ahuramazda (or Ormuzd) the supreme and infinitely good God, a principle of evil, Angra Mainyu (or Ahriman) but without being able to overcome a dualism which falls short of being metaphysically satisfactory, though plausible at a certain level of reality. Buddhism avoids the two dangers—contradiction in God Himself and of a fundamental dualism—but is obliged to sacrifice the personal aspect of God, at any rate in its general doctrine, and this makes it unassimilable for the majority of Westerners and Semites.

its own repercussion.[56] If the existence of creatures is really a proof of God—for those who see through outward appearances—since manifestation is conceivable only in terms of the Principle, just as accidents have meaning only in relation to a substance, analogous things can be said about disequilibria: they presuppose an equilibrium which they have broken and they entail a concordant reaction, whether positive or negative.

To believe that man is "good", that he has the right to ask simply "to be left alone", that moral agitations and eschatological fears are no concern of his, means a failure to see that the limitations which in a sense define man are fundamentally a kind of "abnormality". The mere fact that we do not see what goes on behind our backs and are ignorant of what tomorrow will be like, proves that we are in certain respects very insignificant and shows that we are "accidents" of a "substance" greater than ourselves, but it shows at the same time that we are not our body and not of this world; neither this world nor our body is what we are. And here we would insert a parenthesis: if for thousands of years men could be content with the moral symbolism of reward and punishment it is not because they were stupid—in which case their stupidity would have been infinite and incurable—but because they still had a sense of what equilibrium and disequilibrium means, because they still had an innate feeling of real values, whether of the world or of the soul. They had on the one hand an as it were experiential sense of certitude, since they were contemplative, of divine norms and on the other of human imperfections; a symbolism was enough to recall to them what they already had a natural presentiment of. Spiritually perverted man has, on the contrary, forgotten his initial majesty and the risks it involves; having no desire to concern himself with the fundamentals of his existence he believes that reality is incapable of recalling them to him. And the worst of all absurdities is to believe that the nature of things is absurd, for were it so, whence could we draw light enabling us to recognize that it is so? Or again: man is by definition intelligent and free; in practice he always remains convinced

---

[56] This is one meaning of Christ's saying that "he who draws the sword shall perish by the sword" and also, though from a somewhat different point of view, of the saying that "every house divided against itself shall fall". This last saying is in particular applicable to the man who is unfaithful to his nature "made in the image of God".

of this, for at every opportunity he lays claim both to freedom and to intelligence: to freedom because he does not want to let himself be dominated, and to intelligence because he intends to be the judge of everything himself. But what decides our destiny in the face of the Absolute is our real nature and not our convenience elevated to the status of a norm; it may be that we want to desert our theomorphism while profiting from its advantages, but we cannot escape the consequences that theomorphism implies. It is all very fine for the modernists to despise what may seem to them a worry, a weakness, or a "complex" in traditional people; their own way of being perfect is to ignore that the mountain is collapsing, whereas the apparent imperfection of those they despise includes—or manifests—at least a real possibility of escaping the cataclysm. Everything that has just been said applies equally to whole civilizations: the traditional civilizations include evils that can only be understood—or the scope of which can only be assessed— if one takes account of the fact that these civilizations are based on certainty of the hereafter and therefore on a corresponding indifference to transitory things. Conversely, in order rightly to evaluate the advantages of the modern world, and before seeing in it indisputable values, it must be borne in mind that these "advantages" are mentally conditioned by the denial of the hereafter and by the cult of the things of this world.

Many people today think in such terms as these: "either God exists, or He does not; if He exists and is what people say He is, then He will recognize that we are good and do not deserve punishment." This means that they are prepared to believe in His existence provided He conforms to their own imaginings and recognizes the worth they attribute to themselves. This is to forget on the one hand that we cannot know the standards by which the Absolute judges us, and on the other that the "fire" beyond the tomb is finally nothing but our own Intellect which actualizes itself against our falseness; in other words, it is the immanent truth breaking forth into the full light of day. At death man is confronted by the unimaginable expanse of a reality no longer fragmentary but total and then by the norm of what he has pretended to be, since that norm is part of Reality. Man therefore condemns himself; according to the Koran, it is his bodily members themselves which accuse him; once the lie has been exposed, his violations are transformed into flames; nature, out of balance and falsified, with all its vain assurance proves to be a shirt of Nessus. Man burns not only for his sins; he burns for his majesty as an image of God. It is the choice of setting up the fallen state as a norm and ignorance as a pledge of impunity which the Koran stigmatizes with vehemence—one might almost say by anticipation—by confronting the self-assurance of its contradictors with the terrors of the end of the world.[57]

To summarize, the whole problem of guilt can be reduced to the relation between cause and effect. That man is far from being good is very amply proven both by ancient and by modern history: man does not have the innocence of animals; he is aware of his imperfection, since the idea of imperfection exists for him; thus he is responsible. What is called in moral terminology the fault of man and the chastisement of God is, in itself, nothing other than human disequilibrium coming into collision with the immanent Equilibrium; and this idea is of capital importance.

The notion of an "eternal" hell, after having for many centuries stimulated fear of God and efforts toward virtue, has today rather the opposite effect and contributes to making the doctrine of the hereafter seem implausible; and, by a strange paradox, in a period which is one of contrasts and compensations, and while being on the whole as refractory as possible to pure metaphysics, only sapiential esoterism is in a position to render intelligible the most precarious positions of exoterism and to satisfy certain needs for logical explanations. Now the problem of divine punishment, so difficult for our contemporaries to accept, can be summed up in two questions: first, is it possible for man who is responsible and free to oppose the Absolute either directly or indirectly, even if only in an illusory sense? Certainly he can, since the individual essence can be imbued with any cosmic quality and therefore with states that are "possibilities of impossibility".[58] And the

---

[57] This is indeed one of the most frequently recurring themes of this sacred Book, which sometimes marks, by an almost desperate eloquence, its character of ultimate Message.

[58] "And they say: The Fire will not touch us save for a certain number of days. Say: Have ye received a covenant from *Allāh*—truly *Allāh* will not break His covenant—or tell ye concerning *Allāh* that which ye know not? Nay, but whosoever hath done evil and his sin surroundeth him; such are the rightful owners of the Fire; they will abide therein" (*khālidūn*) (Koran 2:80-81). Here the whole emphasis is on the proposition:

second question is this: can exoteric truth, for instance in regard to hell, be total truth? Certainly not, since it is determined—in a certain sense "by definition"—by a particular moral interest, or by particular reasons of psychological opportuneness. This is what explains the absence of various compensating shades of expression in certain religious teachings; the eschatologies relating to these religious perspectives are of course not "anti-metaphysical", but they are "non-metaphysical" and "anthropocentric",[59] so that in the context of these teachings certain truths would appear "immoral" or at least "ill-sounding": it is therefore not possible for them to discern in infernal states aspects that are more or less positive, or the converse in paradisal states. By this allusion we do not mean to say that there is symmetry between Mercy and Rigor—the former has priority over the latter[60]—but rather that the relationship "Heaven-hell" corresponds by metaphysical necessity to what is expressed in the Far Eastern symbolism of the *yin-yang*, in which the black portion includes a white point and the white portion a black point; if then there are compensations in Gehenna because nothing in existence can be absolute and the Divine Mercy penetrates everywhere,[61] there must also be in Paradise, not indeed sufferings, but

---

". . . and his sin surroundeth him" (*wa ahātat bihi khatī atuhu*), which indicates the essential, and so "mortal" character of the transgression. This passage is a reply to men who believed, not that hell as such is metaphysically limited, but that the duration of the punishment is equal to that of the sin.

[59] Theologians are not in principle unaware that the "eternity" of hell—the case of Paradise is somewhat different—is not on the same level as that of God and could not be identical with it; but they do not draw any inferences from this subtle distinction. If, in the Semitic Scriptures, exoterism is predicated by such ideas as creation *ex nihilo* and a survival both individual and eternal, the exoteric tendency likewise appears in Hindu and Buddhist Scriptures—though in a different fashion—in the sense that these texts appear to place on earth those phases of transmigration which are neither celestial nor infernal; in the climate of Hinduism, exoterism—always averse to subtle explanations—is reduced to the simplicity of the symbols. Certainly one eschatology may be more complete than another, but none could be absolutely adequate by reason of the very limitation of human and earthly imagination.

[60] There is asymmetry between the celestial and infernal states because the former are eminently nearer to pure Being than the latter; their "eternity" is thus on any reckoning different from that of the hells.

[61] Al-Ghazzali relates in his *Durrat al-Fākhirah* that one man, when plunged into the fire, cried out more loudly than all the others: "And he was taken out all burned. And

shadows bearing an inverse testimony to the same principle of compensation and signifying that Paradise is not God, as also that all existences are interdependent. Now this principle of compensation is esoteric—to make a dogma of it would be wholly contrary to the spirit of alternativism so characteristic of Western exoterism—and indeed we find in Sufi writings viewpoints remarkable for their shades of meaning: Jili, Ibn Arabi, and others accept that there is an aspect of enjoyment in the infernal state for, if on the one hand the reprobate suffers from being cut off from the Sovereign Good and, as Avicenna emphasizes, from deprivation of his earthly body although the passions subsist, on the other hand he remembers God, according to Jalal ad-Din Rumi, and "nothing is sweeter than the remembrance of *Allāh*".[62] Here it is perhaps as well to "recall" that those in hell would be *ipso facto* delivered if they had the supreme knowledge—whose potentiality they certainly possess—so that even in hell they hold the key to their liberation. But what must be above all pointed out is that the second death referred to in the Apocalypse, as also the reservation expressed in the Koran where certain sayings about hell are followed by the phrase "unless thy Lord wills otherwise" (*illā mā shā' a 'Llāh*),[63] indicate the point of

God said to him: Why did you cry out more loudly than all the other people in the fire? He replied: Lord, Thou hast judged me, but I have not lost faith in Thy mercy. . . . And God said: Who despaireth of the mercy of his Lord save those who are astray? (Koran 15:56). Go in peace, I have pardoned you." From a Catholic point of view, this would refer to "purgatory". Buddhism knows of *Bodhisattvas*, such as Kshitigarbha, who give relief to the damned with celestial dew or bring them other alleviations, and this is an indication that there are angelic functions of mercy which reach even to hell.

[62] In hell the wicked and the proud know that God is real, whereas on earth they either took no account of this or were always able to bring themselves to doubt it; thus something is changed in them by the mere fact of their death and this something is indescribable from the point of view of earthly life. "The dead alone know the worth of life", say the Muslims.

[63] *Sūrah*s 6:128 and 11:107. The same reservation concerns Paradise: ". . . they will abide there . . . so long as the heavens and the earth endure unless thy Lord willeth otherwise; a gift never failing" (11:108). This last proposition relates most directly to the participation of "those brought nigh" (*muqarrabūn*) in the Divine Eternity by virtue of the supreme union; in their case (that of the *krama-mukti* of Vedantic doctrine) Paradise opens out into Divinity at the end of the cycle ("so long as the heavens and the earth endure"), as is also the case in the Paradises of Vishnu and Amida. As for the reservation mentioned above, it indicates the possibility of changes taking place later

intersection between the Semitic conception of perpetual hell and the Hindu and Buddhist conception of transmigration. In other words the hells are in the final analysis passages to individual non-human cycles and thus to other worlds.[64] The human state—or any other analogous "central" state—is as it were surrounded by a ring of fire: in it there is only one choice, either to escape from the "current of forms" upwards, toward God, or else to leave the human state downwards through the fire, the fire which is like the penalty for the betrayal on the part of those who have not realized the divine meaning of the human condition. If "the human state is difficult to obtain", as is held by Asiatic believers in transmigration, it is—by reason of its centrality and theomorphic majesty—equally hard to leave. Men go to the fire because they are gods and they come out of the fire because they are but creatures: God alone could go to hell eternally, if He could sin. Or again: the human state is very near to the divine Sun, if we can at all speak of "proximity" in such a connection; the fire is the possible price—in reverse—of that privileged situation; how privileged can be gauged by the intensity and inextinguishability of the fire. From the gravity of hell we must infer the grandeur of man, and not conversely infer from the seeming innocence of man the supposed injustice of hell.

What can to a certain extent excuse the common use of the word "eternity" to designate a condition which is in scriptural terms only a

---

which are always beneficial for those who, to use a Sufi expression, "prefer the garden to the Gardener", that is, those whose state is the fruit of action and not of knowledge or pure love. Here may also be mentioned the possibility of the *Bodhisattva*s who, while remaining inwardly in Paradise, enter a particular world which is by analogy "terrestrial" and also—at a much lower level—those non-human beatitudes which, thanks to a particular *karma*, a being may use up passively like a plant absorbing food. But none of this enters into the perspective that is termed monotheistic, a perspective moreover that does not include either the rhythm of the cosmic cycles or, for all the more reason, the rhythm of the universal cycles (the "lives of *Brahmā*"), although certain *ahādīth* and passages in the Bible (doubtless including the "reign of a thousand years") refer to these ideas more or less overtly.

[64] According to the *Mānava Dharma Shāstra*, the *Markendeya Purāna*, and other texts, the transmigration of the "damned" on leaving their hell begins by incarnations as lower animals. Now, the divine infinity requires that transmigration should take place in a "spiroidal" mode: a being can never return to the same earth whatever the content of his new "earthly" existence—"earthly" because compounded of pleasure and suffering.

perpetuity[65]—which is but a "reflection" of eternity—is the fact that analogically speaking eternity is a closed circle, for here there is neither beginning nor end, whereas perpetuity is a circle in the form of a spiral and thus open by reason of its very contingency. On the other hand what clearly shows the inadequacy of current belief in a survival that is both individual and eternal—this survival is necessarily individual in hell but not at the transpersonal peak of Felicity[66]—is the contradictory postulate it involves of an eternity with a beginning in time or of an act—and therefore of a contingency—having an absolute consequence.

This whole problem of survival is dominated by two principles of truth: firstly, that God alone is absolute and that the relativity of cosmic states must consequently be manifested not only "in space" but also "in time", to use an analogy that is perhaps permissible; secondly, that God never promises more than He keeps or never keeps less than

---

[65] "The Greek word *aiōnios* really means 'perpetual' and not 'eternal', for it is derived from *aiōn* (the same word as the Latin *aevum*), which designates an indefinite cycle, and this is, moreover, also the primitive meaning of the Latin word *saeculum*, 'age', by which it is sometimes translated" (René Guénon, *Man and His Becoming According to the Vedānta*). In the same way, the hereafter of the Koran has the quality of an unlimited duration, or of "immortality" (*khuld*), or of a very long time (*abad, abadan*) and not that of eternity (*azal*).

[66] As al-Ghazzali recalls in his *Ihya 'Ulūm ad-Dīn*, the vision of God makes "those who are brought nigh" (*muqarrabūn*) forget the houris and ends in the supreme union. Such too is the case of those who, having entered into the "paradise of Amitabha", there achieve the realization of *Nirvāna*, or in other words are reintegrated into the Principle at the great dissolution marking the end of the whole human cycle. ". . . On obtaining 'Deliverance', the being is not 'absorbed', though such may seem to be the case from the point of view of manifestation, for which the 'transformation' appears to be a 'destruction'; if one places oneself in the absolute reality, which alone remains for such a being, he is on the contrary expanded beyond all limits, if one can use such a figure of speech (which exactly translates the symbolism of steam from water spreading indefinitely into the atmosphere), since it has effectively realized the fullness of its possibilities" (René Guénon, *Man and His Becoming According to the Vedānta*, chap. 20, end). "This is the state of abiding in *Brahma*. . . . He that has come to abide therein even at the end of life can attain to extinction in *Brahma* (*brahmanirvāna*)" (*Bhagavad Gītā*, 2:72). If *Nirvāna* is "extinction" only in relation to existential "illusion", this illusion is itself "extinction" or "void" in relation to *Nirvāna*; as for him who enjoys this "state"—if indeed such a term is still applicable—we must bear in mind the doctrine of the three simultaneous and hierarchically situated "bodies" of the Buddhas: the earthly, the heavenly, and the divine.

He promises—though He may always exceed His promises—and so the eschatological mysteries cannot give the lie to what the Scriptures say, though they can reveal things on which the Scriptures are silent as the case may be; "and God is more knowing" (*wa 'Llāhu a'lam*). From the point of view of transmigration the whole emphasis is on the idea that all that is not the "Self" or the "Void" is relative, and it is added that what is limited in its fundamental nature must also be so in its destiny in one way or another,[67] so that it is absurd to talk of a state that is contingent in itself but delivered from every contingency in "duration". In other words, if the Hindu and Buddhist perspectives differ from that of monotheism, it is because being centered on the pure Absolute[68] and on Deliverance, they emphasize the relativity of conditioned states and do not dwell on them; therefore, they insist on transmigration as such, the relative then being synonymous with movement and instability. During a spiritually normal period and in a setting that is traditionally homogeneous, all these considerations on the different ways of looking at survival would in practice be superfluous or even harmful—and moreover everything is implicitly contained in certain scriptural statements[69]—but for the world in dissolution in which we live it has become indispensable to show the meeting point where the divergences between Semitic and Western monotheism and the great traditions that originated in India are attenuated or are resolved. It is true that such direct comparisons are rarely entirely satisfactory—insofar as they concern cosmology—and every time a point is clarified there is a risk of raising fresh problems; but these difficulties really only serve to show that we are dealing here with an infinitely complex

---

[67] Nonetheless: "O, Partha, neither here nor hereafter is there destruction for him; for none that does righteousness, my son, comes to evil estate" (*Bhagavad Gītā*, 6:40). On this Shankara comments: "He who has not succeeded in his *yoga* will not be subjected to an inferior birth."

[68] This is not merely a pleonasm, for the personal aspect of God is absolute in relation to man as such while being at the same time the first contingency in relation to the Self and, what amounts to the same thing, in respect of "our" transontological Intellect.

[69] In the case of Islam, everything is strictly contained in the *Shahādah*, which provides a key to prevent any relativity whatsoever being set on the same level of reality as the Absolute. Other less fundamental formulas include allusions that are even more precise.

domain which will never be adequately revealed to our earthly understanding. In a sense the Absolute is less difficult to "grasp" than the immeasurable abysses of its manifestation.

There is another point which can hardly be overemphasized. The Scriptures termed "monotheistic" have no need to speak explicitly of certain seemingly paradoxical possibilities of survival given the perspective to which their providential field of expansion restricts them; their quality of *upāya*—of "provisional" and "opportune truth"—obliges these Sacred Books to pass over in silence, not only the compensatory dimensions of the hereafter, but also those prolongations which lie outside the "sphere of interest" of the human being. It is in this sense that it was stated above that exoteric truth could only be partial,[70] leaving aside the polyvalence of its symbolism. The limiting definitions proper to exoterism are comparable to descriptions of an object of which only the form and not the colors can be seen.[71] The "ostracism" of sacred Scriptures is often a function of man's malice; it was efficacious so long as, despite everything, men still had a sufficient intuition of their own imperfection and of their ambiguous situation in face of the Infinite. But today everything is called into question, on the one hand by reason of the loss of this intuition and on the other because of the inevitable confrontations between very different religions, not to mention the scientific discoveries wrongly deemed capable of invalidating religious truths.

[70] The atrocities traditionally committed in the name of religion are a proof of this; in this respect only esoterism is beyond reproach. That there are necessary evils does not mean that they are blessings in the intrinsic sense of the word.

[71] There are *ahādīth* which occupy as it were an intermediate position between the two perspectives in question—the literal and the universal. For example: "He (*Allāh*) will save men from hell when they are burnt like charcoal." Similarly: "By the God in whose hands is my soul, a time shall come when the gates of hell shall be closed and watercress [symbol of coolness] will grow on its soil." Or again: "And God will say: the Angels, the Prophets, and the believers have all interceded for sinners; now there remains none to intercede for them save the Most Merciful of the merciful [*Arham ar-Rāhimīn*, God]. And He will take a handful of fire and withdraw a people who never did any good." To this mercy occurring in time, the Sufis, as we have seen, add a mercy occurring in the very actuality of the state of those in hell.

It should be clearly understood that sacred Scriptures "of the first rank"[72] are never exoteric in themselves,[73] whatever their expressions or their silences; they always leave a possibility of reconstituting the total truth, be it from some minute element, which means that they always let it shine through them; they are never entirely compact crystallizations of partial perspectives.[74] This transcendence of the sacred Scriptures in relation to their concessions to a particular mentality appears in the Koran notably in the form of the esoteric story of the meeting between Moses and al-Khidr: in this story we find, not just the idea that the viewpoint of the Law is always only fragmentary, though fully efficacious and sufficient for the individual as such—he being only a part and not a totality—but also the doctrine found in the *Bhagavad Gītā*,[75] according to which neither good nor bad actions concern the Self directly; that is to say, only knowledge of the Self and, in terms of that knowledge, detachment in relation to action have absolute value.[76] Moses represents the Law, the particular and exclusive form, and al-Khidr universal Truth, which cannot be grasped from the standpoint of the "letter", like the wind of which thou "canst not tell whence it cometh, and whither it goeth".

What matters for God as regards men is, not so much to supply scientific explanations of things that most men cannot understand, as to unleash a "shock" by means of a symbolical concept; and that is precisely the role of the *upāya*. And in this sense the part played by the

---

[72] This reservation means that it is a question here of universal Revelations founding whole civilizations and not of secondary inspirations destined for a particular school and having, for example, a narrowly Vaishnavite tendency.

[73] In their immediate meaning they incontestably expound a "dualistic" and anthropomorphic perspective with a limited eschatology; but, as Meister Eckhart has pointed out, every true meaning is a "literal meaning". According to a *hadīth nabawwi* (a saying of the Prophet himself) the verses of the Koran enclose, not merely an exoteric and an esoteric meaning, but also within the latter many other possible meanings, at least seven and at most seventy; their profusion has been compared to "the waves of the sea".

[74] "Heaven and earth shall pass away, but my words shall not pass away", says the Gospel; and the Koran says: "All things are ephemeral save the Face of *Allāh*."

[75] The *Bhagavad Gītā* is like the "Bible" of *gnosis*; and it is not without reason that Hindus often consider it as an *Upanishad*.

[76] Although it is clear that salvation in the most elementary sense can be obtained short of that value.

violent alternative "Heaven-hell" in the consciousness of the monotheist is very instructive: the "shock", with all it implies for man, reveals far more of the truth than some account that is "more true" but less easy to assimilate and less effective, and therefore in fact "more false" for a particular understanding. It is a matter of "understanding", not with the brain alone, but with our whole "being", and so also with our will; dogma is addressed to the personal substance rather than to thought alone, at any rate in cases where thought is liable to be only a superstructure; it speaks to thought only insofar as thought is capable of communicating concretely with our whole being, and in this respect men are not all the same. When God speaks to man He does not converse, He commands; He wishes to inform man only insofar as He can change him; now ideas do not act in the same way on everyone, hence the diversity of the sacred doctrines. Those perspectives which are *a priori* dynamic—those of Semitic and Western monotheism—envisage the posthumous states, by a kind of compensation, in a static aspect, and thus as definitive; on the other hand those which are *a priori* static, which means more contemplative and thus less anthropomorphic— those of India and the Far East—view these states under an aspect of cyclic movement and cosmic fluidity. Or again: if the Semitic West represents the *post mortem* states as something definitive, it is implicitly correct in the sense that before us lie as it were two infinities, that of God and that of the macrocosm or of the immeasurable and indefinite labyrinth of the *samsāra*; it is the latter which is in the last analysis the "invincible" hell and it is God who in reality is the positive and blissful Eternity. If the perspective of Hinduism and of Buddhism insists on the transmigration of souls, that is, as has already been stated, because its profoundly contemplative character enables it not to limit itself to the human condition alone, and because on this account it inevitably emphasizes the relative and inconstant nature of all that is not the Absolute; for this perspective, the *samsāra* can only be an expression of relativity. Whatever these divergences, the meeting point between the different perspectives becomes visible in such concepts as "the resurrection of the body", which is precisely a "re-incarnation".

One other question which must also be answered here is the following, to which the Koran gives only an implicit answer: why is the Universe made up on the one hand of worlds and on the other of beings which pass through these worlds? This is like asking why there is a shuttle passing through the warp, or why there is warp and weft; or again, why the same relationship of crossing is produced when a cross or a star is inscribed in a system of concentric circles, that is, when the principle of weaving is applied in a concentric way. What we want to show is this: just as the relationship of the center to space cannot be conceived except in this form of the spider's web with its two modes of projection—one continuous and the other discontinuous—so the relationship of the Principle to manifestation—which makes up the Universe—is only conceivable as a combination between worlds arranged according to gradation around the Divine Center and beings who pass through them.[77] To speak of "Existence" is to express the relationship between receptacle and content, or between the static and the dynamic; the journey of souls through life, death, and resurrection is nothing other than the very life of the macrocosm; even in our experience in this world we pass through days and nights, summers and winters; essentially we are beings who pass through states; and Existence cannot be conceived of otherwise. Our whole reality converges toward that unique "moment" which alone matters: our confrontation with the Center.

What was said above about divine sanctions and their root in human nature or in its state of disequilibrium is equally applicable, from the point of view of their deep causes, to the calamities of this world and to death: both are explained by the necessity of a counter shock after a loss of equilibrium.[78] The cause of death is the disequilibrium that brought about our fall and the loss of Paradise, and the trials of life arise, consequently, from the disequilibrium of our personal nature.

---

[77] The symbolism of the spider's web—the symbolism of cosmic compartments and their contents—is found in Buddhist pictures of "the Round of Existence". The Koran is itself an image of the cosmos: the *sūrahs* are the worlds and the verses (*āyāt*) are the beings.

[78] According to the Koran, all earthly ills "come from yourselves" (*min anfusikum*), which does not mean that "everything" does not "come from God" (*kullun min 'indi 'Llāhi*).

In the case of the gravest sanctions beyond the tomb this disequilibrium is in our very essence and reaches the point of an inversion of our deiformity; man "burns" because he does not want to be what he is—because he is free not to want to be so; now, "every house divided against itself shall fall". From this it follows that every divine sanction is the inversion of an inversion, and since sin is an inversion in relation to the primordial equilibrium, we can speak of "offences" committed against God, although very clearly there is no possible psychological meaning in the phrase despite the inevitable anthropomorphism of exoteric conceptions. The Koran describes with the intense eloquence characterizing its last *sūrahs* the final dissolution of the world; now all this can be transposed to the scale of the microcosm, in which death appears as the end of a world and as a judgment, namely as an absorption of the outward by the inward in the direction of the Center. When Hindu cosmology teaches that the souls of the dead go first of all to the Moon, it suggests indirectly, and aside from other far more important analogies, the experience of incommensurable solitude —"the terrors of death"—through which the soul passes "backwards" on leaving the protective matrix which the earthly world had been for it; the material moon is as it were the symbol of an absolute uprooting, of dark and sepulchral solitude, of the chill of eternity;[79] and it is this terrible

---

[79] In passing, let it be said that this is what raises doubts as to the psychological possibility of a journey to the moon or elsewhere in space; such a journey would amount psychologically to death, for when the soul undergoes such an experience, chances are that the body will follow. Even if we allow for the possibility of unforeseeable mental factors making such an adventure possible—and setting aside here the possibility of satanic aid—it is very unlikely that on his return to earth a man would recover his former equilibrium and his old happiness. There is something analogous in lunacy, which is a death, that is, a collapse or a decomposition, not of the immortal soul, but of its psychological cladding, the empirical ego; lunatics are living-dead, most often a prey to dark influences, but occasionally—in surroundings of great religious fervor—a vehicle on the contrary for some angelic influence, though in this case it is strictly speaking not lunacy, the natural fissure being compensated, and in a way filled, by Heaven. Be that as it may, lunacy is characterized, especially as regards those who fall into it, if not always as regards those already in that condition, by an anguish marking the slide into a terrifying sense of alienation, exactly as is the case at death or, by hypothesis, during an interplanetary journey. In all these instances, the normal limits of human surroundings are superseded and in a general sense this is equally true of modern science; it projects one into a void which leaves no choice but that of materialism or a metaphysical readaptation to which the very principles of that science are opposed.

post mortem isolation which marks the repercussion in relation not to a particular sin but to formal existence.[80]

Our very existence in itself is like a still innocent prefiguration of all transgression— innocent, yet engendering all forms of miseries; at least it is so inasmuch as it is a demiurgic "coming out" from the Principle and not inasmuch as it is a positive "manifestation" of the Principle. If the *philosophia perennis* can combine the truth of Mazdean-Gnostic dualism with that of Semitic monism, the exoterisms for their part are forced to choose between a conception metaphysically adequate but morally contradictory and one that is morally satisfactory but metaphysically fragmentary.[81]

One should never ask why misfortunes befall the innocent: in the sight of the Absolute all is disequilibrium, "God alone is good"; now this truth cannot fail to be manifested from time to time in a direct and violent manner. If the good suffer, this means that all men would merit as much; old age and death prove it, for they spare no man. The apportioning of earthly good and ill fortune is a question of cosmic economy, although immanent justice must also sometimes reveal itself in the light of day by showing the link between causes and effects in human action. Man's sufferings testify to the mysteries of his distance and separation, and they cannot but be, the world not being God.

But the leveling justice of death is infinitely more important for us than the diversity of earthly destinies. The experience of death is somewhat like that of a man who has lived all his life in a dark room and suddenly finds himself transported to a mountain top; there his gaze would embrace all the wide landscape; the works of men would seem insignificant to him. It is thus that the soul torn from the earth and from the body perceives the inexhaustible diversity of things and the incommensurable abysses of the worlds which contain them; for the first time it sees itself in its universal context, in an inexorable

---

[80] At death all assurance and all cleverness fall away like a garment and the being who remains is impotent and like a lost child; nothing is left but a substance we have ourselves woven which may either fall heavily or on the contrary let itself be drawn up by Heaven like a rising star. Red Indians put moccasins with embroidered soles on the feet of their dead, and this is eloquently symbolic.

[81] In the first case God is the cause of all: but then whence comes evil? In the second case evil comes from man: but then what is God?

interlocking of parts and in a network of multitudinous and unsus-
pected relationships, and realizes that life has been but an "instant",
but a "play".[82] Projected into the absolute "nature of things", man will
be inescapably aware of what he is in reality; he will know himself
ontologically and without any deforming perspective in the light of the
normative "proportions" of the Universe.

One of the proofs of our immortality is that the soul—which is
essentially intelligence or consciousness—could not have an end that is
beneath itself, namely matter or the mental reflections of matter; the
higher cannot be merely defined in terms of the lower, it cannot be
merely a means in relation to what it surpasses. Thus it is intelligence
in itself—and with it our freedom—that proves the divine scope of
our nature and our destiny. If we say that it "proves" this, it is said
unconditionally and without any wish to add any rhetorical precaution
for the benefit of those myopic persons who imagine that they hold a
monopoly of the "concrete". Whether people understand it or not, the
Absolute alone is "proportionate" to the essence of our intelligence;
only the Absolute (*al-Ahad*, "the One") is perfectly intelligible in the
strict sense, so much so that it is only in it that the intelligence finds
its sufficient reason and its end. The Intellect, in its essence, conceives
of God because it "is" itself *increatus et increabile*; and it conceives or
knows thereby or *a fortiori* the meaning of contingencies; it knows the
meaning of the world and the meaning of man. In fact the intelligence
knows with the direct or indirect aid of Revelation; Revelation is the
objectivation of the transcendent Intellect and to one degree or another "awakens" the latent knowledge—or elements of knowledge—we
bear within ourselves. Thus "faith" (in the widest sense, *īmān*) has
two poles, one "objective" and "outward" and the other "subjective"
and "inward": grace and intellection. And nothing is more vain than
to raise in the name of the former a barrier of principle against the
latter; the most profound "proof" of Revelation—whatever its name

---

[82] According to a *hadīth*, man sleeps, and when he dies he awakes. But the gnostic
(*'arif*) is always awake, as the Prophet has said: "My eyes slept, but my heart did not
sleep."

may be—is its eternal prototype which we bear within ourselves, in our own essence.[83]

Like every Revelation, the Koran is a flashing and crystalline expression of that which is "supernaturally natural" to man, namely the consciousness of our situation in the Universe, of our ontological and eschatological connections. It is for this reason that the Book of *Allāh* is a "discernment" (*furqān*), a "warning" (*dhikrā*), and a "light" (*nūr*) in the darkness of our earthly exile.

—— ·:· ——

To the "Book" (*Kitāb*) of God is joined the "Practice" (*Sunnah*) of the Prophet; it is true that the Koran itself speaks of the *Sunnah* of *Allāh*, meaning by this God's principles of action with regard to men, but tradition has reserved this word for the ways of acting, customs, or examples of Muhammad. These precedents constitute the norm, at all levels, of Muslim life.

The *Sunnah* comprises several dimensions: physical, moral, social, spiritual, and others besides. Belonging to the physical dimension are the rules of propriety that result from the nature of things: for example, not to engage in intense conversation during meals, nor *a fortiori* to speak while eating; to rinse one's mouth after eating or drinking, not to eat garlic, to observe all the rules of cleanliness, and so on and so forth. Equally a part of this *Sunnah* are the rules relating to dress: to cover one's head and to wear a turban whenever possible and—for men—not to wear silk or gold, and to leave one's shoes at the door. Other rules require that men and women not mix in public gatherings, or that a woman not preside at prayer in front of men; some allege that she should not even do this in front of other women, or that she should not chant the Koran, but these two opinions are belied by traditional precedents. Finally, there are the elementary Islamic gestures which every Muslim knows: ways of greeting, thanking, and so on. It goes

---

[83] This does not in any way profit rationalism or "free thinking", for the domain in which these operate is only a surface that has nothing to do with the transpersonal essence of the intelligence.

without saying that the majority of these rules admit of no exception in any circumstances whatsoever.

There is also, and even above all in the hierarchy of values, the spiritual *Sunnah*, concerning the "remembrance of God" (*dhikr*) and the principles of the "spiritual journey" (*sulūk*); this *Sunnah* is very parsimonious as regards what is truly essential in it. Basically, it contains all the traditions referring to the relationships between God and man; these relationships may be either separative or unitive, exclusive or inclusive, distinctive or participative. There is another domain which must be rigorously distinguished from this spiritual *Sunnah*, although it may sometimes seem to overlap with it, and this is the moral *Sunnah*, which concerns above all the highly complex realm of social relationships with all their psychological and symbolist concomitances. In spite of certain obvious coincidences, this dimension does not enter, strictly speaking, into esoterism; it cannot form part—without abuse of terminology—of the sapiential perspective, for it is clearly alien to the contemplation of essences and to concentration on the one and only Reality. This intermediate *Sunnah* on the contrary goes as it were hand in hand with the specifically devotional or obediential perspective, and it is consequently exoteric, whence its will-bound and individualistic appearance; the fact that certain of its elements contradict one another shows moreover that man can and must make his own choice.

What the *faqīr* (the spiritually poor) will retain of this *Sunnah* will be, not so much the ways of acting as the intentions that are inherent in them, that is, the spiritual attitudes and the virtues which relate to the *Fitrah*,[84] to the primordial perfection of man and thereby to the normative nature (*uswah*) of the Prophet. Every man must possess the virtue of generosity, for this is part of his theomorphic nature; but generosity of soul is one thing, and a particular gesture of generosity characteristic of the Bedouin world is another. It will doubtless be said that every gesture is a symbol; with this we agree, on two express conditions: firstly, that the gesture not proceed from a conventional automatism, oblivious to the possible absurdity of the results; and secondly, that the gesture not be the vehicle or support of a religious sentimentalism incompatible with the perspective of the Intellect and the Essence.

---

[84] The nature of man corresponding to the "Golden Age".

Fundamentally, the moral or social *Sunnah* is a direct or indirect adequation of the will to the human norm; its aim is to actualize, and not to limit, our positive horizontal nature; but as it is addressed to all, it necessarily carries limitative elements from the point of view of vertical perfection. This horizontal and collective character of a certain *Sunnah* necessarily implies that it is a sort of *māyā* or *upāya*,[85] which means that it is both a support and an obstacle and that it may even become a veritable *shirk*,[86] doubtless not for the ordinary believer, but for the *sālik*.[87] The average *Sunnah* prevents the ordinary man from being a wild beast and from losing his soul; but it may also prevent a man of outstanding spiritual gifts from transcending forms and from realizing the Essence. The average *Sunnah* may favor vertical realization just as it may hold a man back in the horizontal dimension; it operates both as an equilibrium and as a weight. It favors ascension, but does not condition it; it contributes to the conditioning of ascension only by its intrinsic and non-formal contents which, precisely, are in principle independent of formal attitudes.

From the point of view of the *Religio Perennis*, the question of the *Sunnah* implies a highly delicate problem, given that the accentuation of the intermediate and social *Sunnah* goes hand in hand with a particular religious psychism, which by definition excludes other equally possible religious psychisms and which fashions, as they do, a particular mentality, one which obviously is not essential to Islamic *gnosis*. Quite apart from this aspect of things, it should not be forgotten that the Prophet, like every man, was obliged to perform all kinds of actions during his life, and that he necessarily performed these in one particular way and not in another, and even in different ways depending on the outward or inward circumstances; he fully intended to serve as a universal model, but he did not always specify whether or not a given action amounted, strictly speaking, to a prescription. Furthermore, the Prophet gave different teachings to different men, without being responsible for the fact that the Companions—of very diverse gifts—later transmitted all that they had heard and seen, and that they

---

[85] A "saving mirage", according to the *Mahāyāna*.

[86] An "association" of something else with God.

[87] The spiritual "traveler".

did so sometimes in divergent ways, depending on individual observations and emphases. The conclusion to be drawn from this is that not every element of the *Sunnah* is applicable in the same way or with the same certainty, and that in many cases the teaching lies in the intention rather than in the form.

Be that as it may, there is a fundamental truth that should not be lost sight of, namely that the plane of actions is in itself entirely human, and insistence on a multitude of forms of action, belonging necessarily to a particular style, constitutes an absorbing *karma-yoga*[88] which has no connection with the Path of metaphysical discernment and concentration on the Essential. In the person of the Prophet there is to be found both the simple and the complex, and amongst men there are diverse vocations; the Prophet necessarily personifies a religious—and therefore human—climate of a particular character, but he likewise personifies, and in a different connection, the Truth in itself and the Path as such. There is an imitation of the Prophet founded on the religious illusion that he is intrinsically better than all the other Prophets, including Jesus, and there is another imitation of the Prophet founded on the prophetic quality in itself, that is, on the perfection of the *Logos* become man; this imitation is necessarily more true, more profound, and consequently less formalist than the first, it is centered less on outward actions but rather on the reflections of the Divine Names in the soul of the human *Logos*.

Niffari, who incarnates esoterism in the truest sense of the word, and not a pre-esoterism still largely exoterist and conditioned by the will, bore the following testimony: "*Allāh* said to me: Formulate thy petition to Me thus: Lord, how must I attach myself firmly to Thee so that on the day of my Judgment Thou wilt not punish me or turn Thy face from me? Then I (*Allāh*) shall answer thee saying: Attach thyself to the *Sunnah* in thine outward doctrine and practice, and attach thyself in thine inward soul to the *Gnosis* which I have given thee; and know that when I make Myself known to thee, I will not accept from thee anything of the *Sunnah* except what My *Gnosis* brings thee, for thou art one of those to whom I speak; thou hearest Me and thou knowest that thou hearest Me, and thou seest that I am the source of

---

[88] A path based on action.

all things." The commentator on the passage remarks that the *Sunnah* has a general application and that it makes no distinction between the seekers of a created reward and the seekers of the Essence, and that it contains what any and every person may have need of. Another saying of Niffari: "And He said to me: My exoteric (*zhāhirī*) Revelation does not support My esoteric (*bātinī*) Revelation." And yet another, of an abrupt symbolism that needs to be understood: "The good actions of the pious man are as the bad actions of the privileged of *Allāh*." Which indicates as clearly as possible the relativity of certain elements of the *Sunnah* and the relativity of the cult of the average *Sunnah*.

Adab—traditional politeness—is in fact a particularly problematical sector of the *Sunnah* because of two factors, namely narrow interpretation and blind convention. *Adab* can be flattened out into a formalism that is so cut off from its profound intentions that formal attitudes supplant the intrinsic virtues which are the whole point of their existence; an ill-understood *adab* can give rise to dissimulation, touchiness, lying, and childishness; on the pretext that one must neither contradict a person with whom one is speaking, nor tell him anything disagreeable, one leaves him in harmful error or one refrains from giving him a necessary piece of information, or one inflicts on him, out of kindness, situations which may, to say the least, be undesirable, and so on. In any case, it is important to know—and to understand—that *adab*, even when well understood, has limits: thus, tradition recommends that one should conceal the faults of a brother Muslim, if it does no harm to the collectivity, but it prescribes reprimanding this brother in private, without regard for *adab*, if there is a chance that the reprimand will be accepted; likewise, *adab* must not prevent the public denunciation of faults and errors which run the risk of contaminating others. As regards the relativity of *adab*, it may be recalled that the Shaykh Darqawi and others have sometimes obliged their disciples to break certain rules, without however going against the Law, the *Sharī'ah*; in this case it is not a question of the path of the *Malāmatiyah*, who seek their own humiliation, but simply the principle of the "breaking of habits" in view of "sincerity" (*sidq*) and "poverty" (*faqr*) before God.

As regards a certain *Sunnah* in general, reference may be made to the following saying of the Shaykh Darqawi, reported by Ibn Ajibah: "The systematic pursuit of meritorious acts and the multiplication of supererogatory practices are habits amongst others; they scatter the heart. Let the disciple therefore hold fast to a single *dhikr*, to a single action, each according to what corresponds to him."

From a slightly different point of view, it might be objected that a quintessential and consequently very free interpretation of the *Sunnah* could only concern a few Sufis and not the *sālikūn*, the "travelers".[89] We would say, rather, that this freedom concerns the Sufis insofar as they have transcended the world of forms; but it also concerns the *sālikūn* insofar as they follow in principle the path of *Gnosis* and that their starting point is of necessity inspired by the perspective that conforms to this Path; by the nature of things, they are aware *a priori* of the relativity of forms, especially of some, so that a social formalism with sentimental undertones cannot be imposed on them.

The relativity of a certain *Sunnah*, in a perspective which is not a *karma-yoga*, still less an exoterism, does not annul the importance which the aesthetic integrity of forms has for a civilization, right down to the objects that surround us; for whereas abstaining from a symbolic action is not in itself an error, the presence of a false form is a permanent error;[90] even he who is subjectively independent of it cannot deny that it is an error, and thus an element contrary in principle to spiritual health and to the imponderables of *barakah*. The decadence of traditional art goes hand in hand with the decay of spirituality.

In Amidism as well as in *japa-yoga*,[91] the initiate must abandon all other religious practices and put his faith in quintessential orison alone; this is the expression, not of an arbitrary opinion, but of an aspect of the nature of things; and this aspect is reinforced in the case of men who, in addition to this reduction as to method, base themselves on pure and total metaphysics. Moreover, knowledge of the various traditional worlds, and so of the relativity of doctrinal formulations and formal perspectives, reinforces the need for essentiality on the one

---

[89] Those who have not yet reached the destination.

[90] Modern churches and priests in civilian dress are irrefutable evidence of this.

[91] The invocatory method, whose Vedic seed lies in the monosyllable *Om.*

hand and universality on the other. The essential and the universal are all the more imperative because we live in a world of philosophical supersaturation and spiritual collapse.

The perspective which allows the actualization of the awareness of the relativity of conceptual and moral forms has always existed in Islam—witness the passage in the Koran about Moses and al-Khidr, and also some *ahādīth* which reduce the conditions of salvation to the simplest attitudes. This perspective is likewise that of primordiality and universality, and so of the *Fitrah*; this is what Jalal ad-Din Rumi expresses in the following terms: "I am neither Christian, Jew, Parsi, nor Muslim. I am neither of the East nor of the West, nor of the land nor of the sea. . . . My place is placeless, my trace is traceless. . . . I have put aside duality, I have seen that the two worlds are one; I seek the One, I know the One, I see the One, I invoke the One. He is the First, He is the Last, He is the Outward, He is the Inward. . .".

The Prophet

To Westerners, and no doubt to most non-Muslims, Christ and the Buddha represent perfections that are immediately intelligible and convincing. By contrast, the Prophet of Islam seems complex and uneven and hardly compels recognition as a symbol outside his own traditional universe. The reason is that, unlike the Buddha and Christ, his spiritual reality is wrapped in certain human and earthly veils, and this because of his function as a legislator "for this world". He is thus akin to the other great Semitic Revealers, Abraham and Moses, and also to David and Solomon. From the Hindu point of view one could add that he is close to Rama and Krishna whose supreme sanctity and saving power did not prevent the occurrence of all sorts of family and political vicissitudes. This allows us to bring out a fundamental distinction: there are not only those Revealers who represent exclusively the "other world", there are also those whose attitude is at the same time divinely contemplative and humanly combative and constructive.

When one has acquired a real familiarity with the life of Muhammad according to the traditional sources,[1] three elements stand out which could be provisionally designated by the following terms: piety, combativeness, and magnanimity. By "piety" we mean wholehearted attachment to God, the sense of the hereafter, absolute sincerity, and thus an altogether general characteristic in saints and *a fortiori* in messengers of Heaven; we mention it because in the life of the Prophet it appears with a particularly salient function, and because it prefigures in a sense the spiritual climate of Islam.[2] There were in this life wars and, standing out against this background of violence, there was a superhuman grandeur of soul; there were also marriages and through them a deliberate entry into the earthly and social sphere—we do not

---

[1] "Traditional sources" because the profane biographers of the Prophet, whether Muslim or Christian, always seek to "excuse" him, the former in a lay and anti-Christian sense and the latter, even in favorable cases, with a sort of psychological condescension.

[2] In the case of Christ and the Buddha, one could not speak of manifestations of piety, that is to say of "fear" and "love"; the human is as it were extinguished in the divine message, whence the "anthropotheism" of the Christian and Buddhist perspectives.

say: into the worldly and profane sphere—and *ipso facto* an integration of collective human life into the spiritual realm given the Prophet's "avataric" nature. On the plane of "piety", we shall mention the love of poverty, fasting, and vigils; some people will no doubt object that marriage and especially polygamy are opposed to asceticism, but that is to forget, firstly, that married life does not remove from poverty, vigils, and fasts their rigor, nor render them easy and agreeable,[3] and secondly, that in the case of the Prophet marriage had a spiritualized or "tantric" character, as indeed has everything in the life of such a being because of the metaphysical transparency which phenomena then assume.[4] Seen from outside, most of the Prophet's marriages had, moreover, a "political" aspect, politics having here a sacred significance connected with the establishing on earth of a reflection of the "City of God". Finally, Muhammad gave enough examples of long abstinences, particularly in his youth when passion is considered to be most strong, to be exempt from superficial judgments on this account. Another re-proach often leveled at him is that of cruelty; but it is rather implac-ability that should be spoken of, and it was directed, not at enemies as such, but only at traitors, whatever their origin; if there was hardness here, it was that of God Himself through participation in the Divine Justice which rejects and consumes. To accuse Muhammad of having a vindictive nature would involve, not only a serious misjudgment of his spiritual state and a distortion of the facts, but also by the same token a condemnation of most of the Jewish Prophets and of the Bible

---

[3] As regards Islam in general, people too easily lose sight of the fact that the prohibition of fermented drinks unquestionably involved a sacrifice for the ancient Arabs and for the other peoples to be brought into Islam, all of whom knew wine. Nor is Ramadan a recreation, and the same is true of the regular—and often nocturnal—practice of prayer; most certainly Islam did not impose itself because it was easy. On our first visits to Arab towns, we were impressed by the austere and even sepulchral atmosphere: a kind of desert-like whiteness was spread like a shroud over houses and people; every-where there was a breath of prayer and of death. In this we see beyond question traces of the soul of the Prophet.

[4] The *Sunnah* transmits this saying of the Prophet: "I have never seen anything without seeing God in it", or, "without seeing God nearer to me than it". On the subject of sex, see *The Wisdom of the Prophets* by Ibn Arabi, and especially the chapters on Muham-mad and Solomon, in the annotated translation by our friend Titus Burckhardt.

itself;[5] in the decisive phase of his earthly mission, at the time of the taking of Mecca, the Messenger of *Allāh* even showed a superhuman forbearance in the face of a unanimous feeling to the contrary in his victorious army.[6]

At the beginning of the Prophet's career there were painful obscurities and uncertainties, and these show that the mission imposed on him arose, not from the human genius of Muhammad—a genius which he himself never suspected—but essentially from the divine choice; in an analogous way, the seeming imperfections of the great Messengers have always had a positive meaning.[7] The complete absence in Muhammad of any kind of ambition leads us moreover to make here a brief digression: it is always astonishing to find that certain people, convinced of their purity of intention, their talents, and of their combative power, imagine that God ought to make use of them, and wait impatiently, even with disappointment and dismay, for a call from Heaven or for some miracle; what they forget—and such forgetfulness is strange in defenders of spirituality—is that God has no need of any man and can well dispense with their natural gifts and their passions. Heaven only makes use of talents provided they have first been broken for God or else when a man has never been aware of them; a direct instrument of God is always raised from the ashes.[8]

Reference was made above to the "avataric" nature of Muhammad, to which it might be objected that for Islam or, what comes to the same thing, by his own conviction Muhammad was not and could not be an *Avatāra*. But this is not really the question because it is perfectly obvious that Islam is not Hinduism and notably excludes any

[5] All these considerations are adduced not to "attenuate" some "imperfections" but simply to explain facts. The Christian Church was also implacable—in the name of Christ—during the period when it was still all-powerful.

[6] Among numerous manifestations of forbearance, let just one *hadīth* be quoted: "God has created nothing He loves better than the emancipation of slaves, and nothing He hates more than divorce."

[7] For instance, in the case of Moses, his difficulty in speaking indicated the divine prohibition to divulge the mysteries, which implies a superabundance of wisdom.

[8] A "direct instrument" is a man conscious of the part he has to play from the moment it is allotted to him; on the other hand, anyone or anything can be an "indirect instrument".

idea of incarnation (*hulūl*); quite simply, and using Hindu terminology, which in this case is the most direct or the least inadequate, we would reply that a certain Divine Aspect took on under particular cyclic circumstances a particular terrestrial form, something in full conformity with what the Envoy of *Allāh* testified as to his own nature, for he said: "He who has seen me has seen God" (*al-Haqq*, "the Truth"); "I am He and He is I, save that I am he who I am and He is He who He is"; "I was a Prophet when Adam was still between water and clay" (before the creation); "I have been charged to fulfill my mission since the best of the ages of Adam (the origin of the world), from age to age down to the age in which I now am."[9]

In any case, if Islam is loath to attribute divinity to a historical personage, that is because its perspective is centered on the Absolute as such, as is shown for instance in the conception of the final leveling before the Judgment: God alone in this conception remains "living" and all else is leveled in universal death including the supreme Angels, hence also the "Spirit" (*ar-Rūh*), the divine manifestation at the luminous center of the cosmos.

It is natural that the upholders of Islamic exoterism (*fuqahā* or *ulama azh-zhāhir*, "wise men of the outer order") should have an interest in denying the authenticity of those *ahādīth* which refer to the "avataric" nature of the Prophet, but the very concept of the "Spirit of Muhammad" (*Rūh muhammadī*)—which is the *Logos*—proves the correctness of these *ahādīth*, whatever their historic value, assuming that this value might be open to doubt. Each traditional form identifies its founder with the Divine *Logos* and looks on the other spokesmen

---

[9] There is an Arabic saying that "Muhammad is a mortal, but not as other mortals; (in comparison with them) he is like a jewel among pebbles". Most profane critics have wrongly interpreted the reply: "What am I, if not a mortal and an Envoy?" (Koran 17:93) given by the Prophet to unbelievers who asked him for absurd and inappropriate wonders, as a denial of the gift of miracles, a gift which Islam in fact attributes to all the prophets. Christ also refused to perform miracles when the tempter urged him to do so, setting aside here the intrinsic meaning of his answers. In fact, Muhammad's saying means—in conformity with the perspective characterizing Islam, which emphasizes that every derogation of natural laws comes about "with God's permission" (*bi-idhni 'Llāh*)—"What, if not a man like yourselves, am I apart from the Grace of God?" It should be added that the *Sunnah* bears witness to a number of miracles in the case of Muhammad which, as arguments to "weaken" (*mu'jizāt*) unbelief, are differentiated from the prodigies of the saints, which are called divine "favors" (*karāmāt*).

of Heaven, insofar as it takes them into consideration, as projections of this founder and as secondary manifestations of the one *Logos*; in the case of Buddhists, Christ and the Prophet can only be envisaged as *Buddhas*. When Christ says that "no man cometh unto the Father but by me", it is the *Logos* as such who speaks, although for a given world Jesus is truly identified with this one and universal Word.

The Prophet is the human norm in respect both of his individual and of his collective functions, or again in respect of his spiritual and earthly functions.

Essentially he is equilibrium and extinction: equilibrium from the human point of view and extinction in relation to God.

The Prophet is Islam; if Islam presents itself as a manifestation of truth, of beauty, and of power—and it is indeed these three elements which inspire it and which, on various planes, it tends by its nature to actualize—the Prophet for his part incarnates serenity, generosity, and strength. These virtues could also be enumerated in the inverse order, that is, according to the ascending hierarchy of their values and by reference to the degrees of spiritual realization. Strength is the affirmation—if need be combative—of Divine Truth both in the soul and in the world, and here lies the distinction drawn in Islam between the two kinds of holy warfare, the greater (*akbar*) and the lesser (*asghar*), or the inner and the outer; as for generosity it compensates the aggressive aspect of strength; it is charity and pardon.[10] These two complementary virtues of strength and generosity culminate—or are in a sense extinguished—in a third virtue: serenity, which is detachment from the world and from the ego, extinction before God, knowledge of the Divine and union with it.

There is a certain, no doubt paradoxical, relationship between virile strength and virginal purity in the sense that both are concerned

---

[10] Al-Ghazzali says that the principle (*asl*) of all good actions (*mahāsin*) is generosity (*karam*). God is "the Generous" (*al-Karīm*).

with the inviolability of the sacred,[11] strength in a dynamic and combative manner and purity in a static and defensive manner; it could also be said that strength, a "warrior" quality, contains a mode or complement that is static or passive, and this is sobriety, love of poverty and of fasting, and incorruptibility, which are "pacific" or "non-aggressive" qualities. In the same way generosity, which "gives", has its static complement in nobility, which "is"; or rather nobility is the intrinsic reality of generosity. Nobility is a sort of contemplative generosity; it is love of beauty in its widest sense; for the Prophet and for Islam it is here that aestheticism and love of cleanliness enter,[12] for cleanliness removes from things, and especially from the body, the mark of their earthliness and fall and so brings them back, both symbolically and in a certain manner even in virtuality, to their immutable and incorruptible prototypes, or to their essences. As for serenity, it also has a necessary complement in veracity which is as it were its active or discriminative aspect; it is the love of truth and of intelligence, so characteristic of Islam, and therefore it is also impartiality and justice. Nobility compensates the aspect of narrowness in sobriety, and these two complementary virtues find their culmination in veracity in the sense that they subordinate themselves to it and, if need be, efface themselves—or seem to do so—in its presence.[13]

The virtues of the Prophet form, so to speak, a triangle: serenity-veracity is the apex of the triangle, and the two other pairs of virtues—generosity-nobility and strength-sobriety—form the base; the two angles of the base are in equilibrium and at the apex they are so to

---

[11] This is what is expressed by the "illiteracy" of the Prophet (*al-ummī*, "the unlettered"); divine "Knowledge" can only be implanted in virgin soil. The purity of the Blessed Virgin is not unconnected with the sword of the Archangel guarding the entrance to Paradise.

[12] The Prophet said that "God detests filthiness and noise" and this is highly characteristic of the aspect of purity and calm in contemplation, an aspect which is found in Islamic architecture, ranging geographically speaking from the Alhambra to the Taj Mahal. In the courtyards of mosques and palaces, their calm and balance are echoed in the murmuring of the fountains, the undulatory monotony of which repeats that of the arabesques. For Islam architecture is, next to calligraphy, the supreme sacred art.

[13] The three virtues of strength, generosity, and serenity—and with them the three other virtues—already find expression in the very sound of the words of the second testimony of faith (*Shahādah*) *Muhammadun Rasūlu 'Llāh* ("Muhammad is the Messenger of God").

speak reduced to unity. As was said above, the soul of the Prophet is in its essence equilibrium and extinction.[14]

Imitation of the Prophet implies: strength toward oneself; generosity toward others; serenity in God and through God. We could also say: serenity through piety, in the most profound sense of that term.

Such imitation moreover implies: sobriety in relation to the world; nobility in ourselves, in our being; veracity through God and in Him. But we must not lose sight of the fact that the world is also within us, and that, conversely, we are not other than the creation which surrounds us and, finally, that God created "by the Truth" (*bi 'l-Haqq*); the world is, both in its perfections and in its equilibrium, an expression of the Divine Truth.[15]

The aspect "strength" is at the same time, and indeed above all, the active and affirmative character of the spiritual means or method; the aspect "generosity" is also the love of our immortal soul; while the aspect "serenity", which *a priori* is seeing all things in God, is also seeing God in all things. One may be serene because one knows that "God alone is", that the world and its troubles is "non-real", but one also may be serene because—admitting the relative reality of the world— one realizes that "all things are willed by God", that the Divine Will acts in all things, that all things symbolize God in one or another respect and that symbolism is for God what might be called a "manner of being". Nothing is outside God; God is not absent from anything.

Imitation of the Prophet means actualizing a balance between our normal tendencies, or more exactly between our complementary

---

[14] It would be wrong to seek to enumerate the virtues of Christ in this way for they cannot be said to characterize him, given that Christ manifests divinity and not human perfection, at any rate not expressly and explicitly so as to include also the collective functions of earthly man. Christ is divinity, love, sacrifice; the Virgin is purity and mercy. Similarly the Buddha could be characterized in the following terms: renunciation, extinction, and pity, for it is indeed those qualities or attitudes which in a special sense he incarnates.

[15] An expression, that is to say, of the pure Spirit or, in Hindu terms, of pure "Consciousness" (*Chit*) which objectifies itself in *Māyā* through Being (*Sat*).

virtues and, following from this and above all, it is extinction in the Divine Unity on the basis of this harmony. It is thus that the base of the triangle is in a certain sense absorbed into its apex, which appears as its synthesis and its origin or as its end and the reason for its existence.

———— .:. ————

If we now return to the description given above but formulate it somewhat differently, we shall say that Muhammad is the human form turned toward the Divine Essence; this "form" has two chief aspects, corresponding respectively to the base and to the apex of the triangle, namely nobility and piety. Now nobility is compounded of strength and generosity, while piety—at the level here in question—is compounded of wisdom and sanctity; it should be added that by "piety" we must understand the state of spiritual servitude (*'ubūdiyah*) in the highest sense of the term, comprising perfect "poverty" (*faqr*, whence the word *faqīr*) and "extinction" (*fanā*) before God, and this is not unrelated to the attribute "unlettered" (*ummī*) which is applied to the Prophet. Piety is what links us to God; in Islam this something is first of all an understanding, inasmuch as this is possible, of the evident Divine Unity—for one who is "responsible" must grasp this evidentness and there is here no sharp demarcation between "believing" and "knowing"—and next it is a realization of the Unity that goes beyond our provisional and "unilateral" understanding which is itself ignorance when regarded in the light of plenary knowledge: there is no saint (*walī*, "representative", thus "participant") who is not a "knower through God" (*'arīf bi'Llāh*). This explains why in Islam piety—and all the more the sanctity which is its flower—has an air of serenity;[16] it is a piety that essentially opens onto contemplation and *gnosis*.

Or again, the phenomenon of Muhammad could be described by saying that the soul of the Prophet is made of nobility and serenity, the latter comprising sobriety and veracity and the former strength and generosity. The Prophet's attitude to food and sleep is determined by

[16] It is on this account that some have reproached this piety with being "fatalistic" or "quietist". The tendencies actually in question already show in the term *islām* which means "abandonment" (to God).

sobriety and his attitude to woman by generosity; here the real object
of generosity is the pole of "substance" in humankind, this pole—
woman—being envisaged in its aspect as a mirror of the beatific infinitude of God.

Love of the Prophet constitutes a fundamental element in Islamic
spirituality, although this love must not be understood in the sense of a
personalistic *bhakti* which would presuppose divinizing the hero in an
exclusive way.[17] It arises because Muslims see in the Prophet the prototype and model of the virtues which constitute the theomorphism of
man and the beauty and equilibrium of the Universe, and which are so
many keys or paths toward liberating Unity—this is why they love him
and imitate him even in the very smallest details of his daily life; the
Prophet, like Islam as a whole, is as it were a heavenly mold ready to
receive the influx of the intelligence and will of the believer, and one
wherein even effort becomes a kind of supernatural repose.

"Verily God and His angels bless the Prophet; O ye who believe! Bless
him and give him salutation" (Koran 33:56). This verse forms the scriptural foundation of the "Prayer on the Prophet"—or more precisely
the "Blessing of the Prophet"—a prayer which is in general use in Islam
because both the Koran and the *Sunnah* recommend it, though it takes
on a special character in esoterism where it becomes a basic symbol.
The esoteric meaning of this verse is as follows: God, Heaven, and
Earth—or, the Principle (which is unmanifest), the supra-formal manifestation (the angelic states), and formal manifestation (comprising
both men and the *jinn*, in other words the two categories of corrupt-

---

[17] By "exclusive" is meant seeing the Divine in practice only in a human form, and not
apart from it, as is the case in the cult of Rama or of Krishna. In this connection let
us recall the analogy between the Hindu *Avatāra*s and the Jewish Prophets: the latter
remained within the Judaic framework as did the former within the Hindu framework save for one single great exception in each case: the Buddha and Christ. David
brought the Psalms and Solomon the Song of Songs, as Rama inspired the *Rāmāyana*
and the *Yoga Vasishta* (or *Mahārāmāyana*) and Krishna the *Mahābhārata*, including
the *Bhagavad Gītā*, and also the *Srīmad Bhāgavatam.*

ible beings,[18] whence the need for an injunction)—confer (or transmit, as the case may be) vital graces on universal Manifestation, or, in another respect, on the center of that Manifestation, namely the cosmic Intellect.[19] One who blesses the Prophet blesses by implication the world and the universal Spirit (*ar-Rūh*),[20] the Universe, and the Intellect, both the Totality and the Center, so that the blessing, multiplied tenfold, falls back from each of these manifestations of the Principle,[21] on him who has truly put his heart into this prayer.

The terms of the "Prayer on the Prophet" are generally as follows, though there are many variants and developments of it: "O, (my) God (*Allāhumma*), bless our Lord Muhammad, Thy Servant (*'Abd*) and Thy Messenger (*Rasūl*), the unlettered Prophet (*an-Nabī al-ummī*), and his family and his companions, and salute them." The words "salute" (*sallam*), "salutation" (*taslīm*), or "peace" (*salām*)[22] signify a reverential

---

[18] These are the two "weights" or "species having weight" (*ath-thaqalān*) of which the Koran speaks in the *Sūrah* "The Beneficent", verse 31. Men are created of "clay" (*tīn*), that is of matter, and the *jinn* of "fire", or an immaterial, animic or—as the Hindus would say—"subtle" (*sukshma*) substance. As for the angels, they are created of light (*nūr*), of a non-formal substance; the differences between angels are like those between colors, sounds, or perfumes, not those between forms, which to them appear as petrifactions and fragmentations.

[19] This prayer is thus as least partly equivalent to the Buddhist wish "May all beings be happy!"

[20] Also called the "First Intellect" (*al-'Aql al-awwal*); it is either "created" or "uncreated", according to the way it is envisaged.

[21] The Prophet said: "He who blesses me once shall be ten times blessed by God. . .". Another *hadīth* says: "Truly the Archangel Gabriel came to me and said: 'O Muhammad, none of thy community shall bless thee without my blessing him ten times and none of thy community shall greet thee without my greeting him ten times.'" According to another *hadīth*, God created an angel from every prayer on the Prophet, and this is full of meaning from the point of view of the economy of spiritual and cosmic energies. Our regular readers are familiar with the following Vedantic classification, also found in the writings of René Guénon: gross or "material" manifestation and subtle or "animic" manifestation, these two together constituting formal manifestation; formless (supra-formal) or "angelic" manifestation which, together with formal manifestation, makes up manifestation as such; and finally, the unmanifest which is the Principle and comprises both Being and Non-Being (or Beyond- Being). The basis of these categories is the primary distinction between the Principle and manifestation.

[22] To greet in Arabic is "to give peace"; it is to say: "Peace be with you" (*as-salāmu 'alaykum*).

homage on the part of the believer (the Koran says: "And give him greeting" or "salutation") and thus a personal attitude, whereas the blessing brings in the Divinity, for it is He who blesses; on the part of God, "salutation" is a "look" or a "word", that is to say an element of grace which is not "central", as in the case of the "blessing" (*salāt: sallā 'alā*, "pray on"), but "peripheral" and so relating to the individual and to life, not to the Intellect and to *gnosis*. That is why the Name of Muhammad is followed by both "blessing" and "salutation" whereas the names of the other divine "Messengers" and of the Angels are followed only by the "salutation": from the point of view of Islam it is Muhammad who incarnates the Revelation "actually" and "definitively", and Revelation corresponds to the "blessing", not to the "salutation". In the same more or less exoteric sense, it could be said that the "blessing" refers to the prophetic inspiration and to the "relatively unique" and "central" character of the *Avatāra* envisaged, while the "salutation" refers to the human, cosmic, and existential perfection common to all the *Avatāra*s or to the perfection of the Angels.[23] The "blessing" is a transcendent, active, and "vertical" quality whereas the "salutation" is an immanent, passive, and "horizontal" quality; or again, the "salutation" concerns the "outward", the "support", whereas the blessing concerns the inward or the "content", whether in the case of divine acts or of human attitudes. Herein lies the whole difference between the "supernatural" and the "natural": the "blessing" signifies the divine presence inasmuch as it is an unceasing influx, which in the microcosm—in the Intellect—becomes intuition or inspiration and, in the case of the Prophet, Revelation; on the other hand the "peace", or "salutation", signifies the divine presence inasmuch as it is inherent in the cosmos, becoming, in the microcosm, intelligence, virtue, and wisdom; it pertains to existential equilibrium, the cosmic economy. It is true that intellective inspiration—or innate knowledge—is also

---

[23] The Spirit (*ar-Rūh*) is here an exception because of its central position among the Angels, which confers on it the "prophetic" function in the highest sense; the Koran mentions it separately from the angels and it is also said that the Spirit was not required to prostrate before Adam as they were; in Muslim logic it would merit, like Muhammad, both the *salāt* and the *salām*. The Archangel Gabriel is a personification of a function of the Spirit, the celestial ray which reaches the Prophets on earth.

"supernatural", but it is so, as it were, in a "natural" manner within the framework and in accordance with the possibilities of "Nature".

According to the Shaykh Ahmad al-Alawi, the divine act (*tajallī*) expressed by the word *salli* ("bless") is like lightning in instantaneity, and it includes the extinction to some degree of the human receptacle undergoing it, whereas the divine act expressed by the word *sallim* ("salute") spreads the divine presence into the modalities of the individual himself; the Shaykh said this is why the *faqīr* should always ask for *salām* ("peace") which corresponds to the divine "salutation",[24] in order that revelations or intuitions should not vanish like flickers of lightning but become fixed in his soul.

In the verse of the Koran which instituted the blessing of Muhammad, it is said that "God and His angels bless the Prophet", but the "salutation" is mentioned only at the end of the verse, where it is a question of the believers; the reason for this is that the *taslīm* (or *salām*) is here taken to be implied, which means that at root it is an element of the *salāt* and is only dissociated from it *a posteriori* and because of the contingencies of the world.

The initiatic intention of the "Prayer on the Prophet" is the aspiration of man towards his totality. Totality is that of which we are a part; now we are a part, not of God who is without parts, but of Creation, which, taken as a whole, is the prototype and norm of our being, while its center, *ar-Rūh*, is the root of our intelligence; this root is a vehicle for the "Uncreated Intellect", *increatus et increabile* according to Meister Eckhart.[25] The totality is perfection while the part as such is imperfect, for it manifests a rupture of the existential equilibrium and so of the totality. In the sight of God we are either "nothing" or "everything", depending on the point of view,[26] but we are never a "part"; we are,

---

[24] And this is precisely what he does through the "Prayer on the Prophet".

[25] According to the perspective of unity of essence, this root is also identified with the "Uncreated Intellect".

[26] "Nothing" from the ordinary, "separative" point of view and "everything" from the "unitive" point of view, that of the "oneness of the Real" (*wahdat al-Wujūd*).

on the other hand, a part in relation to the Universe, which is the archetype, the norm, equilibrium, perfection; it is "Universal Man" (*al-Insān al-Kāmil*)[27] of which the human manifestation is the Prophet, the *Logos*, the *Avatāra*. The Prophet—still envisaged in the esoteric and universal meaning of the term—is thus the totality of which we are a fragment. But this totality is also manifested in us, and in a direct manner: it is the intellectual center, the "Eye of the Heart", seat of the "Uncreated", the celestial or divine point in relation to which the ego is the microcosmic periphery;[28] thus we are "peripheral" in relation to the Intellect (*ar-Rūh*) and a "part" in relation to Creation (*al-Khalq*). The *Avatāra* represents both these poles at once: he is our totality and our center, our existence and our knowledge; the "Prayer on the Prophet"—like every analogous formula—has consequently not only the meaning of an aspiration towards our existential totality, but also by that very fact the meaning of an "actualization" of our intellectual center, these two points of view being moreover inseparably linked together. Our movement towards totality—a movement whose most elementary expression is charity in the sense of the abolition of the illusory and passional division between "I" and "other than I"—this movement at the same time purifies the heart, or in other words it frees the Intellect from the obstructions standing in the way of unitive contemplation.

In the Muhammadan blessing—the Prayer on the Prophet—the attributes given the Prophet apply also—or even more so—to the totality and the Center of which Muhammad is the human expression, or rather "an expression" if we take into account the whole of humanity in all places and at all periods. The name Muhammad itself means the "Glorified" and indicates the perfection of Creation, affirmed also in Genesis in the words: "And God saw that it was good"; moreover

---

[27] See *De l'Homme Universel* by Abd al-Karim Jili (translated from Arabic to French and commented upon by Titus Burckhardt).

[28] In the same way the lotus on which the Buddha rests is both the manifested Universe and the heart of man, each of these being envisaged as a support of *Nirvāna*. In the same way too, the Blessed Virgin is both pure universal Substance (*Prakriti*), the womb of the manifested divine Spirit and of all creatures in respect of their theomorphism, and the primordial substance of man, his original purity, his heart as the support of the Word which delivers.

the words "our Lord" (*Sayyidunā*) used before the name Muhammad indicate the primordial and normative quality of the Cosmos in relation to ourselves.

The attribute following the name of Muhammad in this prayer is "Thy servant" ('*abduka*): the Macrocosm is the "servant" of God because manifestation is subordinate to the Principle, or the effect to the Cause; Creation is "Lord" in relation to man and "Servant" in relation to the Creator. Thus the Prophet is—like Creation—essentially an "isthmus" (*barzakh*), a "line of demarcation" and at the same time a "point of contact" between two degrees of reality.

Next comes the attribute "Thy Messenger" (*rasūluka*): this attribute concerns the Universe inasmuch as it transmits the possibilities of Being to its own parts—to the microcosms—through the medium of the phenomena or symbols of nature; these symbols are the signs (*āyāt*) spoken of in the Koran,[29] the proofs of God which the Sacred Book recommends for meditation by those "endowed with understanding".[30] The possibilities thus manifested transcribe in the outward world the "principial truths" (*haqā'iq*) just as intellectual intuitions and metaphysical concepts transcribe them in the human subject; the Intellect, like the Universe, is "Messenger", "Servant", "Glorified", and "our Lord".

The "Prayer on the Prophet" sometimes includes the following two attributes: "Thy Prophet" (*Nabīyuka*) and "Thy Friend" (*Habībuka*); this second qualification expresses intimacy, the generous proximity—not the opposition—between manifestation and the Principle; as for the word "Prophet" (*Nabī*), this indicates a particular message, not the universal message of the Messenger (*Rasūl*):[31] in the world it stands for

---

[29] It has already been pointed out that the word "sign", when it does not relate to phenomena of this world, is applied to the verses of the Koran, and this clearly shows the analogy between Nature and Revelation.

[30] It is therefore quite possible for a tradition to be founded wholly on this symbolism; this is notably true of Shinto and of the tradition of the Sacred Pipe among the North American Indians.

[31] The *Nabī* is such not because he receives and transmits a particular message, namely one that is limited to particular circumstances, but because he possesses *nubuwwah*, the mandate of prophecy; every *Rasūl* is a *Nabī*, but not every *Nabī* is a *Rasūl*; it is somewhat like saying that every eagle is a bird, but not every bird an eagle. The mean-

the whole of cosmic determinations concerning man, including natural laws; and within ourselves it is awareness of our final end, together with all this awareness implies for us.

As for the next attribute, "the unlettered Prophet" (*an-Nabī al-ummī*), this expresses the "virginity" of the receptacle, whether universal or human: with regard to inspiration, it is determined by nothing but God; before the divine Pen it is a blank page; none but God fills the Creation, the Intellect, the *Avatāra*.

The "blessing" and the "salutation" apply, not only to the Prophet, but also to his "family and his companions" (*'alā ālihi wa sahbihi*), that is, in the macrocosmic order, to Heaven and Earth or to non-formal and formal manifestation, and in the microcosmic order, to soul and body, the Prophet being in the first case the Divine Spirit (*ar-Rūh*) and in the latter the Intellect (*al-'Aql*) or the "Eye of the Heart" (*'Ayn al-Qalb*); Intellect and Spirit coincide in their essence in that the former is like a ray of the latter. The Intellect is the "Spirit" in man; the "Divine Spirit" is nothing other than the universal Intellect.

The attributes applied to the Prophet mark the spiritual virtues, the chief of which are: "poverty" (*faqr*, which is a quality of the *'abd*),[32] then "generosity" (*karam*, a quality of the *Rasūl*),[33] and finally "veracity" or "sincerity" (*sidq, ikhlās*, a quality of the *Nabī al-ummī*).[34] "Poverty" is spiritual concentration, or rather its negative and static aspect, non-expansion, and consequently "humility" in the sense of the "cessation of the fire of the passions" (in the words of Tirmidhi); as for "generosity", it is akin to "nobility" (*sharaf*); it is the abolishing of egoism and this implies "love of one's neighbor" in the sense that the passional distinction between "I" and "other" is then transcended; finally,

---

ing "particular message" is called for, not just by the fact that the man is a *Nabī*, but by the fact that he is so without being a *Rasūl*. It is as a *Nabī* and not as a *Rasūl* that Muhammad is "unlettered", just as—to return to our comparison above—it is because it is a bird that the eagle can fly, not because it is an eagle.

[32] In the sense that the *'abd* has nothing that belongs to him as his own.

[33] The *Rasūl* is indeed a "mercy" (*rahmah*); he is disinterestedness itself, the incarnation of charity.

[34] Veracity is inseparable from virginity of spirit in the sense that the spirit must be free from all artifice, from all prejudice, and from any passional interference.

"veracity" is the contemplative quality of the intelligence and, on the plane of reason, is logic or impartiality, in a word, "love of truth".

From the initiatic point of view, the "Prayer on the Prophet" relates to the "intermediate stage", namely to the "expansion" which follows "purification" and precedes "union"; herein lies the deepest meaning of the *hadīth*: "No man will meet God who has not first met the Prophet."[35]

The Prayer on the Prophet can be likened to a wheel; the prayer of blessing is its axle; the Prophet is its hub; his family make up the spokes; his Companions are the rim.

In the broadest interpretation of this prayer, the Blessing corresponds to God, the name of the Prophet to the Universal Spirit,[36] the Family to the beings who participate in God—through the Spirit—in a direct manner, and the Companions to those beings who participate in God indirectly but likewise thanks to the Spirit. This extreme limit can be defined in various ways according to whether we envisage the Muslim world, or the whole of humanity, or all creatures on earth, or even the whole Universe.[37]

The individual will, which is both egocentric and dispersed, must be converted to the universal Will which is "concentric" and transcends earthly humanity.

As a spiritual principle, the Prophet is not only the Totality of which we are separate parts or fragments, he is also the Origin in relation to which we are so many deviations;[38] in other words, the Prophet as

---

[35] This is also the initiatic meaning of the saying in the Gospels: "No man cometh unto the Father, but by me." Nonetheless the difference of "accent" which distinguishes the Christian perspective from Sufism must be taken into account.

[36] *Ar-Rūh*, which includes the four archangels; on the earthly plane and in the Muslim cosmos, it is the Prophet and the first four Caliphs.

[37] The symbolism of the Prayer on the Prophet closely corresponds to that of the Tibetan prayer wheels: a prayer, inscribed on a band of paper, blesses the universe by its rotation.

[38] It is in this sense that, according to Saint Bernard, our ego should seem to us "some-

Norm is not only the "Whole Man" (*al-Insān al-Kāmil*) but also the "Ancient Man" (*al-Insān al-Qadīm*). Here there is a sort of combination of a spatial with a temporal symbolism: to realize the "Whole" or "Universal Man" means to come out from oneself, to project one's will into the absolute "other", to extend oneself into the universal life which is that of all beings; while to realize the "Ancient" or "Primordial Man" means to return to the origin which we bear within us; it means to return to eternal childhood, to rest in our archetype, our primordial and normative form, in our theomorphic substance. According to the spatial symbolism, the path towards realization of the "Whole Man" is height, the ascending vertical which expands into the infinity of Heaven; according to the temporal symbolism, the path towards the "Ancient Man" is the past in a quasi-absolute sense, the divine and eternal origin.[39] The "Prayer on the Prophet" refers to the spatial symbolism in the designation *Rasūl*, "Messenger"—though here the dimension is designated in a descending direction—and to the temporal symbolism in the attribute *Nabī al-ummī*, "unlettered Prophet", which clearly is connected with the origin.

The term "the Ancient Man" thus more particularly refers to the Intellect, to perfection of "consciousness", and the term "the Whole Man" to Existence, to perfection of "being"; but at the same time, on the plane of the spatial symbolism itself, the center refers to the Intellect, whereas on the plane of the temporal symbolism duration refers to Existence, for it extends indefinitely. We can establish a connection between the origin and the center on the one hand and between duration and the totality—or limitlessness—on the other; it could even be said that the origin, which in itself cannot be grasped, is for us situated at the center and that duration, which everywhere eludes us, coincides for us with totality. In the same way, starting from the idea that the "Whole Man" particularly concerns the macrocosm and the "Ancient Man" the microcosm, it could be said that in its totality the world is Existence, whereas at the origin the human microcosm is Intelligence,

---

thing to be despised" and that, according to Meister Eckhart, one must "hate one's soul".

[39] This sheds a revealing light on the meaning of tradition as such and also in a more particular sense on the worship of ancestors.

though only in a sense, since we do not go beyond the realm of the created and of contingencies.

On the plane of the "Whole Man", two dimensions can be distinguished: "Heaven" and "Earth", or "height" (*tūl*) and "breadth" (*'ardh*): "height" links the earth to Heaven, and, in the case of the Prophet, this link is the aspect of *Rasūl* ("Messenger" and so also "Revealer") while the earth is the aspect of *'Abd* ("Servant"). These are the two dimensions of charity: love of God and love of the neighbor in God.

On the plane of the "Ancient Man", we shall not distinguish two dimensions for, in the origin, Heaven and Earth were one; as we have already seen, this plane is related to the "unlettered Prophet". His virtue is humility or poverty: to be only what God has made us, to add nothing; pure virtue is apophatic.

Let us sum up this doctrine as follows: the nature of the Prophet comprises the two perfections of totality[40] and of origin:[41] Muhammad incarnates the theomorphic and harmonious totality[42] of which we are fragments and also the origin in relation to which we are states of degeneration, when considered as individuals. For the Sufi, to follow the Prophet means extending the soul to the life of all beings, to "serve God" (*'ibādah*) and to "pray" (*dhakara*) with all and in all;[43] but it also means reducing the soul to the "divine remembering" (*dhikru 'Llāh*) of the one and primordial soul.[44] In the final analysis and through the various poles envisaged—the poles of totality and origin, of plenitude and simplicity—it means realizing both the "infinitely Other" and the "absolutely Oneself".

---

[40] "God said: O Adam! Cause them to know their names!" (Koran 2:33). "And when We said to the angels: Prostrate yourselves before Adam!" (2:34).

[41] "Assuredly we have created man in the most fair form" (Koran 95:4).

[42] These two qualities are essential. The creation is "good" because it is made in the image of God and because it compensates its disequilibriums—which are ontologically necessary, otherwise creation would not exist—by the total equilibrium, which indirectly "transmutes" them into factors of perfection.

[43] "The seven Heavens and the earth and those in them praise Him; and there is nothing that does not chant His praises, but ye understand not their song. . ." (Koran 17:44).

[44] "And every time they shall receive a fruit (in Paradise) they shall say: this is what we have received aforetime. . ." (Koran 2:25).

The Sufi, following the example of the Prophet, wants neither "to be God" nor "to be other than God": and this is not unconnected with all that has been said above and with the distinction between "extinction" (*fanā*) and "permanence" (*baqā*). There is no extinction in God without universal charity and there is no permanence in Him without that supreme poverty which is submission to the origin. As we have seen, the Prophet represents both universality and primordiality, just as Islam in its deepest meaning is "that which is everywhere" and "that which has always been".

All these considerations enable us to understand to what degree the Islamic way of envisaging the Prophet differs from the Christian or Buddhist cults of the God-Man. The sublimation of the Prophet is effected, not by starting out from the idea of an earthly divinity, but by means of a kind of metaphysical mythology: Muhammad is either man among men—we do not say "ordinary man"—or Platonic idea, cosmic and spiritual symbol, unfathomable *Logos*;[45] never is he God incarnate.

The Prophet is above all a synthesis combining human "smallness" with the divine mystery. This aspect of being a synthesis, or a reconciliation of opposites, is characteristic of Islam and expressly results from its being the "last Revelation": if the Prophet is the "Seal of Prophecy" (*khātam an-nubuwwah*) or of "the Messengers" (*al-mursalīn*), this implies that he should appear as a synthesis of all that came before him; hence his aspect of "leveling", that something "anonymous" and "countless" which is apparent also in the Koran.[46] Those who, by ref-

---

[45] It is said that, without Muhammad, the world would not have been created; thus he is indeed the *Logos*, not as man, but in his "inner reality" (*haqīqah*) and as the "Muhammadan Light" (*Nūr muhammadīyah*). It is also said that the virtues of the Prophet are created, since they are human, but that they are "nonetheless eternal insofar as they are qualities of Him of whom eternity is the attribute" (according to the *Al-Burdah* by the Shaykh al-Busiri). In the same way, the Prophet is named *Haqq* ("Truth") while *al-Haqq* ("the Truth") is a Divine Name. The *haqīqah* of Muhammad is described as a mystery; it is either hidden or blindingly bright and can only be interpreted from afar.

[46] Aishah, the favorite wife of Muhammad, said that the Koran reflects or prefigures the soul of God's Messenger.

erence to the example of Jesus, find Muhammad too human to be a spokesman of God, are following a line of reasoning just like that of those who, by reference to the extremely direct spirituality of the *Bhagavad Gītā* or the *Prajnā Pāramitā Hridaya Sūtra*, would consider the Bible too human to have any title to the dignity of Divine Word.

The virtue—claimed by the Koran—of being the last Revelation and the synthesis of the prophetic cycle, reveals itself not only in the outward simplicity of a dogma which is inwardly open to every degree of profundity, but also in the capacity Islam has of integrating all men as it were into its center, of conferring on all the same unshakable and if need be combative faith and of making them participate, at least virtually though effectively, in the half-celestial, halfterrestrial nature of the Prophet.

The Path

Our aim in this section is not so much to treat of Sufism exhaustively or in detail—other writers have had the merit of doing so with varying degrees of success—but rather to envisage the "path" (*Tarīqah*) in its general aspects or in its universal reality; therefore the terms used will not always be those proper to Islam alone. Now, when considered from this very general aspect, the "path" presents itself first of all as the polarity of "doctrine" and "method", or as metaphysical truth accompanied by contemplative concentration. As a matter of fact, everything in it is reducible to these two elements: intellection and concentration or discernment and union. For us, who are in the realm of relativity since we exist and think, metaphysical truth is in the first place discrimination between the Real and the unreal or the "less real"; and concentration or the operative act of the spirit—prayer in the very broadest sense—is in a way our response to the truth which offers itself to us; it is Revelation entering into our consciousness and becoming in some degree assimilated by our being.

For Islam, or to be more precise for Sufism which is its kernel,[1] the metaphysical doctrine is—as we have many times pointed out—that "there is no reality save the One Reality" and that, insofar as we are obliged to take account of the existence of the world and of ourselves, "the cosmos is the manifestation of Reality".[2] Vedantists will say, to repeat this once more, that "the world is false; *Brahma* is true", but that "all things are *Ātmā*"; all eschatological truths are contained within this second statement. It is by virtue of this second truth that we are saved; according to the first we even "are not" although we do "exist"

---

[1] Since we do not wish to attribute to a religious faith as such sapiential theses which it can enunciate only implicitly. For the "science of religions", esoterism comes after dogma, of which it is supposed to be an artificial development and even one borrowed from foreign sources. In reality, the sapiential element must precede the exoteric formulation, for being a metaphysical perspective it determines the form. Without a metaphysical foundation there can be no religion; doctrinal esoterism is only the development, starting from the Revelation itself, of what "was before" the beginning.

[2] The cosmos in the perfection of its symbolism, *Muhammad*; here the reader will recognize the second *Shahādah*.

in the field of reverberations of the contingent. It is as if we were saved beforehand because we are not and because "all things are ephemeral save the Face of *Allāh*".

The distinction between the Real and the unreal coincides in a sense with that between Substance and accidents; the Substance-accident relationship makes it easy to understand the "less real"—or "unreal" nature—of the world and reveals to those capable of grasping it the inanity of the error which attributes an absolute character to phenomena. Moreover the common meaning of the word "substance" clearly shows that there are intermediate substances which are "accidental" by comparison with pure Substance but nonetheless play the part of substances in relation to what is accidental for them: these substances are, in ascending order, matter, ether, the animic substance, supraformal and macrocosmic substance—which could also be termed "angelic"—and finally universal, metacosmic Substance which is one of the poles of Being, or its "horizontal dimension" or feminine aspect.[3] The anti-metaphysical error of the *asura*s is that they take accidents for reality and deny Substance by describing it as "unreal" or "abstract".[4]

To perceive the unreality—or the lesser or relative reality—of the world means at the same time to perceive the symbolism of phenomena; to know that the "Substance of substances" is alone absolutely real—or strictly speaking that it alone is real—means to see Substance in every accident and through them; thanks to this initial knowledge of Reality, the world becomes metaphysically "transparent". When it is said that a *Bodhisattva* sees only space and not its contents, or that he looks on the latter as being space, this means that he sees only Substance, which in relation to the world appears as a "void" or, on the contrary, that the world appears as a "void" in terms of the principial Plenitude; there are here two "voids"—or two "plenitudes"—and they

---

[3] Being is the relative Absolute, or God as "relatively absolute", that is to say insofar as He creates. The pure Absolute does not create; if one wished to introduce here the ideas of "substance" and "accidents", one would have to think of the essential divine qualities arising from Beyond-Being or from the Self and crystallizing in Being, but such an application would nonetheless be inadequate.

[4] We believe the attribution to Heraclitus of the modern "actualism" (*Aktualitäts-Theorie*) to be mistaken, since a theory of the cosmic play of the All-Possibility is not necessarily a materialistic pantheism.

are mutually exclusive, just as in an hourglass the two compartments cannot be simultaneously empty or full.

Once it has been fully grasped that the relationship between water and drops of water parallels that between Substance and the accidents which are the contents of the world, the "illusory" nature of these accidents cannot be a matter of doubt or present any difficulty. If it is said in Islam that creatures are a proof of God this means that the nature of phenomena is that of "accidents" and that they therefore disclose the ultimate Substance. The comparison with water is nonetheless imperfect in that it takes no account of the transcendence of Substance; but matter cannot offer any less inadequate picture because transcendence melts in its reflections to the very degree that the plane in question partakes of accidentality.

There is discontinuity between accidents and Substance, although from Substance to accidents there is an extremely subtle continuity in the sense that, Substance alone being fully real, accidents must necessarily be aspects of it; but in that case they are being considered only in terms of their cause and not in any other terms and the irreversibility of relationship is therefore maintained. In other words, the accident is then reduced to Substance; as accident it is an "exteriorization" of Substance and to this corresponds the Divine Name *azh-Zhāhir* ("the Outward"). All errors concerning the world and God consist either in a "naturalistic" denial of the discontinuity and hence also of transcendence[5]—whereas it is on the basis of this transcendence that the whole edifice of science should have been built—or else they consist in a failure to understand the metaphysical and "descending" continuity which in no way abolishes the discontinuity starting from the rela-

---

[5] It is more or less this "scientific" prejudice, going hand in hand with a falsification and impoverishment of speculative imagination, which prevents a man like Teilhard de Chardin from conceiving the overriding discontinuity between matter and the soul, or between the natural and the supernatural orders and so leads to the evolutionary outlook, which—inverting the truth—makes everything begin with matter. A "minus" always presupposes an initial "plus", so that a seeming evolution is no more than the quite provisional unfolding of a pre-existing result; the human embryo becomes a man because that is what it already is; no "evolution" will produce a man from an animal embryo. In the same way, the whole cosmos can spring only from an embryonic state which contains the virtuality of all its possible unfolding and simply makes manifest on the plane of contingencies an infinitely higher and transcendent prototype.

tive. "*Brahma* is not in the world" but "all things are *Ātmā*"; "*Brahma* is true, the world is false" and "He (the delivered one, the *mukta*) is *Brahma*". In these statements the whole of *gnosis* is contained, just as it is also contained in the *Shahādah* or in the two Testimonies, or again in the Christic mysteries.[6] And the following idea is crucial: metaphysical truth with all it comprises lies in the very substance of intelligence; any denial or limitation of truth is always a denial or limitation of the Intellect; to know the Intellect is to know its consubstantial content and thus the nature of things, and this is why Greek *gnosis* says "Know thyself" and the Gospels say, "The kingdom of heaven is within you"; and likewise Islam: "Whoso knoweth himself knoweth his Lord."

Revelation is an objectivization of the Intellect and that is why it has the power to actualize the intelligence which has been obscured—but not abolished—by man's fall. This obscuring of the intelligence may be only accidental, not fundamental, and in such a case the intelligence is in principle destined for *gnosis*.[7] If elementary belief cannot consciously and explicitly attain to total truth that is because in its own way it too limits the intelligence; it is moreover inevitably and paradoxically allied to a certain rationalism—Vishnuism shows in this respect the same phenomenon as the West—without however becoming lost in it, unless there is a weakening of the faith itself.[8] Be

---

[6] Trinity, Incarnation, Redemption. It is the supraontological and gnostic Trinity which is meant here, conceived either "vertically" (the hierarchy of the *hypostases*: Beyond-Being, Being, Existence; *Paramātmā, Īshvara, Buddhi*) or "horizontally" (the intrinsic "aspects" or "modes" of the Essence: Reality, Wisdom, Beatitude; *Sat, Chit, Ānanda*).

[7] To say that there is a Christian *gnosis* means that there is a Christianity, centered on Christ as the Intellect, which defines man primarily as intelligence and not merely as fallen will or as passion. If total truth lies in the very substance of the intelligence, then for Christian *gnosis*, the intelligence will be the immanent Christ, "the Light of the World". To see in all things the Divine Substance, which means to see in all things an objectivation—and in some respects a refraction—of Intelligence is to realize that "God became man" and this without any detriment whatsoever to the literal meaning of the dogma.

[8] Cartesianism—perhaps the most intelligent way of being unintelligent—is the classic example of a faith which has become the dupe of the groping of reasoning; this is a "wisdom from below" and history shows it to be deadly. The whole of modern philosophy, including "science", starts from a false conception of intelligence; for instance, the modern cult of life errs in the sense that it seeks the explanation and goal of man at a level below him, in something which could not serve to define the human creature.

that as it may, a perspective which attributes an absolute character to relative situations, as does Semitic exoterism, cannot be intellectually complete; but to speak of exoterism is to speak also of esoterism, and this means that the statements of the former are the symbols of the latter.

Exoterism transmits aspects or fragments of metaphysical truth—which is nothing other than the whole truth—whether about God, about the universe, or about man: in man it chiefly envisages the passional and social individual, and in the universe it discerns only what affects that individual; in God it hardly sees anything more than what has to do with the world, creation, man and his salvation. Consequently—and at the risk of repetition, this must be emphasized—exoterism takes no account either of the pure Intellect, which transcends the human plane and opens out onto the divine, or of pre-human and post-human cycles, or of Beyond-Being which is beyond all relativity and thus also beyond all distinctivity. Such a perspective is comparable to a skylight, which gives the sky a certain form, round, square, or some other; through this the view of the sky is fragmentary, though it certainly does not prevent the sky from filling the room with light and life. The danger of a religious outlook based on the will is that it comes very close to insisting that faith include a maximum of will and a minimum of intelligence; indeed intelligence is blamed, either for diminishing merit by its very nature, or for illusorily arrogating to itself both the value of merit and a knowledge such as is in reality unattainable.[9]

But in a much more general way, all rationalism—whether direct or indirect—is false from the sole fact that it limits the intelligence to reason or intellection to logic, or in other words cause to effect.

[9] The individualism and sentimentality of a certain passional type of mysticism are undeniable facts, whatever may be the spiritual virtualities of the framework taken as a whole; in this type of mysticism the intelligence has no operative function despite the possibilities of its inmost nature; the absence of metaphysical discernment brings in its wake an absence of methodical concentration, the latter being the normal complement of the former. From the point of view of *gnosis*, the intelligence is not a part but the center and it is the starting point for a consciousness embracing our whole being. One thing very characteristic of the mental climate of the traditional West—though in no way does it compromise true intellectuality—is the association of ideas formed between intelligence and pride, as also between beauty and sin, an association that explains many deadly reactions, beginning with the Renaissance.

Be that as it may, it could be said of religions: "like man, like God"; in other words, the way in which man is envisaged influences the way in which God is envisaged, and vice versa, depending on the situations.

One point which needs to be brought out here is that the criterion of metaphysical truth or of its depth lies, not in the complexity or difficulty of its expression, but in the quality and effectiveness of its symbolism, with respect to a particular capacity of understanding or style of thinking.[10] Wisdom does not lie in any complication of words but in the profundity of the intention; assuredly the expression may according to the circumstances be subtle and difficult, but it may also not be so.

At this point and before going further, we would allow a digression. It is said that a great number of youths today no longer want to hear any talk of religion or philosophy or indeed of any doctrine, that they feel everything of the kind to be outworn and discredited and that they will respond only to what is "concrete" and "lived", or even only to what is "new". The answer to this mental deformation is simple enough: if the "concrete" has value,[11] it cannot go along with a false attitude—one which consists in rejecting all doctrine—nor could it be wholly new; there have always been religions and doctrines, which proves that their existence is in man's nature; for thousands of years the best of men, whom we cannot despise without making ourselves despicable, have promulgated and propagated doctrines and lived according to them or died for them. The ill certainly does not lie in the hypothetical vanity of all doctrine but solely in the fact that too many

---

[10] That is why it is absurd to maintain—be it said in passing—that China produced no "metaphysical systems" comparable to those of India or of the West; for this is to overlook the fact that the yellow race is preponderantly visual and not, like the white race, auditive and verbal, this psychic difference having absolutely nothing to do with the level of pure intelligence.

[11] When people today talk of what is "concrete", it is usually as if one were to call foam "concrete" and water "abstract". This is the classic confusion between accidents and substance.

men either have not followed—or do not follow—true doctrines, or have on the contrary followed—or are following—false doctrines; it lies in the fact that brains have been exasperated and hearts deceived by too many inconsistent and erroneous theories; and it lies in the fact that innumerable errors,[12] both garrulous and pernicious, have cast discredit on truth, truth which necessarily is expressed in words and is always there, but which no one heeds. All too many people no longer even know what an idea is, what its value and what its function is; they do not so much as suspect that perfect and definitive theories have always existed, theories which are therefore on their own level fully adequate and effective, and that there is nothing to add to what has been said by the sages of old except effort on our own part to understand it. If we are human beings, we cannot abstain from thought, and if we think then we are choosing a doctrine; the weariness, the lack of imagination, and the childish arrogance of disillusioned and materialistic young people does not alter this. If it is modern science which has created the abnormal and disappointing conditions which afflict youth today, that is because this science is itself abnormal and disappointing. No doubt it will be said that man is not responsible for his nihilism, that it is science which has slain the gods; but this is an avowal of intellectual impotence, not something to be proud of, for he who knows what the gods signify will not let himself be unhorsed by the discoveries in the physical realm—which merely displace sensory symbols, but do not abolish them[13]—and still less by gratuitous hypotheses and the errors of psychology.

Existence is a reality in some respects comparable to a living organism; it cannot with impunity be reduced, in man's consciousness and in his modes of action, to proportions that violate its nature; pulsations of the "extra-rational"[14] pass through it from every quarter. Now

---

[12] "My name is Legion", said a devil in the story of the Gadarene swine in the Gospel.

[13] Even if we know that space is an eternal night sheltering galaxies and nebulae, the sky will still stretch blue above us and symbolize the realm of angels and the kingdom of Beatitude.

[14] Ordinarily and in every sort of context, people speak of the "irrational", but this is a dangerous abuse of terminology all too liable to reduce the supra-rational to the infra-rational.

religion and all forms of wisdom[15] belong to this "extra-rational" order, the presence of which we observe everywhere around us, if we are not blinded by a mathematician's prejudice; to attempt to treat existence as a purely arithmetical and physical reality is to falsify it in relation to ourselves and within ourselves, and in the end it is to blow it to pieces.

In a similar vein of thought, we must take note of the abuse of the idea of intelligence. For us, intelligence can have no other object than truth, just as love has beauty or goodness for its object. Certainly there can be intelligence in error—since intelligence is mingled with contingency and denatured by it, and error, being nothing in itself, has need of the Spirit—but in any case we must never lose sight of what intelligence is in itself, nor believe that a work compounded of error could be the product of a healthy or even transcendent intelligence; and above all, cleverness and cunning must not be confused with pure intelligence and with contemplation.[16] Intellectuality essentially comprises an aspect of "sincerity"; now perfect sincerity of intelligence is inconceivable apart from disinterestedness; to know is to see, and seeing is an equating of subject with object and not a passional act. "Faith", or the acceptance of truth, has to be sincere, that is to say it should be contemplative: for it is one thing to accept an idea—whether true or false—because one has some material or sentimental interest in it, and quite another to accept it because one knows or believes it to be true.

Science, some people will say, has long since shown the inconsistency of the Revelations, which arise—as they would argue—from our inveterate nostalgia as timid and unsatisfied earthlings.[17] In a context

---

[15] In which case, it is a question of the "supra-rational".

[16] As we pointed out in *Stations of Wisdom*, in the chapter "Orthodoxy and Intellectuality", lack of intelligence and vice may be only superficial and thus in a sense "accidental" and therefore remediable, just as they may also be relatively "essential" and virtually incurable. But an essential lack of virtue is nevertheless incompatible with transcendent intelligence, just as outstanding virtue is hardly ever found in a fundamentally unintelligent person. We might add that there are those who despise intelligence, either in the name of "humility" or in the name of the "concrete", while others confuse it for all practical intent with malice; to this, Saint Paul has replied in anticipation (1 Cor. 14:20): "Brethren, be not children in understanding: howbeit in malice be ye children, but in understanding be men."

[17] And incurably stupid earthlings, we would add, were this hypothesis true.

such as that of this book, there is no need to reply yet again to such a thesis, but let us nevertheless take the opportunity to add one more image to those already given elsewhere. Imagine a radiant summer sky and imagine simple folk who gaze at it, projecting into it their dream of the hereafter; now suppose that it were possible to transport these simple folk into the dark and freezing abyss of the galaxies and nebulae with its crushing silence. In this abyss all too many of them would lose their faith, and this is precisely what happens as a result of modern science, both to the learned and to the victims of this popularization. What most men do not know—and if they could know it, why should they be called on to believe?—is that this blue sky, though illusory as an optical error and belied by the vision of interplanetary space, is nonetheless an adequate reflection of the Heaven of the Angels and the Blessed and that therefore, despite everything, it is this blue mirage, flecked with silver clouds, which is right and will have the final say; to be astonished at this amounts to admitting that it is by chance that we are here on earth and see the sky as we do. Of course the black abyss of the galaxies also reflects something, but the symbolism is then shifted and it is no longer a question of the Heaven of the Angels; it is then—to remain faithful to our point of departure—doubtless first a question of the terrors of the divine mysteries, in which he is lost who seeks to violate them by means of his fallible reason and without adequate motive; in a positive sense, it is the *scientia sacra* which transcends the faith of the simple and is, *Deo juvante*,[18] accessible to the pure Intellect;[19] but it is also a question, according to the immediate symbolism of appearances, of the abysses of universal manifestation, of this *samsāra* whose limits infinitely elude our ordinary experience. Finally, extra-terrestrial space likewise reflects death, as has already been pointed out above; it is a projection outside our earthly security into a vertiginous void and an unimaginable estrangement; this is something which can also be understood in a spiritual sense since we must "die before we die". What we would chiefly emphasize here is the error of

[18] But nothing is possible apart from divine aid, the *tawfiq*; the Sufis insist on this. Higher intelligence is not of itself a sufficient guarantee in what concerns our final goal.

[19] It is precisely this *scientia sacra* which enables us to grasp that this "faith" is right and that "children" are not wrong when they pray turning to the blue sky, though in another fashion grace too enables us to grasp this.

believing that by the mere fact of its objective content "science" possesses the power and the right to destroy myths and religions and that it is thus some kind of higher experience, which kills gods and beliefs; in reality, it is human incapacity to understand unexpected phenomena and to resolve certain seeming antinomies, which is smothering the truth and dehumanizing the world.

But one further ambiguity still remains to be cleared up once and for all. The word *gnosis*, which appears in this book and in our previous works, refers to supra-rational, and thus purely intellective, knowledge of metacosmic realities. Now this knowledge cannot be reduced to the Gnosticism of history, otherwise it would be necessary to say that Ibn Arabi or Shankara were Alexandrine "gnostics"; in short, *gnosis* cannot be held responsible for every association of ideas or every abuse of terminology. It is humanly admissible not to believe in *gnosis*; what is quite inadmissible in anyone claiming to understand the subject is to include under this heading things having no relation—whether of kind or of level—with the reality in question, whatever the value attributed to that reality. In place of *gnosis*, the Arabic term *ma'rifah* or the Sanskrit term *jnāna* could just as well be used, but a Western term seems more normal in a book written in a Western language; there is also the term "theosophy", but this has even more unfortunate associations, while the term "knowledge" is too general, unless its meaning is made specific by an attribute or by the context. All that we wish to underscore and make clear is that the term *gnosis* is used by us exclusively in its etymological and universal sense and therefore cannot be reduced to meaning merely the Greco-Oriental syncretism of later classical times;[20] still less can it be applied to some pseudo-religious or pseudo-yogic or even merely literary fantasy.[21] If for example, Catho-

---

[20] Even though we do not reduce the meaning of this word to that syncretism, we nevertheless admit for clear and historical reasons that one also calls "gnostics" the heretics indicated by this term. Their first fault lay in misinterpreting *gnosis* in a dogmatic mode, thus giving rise to errors and to a sectarianism incompatible with a sapiential perspective; despite this, the indirect connection with genuine *gnosis* can, if need be, justify the use of the term "gnostic" in this case.

[21] As is more and more often done since psychoanalysts have arrogated to themselves a monopoly in all that concerns the "inner life", where they mix together the most diverse and irreconcilable things in a common process of leveling and relativization.

lics can call Islam, in which they do not believe, a religion and not a pseudo-religion, there seems no reason why a distinction should also not be made—apart from any issue of Catholicism and non-Catholicism—between a genuine *gnosis* having certain precise or approximate characteristics and a pseudo-*gnosis* devoid of them.

In order to bring out clearly that the difference between Islam and Christianity is indeed a difference of metaphysical perspectives and symbolism—which is to say that the two spiritualities converge—let us attempt to characterize Christian *gnosis* succinctly by starting from the key idea that Christianity means "God became what we are, in order that we might become what He is" (Saint Irenaeus); Heaven became earth that earth might become Heaven. Christ re-enacts in the outward historical world what is being enacted from time immemorial in the inner world of the soul. In man the Spirit becomes the ego in order that the ego may become pure Spirit; the Spirit or the Intellect (*Intellectus,* not *mens* or *ratio*) becomes ego by incarnating itself in the mind in the form of intellection, of truth, and the ego becomes the Spirit or Intellect through uniting with it.[22] Thus Christianity is a doctrine of union, or the doctrine of Union, rather than of Unity: the Principle unites itself to manifestation so that it may become united to the Principle; hence the symbolism of love and the predominance of the "bhaktic" Path. "God became man", says Saint Irenaeus, "because of the immensity of His love", and man must unite himself with God also through "love", whatever meaning—volitive, emotional, or intellectual—be given to that term. "God is Love": as Trinity, He is Union and He wishes Union.

---

[22] "The Spirit searcheth all things, yea the deep things of God. For what man knoweth the things of a man, save the spirit of man which is in him? Even so the things of God knoweth no man, but the Spirit of God. Now we have received, not the spirit of the world, but the spirit which is of God; that we might know the things that are freely given to us of God" (1 Cor. 2:10-12). For Dante, the damned are those "who have lost the good of the Intellect" (*Inferno*, 3:18) and this can be related to the microcosmic and human reflection of the Divine Intellect as well as to that Intellect itself.

Now, what is the content of the Spirit; in other words, what is Christ's sapiential message? For that which is this message is also, in our microcosm, the eternal content of the Intellect. This message or content is: love God with all your faculties and, by virtue of this love, love your neighbor as yourself; that is, become united—for in essence to "love" means to "become united"—with the Heart-Intellect and, according to or as a condition of this union, abandon all pride and all passion and discern the Spirit in every creature. "What ye shall have done unto the least of these my little ones, ye shall have done it unto Me." The Heart-Intellect, the "Christ in us", is not only light or discernment but also warmth or bliss and thus "love": the "light" becomes "warm" to the degree that it becomes our being.[23]

This message—or this innate truth—of the Spirit prefigures the cross since there are here two dimensions, one "vertical" and the other "horizontal": namely love of God and love of the neighbor, or union with the Spirit and union with the human setting, this setting being envisaged as a manifestation of the Spirit or as the "mystical body". From a slightly different point of view, these two dimensions are represented respectively by knowledge and love: man "knows" God and "loves" his neighbor, or again: man loves God most through knowing Him and knows his neighbor best by loving him. As for the grievous aspect of the cross, it must be said that from the point of view of *gnosis* more than from any other, both in ourselves and among men, it is profoundly true that "the light shineth in darkness; and the darkness comprehended it not".[24]

The whole of Christianity is expressed in the doctrine of the Trinity, and fundamentally this doctrine represents a perspective of union;

---

[23] That is why the love (*mahabbah*) of the Sufis does not at all presuppose a bhaktic Path, any more than the use by Shivaite Vedantists of the term *bhakti* implies any Vaishnavite dualism in their outlook.

[24] The gnostic dimension—and again this term is to be taken in its etymological and timeless meaning—stands out in the clearest possible way in a passage in the recently discovered Gospel of Thomas which relates how Christ, after speaking to the Apostles, went out with Saint Thomas and spoke three words or sentences to him. When Thomas returned alone, the other disciples pressed him with questions, and he said that were he to confide to them even one of these sayings they would stone him and that fire would then leap forth from the stones to devour them.

it sees union already *in divinis*. God prefigures in His very Nature the relationships between Himself and the world, these relationships becoming "external" only in an illusory mode.

As has been pointed out already, the Christian religion lays stress on the "phenomenal" content of faith rather than on its intrinsic and transforming quality; we say "lays stress" and "rather than" to show that this definition is not unconditional; the Trinity does not belong to the phenomenal order, but nonetheless depends on the phenomenon of Christ. Insofar as the object of faith is "principial", it coincides with the "intellectual" or contemplative nature of faith,[25] but insofar as its content is "phenomenal", faith will be "volitive". Broadly speaking Christianity is an "existential" Path[26]—"intellectualized" in *gnosis*—whereas Islam is on the contrary an "intellectual" Path "phenomenalized", which means that it is *a priori* intellectual, either directly or indirectly according to whether we are speaking of the *Sharīʿah* or of the *Haqīqah*. The Muslim, on the strength of his unitary conviction—wherein certitude coincides finally with the very substance of intelligence and thus with the Absolute[27]—readily sees in phenomena temptations to "associations" (*shirk, mushrik*) whereas the Christian, centered as he is on the fact of Christ and on the miracles flowing in essence from that fact, feels an innate distrust of intelligence—which he readily reduces to the "wisdom after the flesh" in opposing it to Pauline charity—and of what he believes to be the pretensions of the "human spirit".

Now if from the point of view of "realization" or of the "path", Christianity operates through "love of God"—a love which responds to the divine love for man, God being Himself "Love"—Islam, as we have already seen, proceeds through "sincerity of unitary faith", and

---

[25] This is what is meant by the saying that at birth the soul is "Christian"—or "Muslim", according to the religion—and that it is men who turn it away, as the case may be, from its innate faith or on the contrary "confirm" that faith. This recalls the "recollection" of Plato.

[26] Since it is founded on the element *Sat*, "Being" of the Vedantic terminology and not directly on the element *Chit*, ("Consciousness"), although the *Logos* intrinsically relates to the latter element, and this opens up the dimension of *gnosis*. The Intellect became phenomenal in order that the phenomenal might become Intellect.

[27] But it goes without saying that this definition is applicable to all *gnosis*.

we know this faith must imply all the consequences logically follow-ing from its content—which is Unity, or the Absolute. First there is *al-īmān*, the accepting of Unity by man's intelligence; then—since we exist both individually and collectively—there is *al-islām*, the submis-sion of the will to Unity, or to the idea of Unity; this second element relates to Unity insofar as it is a synthesis on the plane of multiplicity; finally there is *al-ihsān*, which expands or deepens the two previous elements to the point of their ultimate consequences. Under the influ-ence of *al-ihsān*, *al-īmān* becomes "realization" or a "certitude that is lived"—"knowing" becomes "being"—while *al-islām*, instead of be-ing limited to a certain number of prescribed attitudes, comes to in-clude every level in our nature; *a priori* faith and submission are hardly more than symbolic attitudes, although nonetheless efficacious at their own level. By virtue of *al-ihsān*, *al-īmān* becomes *gnosis*, or "participa-tion" in the Divine Intelligence, and *al-islām* becomes "extinction" in the Divine Being. Since participation in the divine is a mystery, no man has a right to proclaim himself a *mu'min* ("believing", one possessing *īmān*) though he can perfectly well call himself *muslim* ("submitted", one conforming to *islām*); *īmān* is a secret between the servant and his Lord, like the *ihsān* which determines its degree (*maqām*) or "secret" (*sirr*), its ineffable reality. In unitary faith—with the fullness of its con-sequences—as in total love of God, it is a question of escaping from the dispersing and mortal multiplicity of all that—being "other than He"—is not; one needs to escape from sin because it implies in prac-tice a "total" love for the creature or the created, hence a love turned away from God-Love and squandered into what is inferior to man's immortal personality. Here there is a criterion that clearly shows the meaning of religions and modes of wisdom: it is "concentration" based on truth and in view of rediscovering, beyond death and this world of death, all we have loved here below; but all this is for us hidden in a ge-ometrical point, which at the outset appears to us like an utter impov-erishment and indeed is so in a certain relative sense and in relation to our world of deceptive richness, of sterile segmentation into a myriad of facets or refractions. The world is a movement which already bears within itself the principle of its own exhaustion, an unfolding which displays at every point the stigmata of its narrowness and in which Life and the Spirit are astray, not by some absurd chance but because this encounter between inert Existence and living Consciousness is a possibility and thus something which cannot but be, something posited by the very infinitude of the Absolute.

At this point, something must be said about the priority of contemplation. As one knows, Islam defines this supreme function of man in the *hadīth* about *ihsān* which orders man to "worship *Allāh* as though thou didst see Him", since "if thou dost not see Him, He nonetheless seeth thee". Christianity, for its part, enunciates first the total love of God and then love of the neighbor; now it must be insisted, in the interest of the love of God, that this second love could not be total because love of ourselves is not so; whether *ego* or *alter*, man is not God.[28] Be that as it may, it follows from all traditional definitions of man's supreme function that he who is capable of contemplation has no right to neglect it but is on the contrary "called" to dedicate himself to it; in other words, he sins neither against God nor against his neighbor—to say the least—in following the example of Mary in the Gospels and not that of Martha, for contemplation contains action and not the reverse. If in point of fact action can be opposed to contemplation, it is nevertheless not opposed to it in principle, nor is action called for beyond what is necessary or required by the duties of a man's station in life. In abasing ourselves from humility, we must not also abase things which transcend us, for then our virtue loses all its value and meaning; to reduce spirituality to a "humble" utilitarianism—thus to a latent materialism— is to give offense to God, on the one hand because it is like saying it is not worthwhile to be overly preoccupied with God, and on the other hand because it means relegating the divine gift of intelligence to the rank of the superfluous.

Apart from this, and on a vaster scale, it must be understood that the "metaphysical point of view" is synonymous with "inwardness": metaphysics is not "external" to any form of spirituality, it is thus impossible to consider something both metaphysically and from the

---

[28] As for the *hadīth* just cited, it does not keep silent on human charity since before defining *ihsān*, it defines *islām* and this consists, among other things, in "the paying of the tithe" or *zakāt*.

outside at one and the same time. Furthermore, those who uphold the extra-intellectual principle according to which any possible competence would derive exclusively from a practical participation, do not refrain from legislating "intellectually" and in "full awareness" of what they are doing[29] about forms of spirituality in which they do not participate in any way whatever.

Intelligence can be the essence of a path provided there is a contemplative mentality and a thinking that is fundamentally non-passional; an exoterism could not, as such, constitute this path but can, as in the case of Islam, predispose to it by its fundamental perspective, its structure, and its ambience. From the strictly Shariite point of view, intelligence is reduced—for Islam—to responsibility; viewed thus, every responsible person is intelligent; in other words a responsible person is defined in relation to intelligence and not in relation to freedom of the will alone.[30]

—— ·:· ——

At the beginning of this book we saw that Islam is founded on the nature of things in the sense that it sees the condition for salvation in our deiformity, namely in the total character of human intelligence, then in the freedom of the will, and finally in the gift of speech, provided these faculties be respectively—thanks to an "objective" divine intervention—vehicles for certitude, for moral equilibrium, and for unitive prayer. We have further seen that these three modes of deiformity and their contents are, broadly speaking, represented in the Islamic tradition by the triad *Imān-Islām-Ihsān* ("Faith-Law-Path"). Now to speak of something as theomorphic is to refer to characteristics proper to

---

[29] For example, by maintaining that the Absolute of the *Vedānta* or of Sufism is only a "natural" (?) absolute, "devoid of life" and therefore "misleading" and so on.

[30] "They will say: Had we but listened or had we but understood [*na'qilu* with the intelligence: *'aql*] we would not be among the guests of the furnace" (Koran 67:10). Islamic appreciation for the intelligence is also revealed in this *hadīth* among others: "Our Lord Jesus said: It was not impossible for me to raise the dead, but it was impossible for me to cure the stupid."

the Divine Nature, and in fact God is "Light" (*Nūr*),[31] "Life" (*Hayāt*) or "Will" (*Irādah*), and "Word" (*Kalām, Kalimah*); this Word is the creative word *kun* ("be!").[32] But what with God is creative power is, with man, transmuting and deifying power; if the Divine Word creates, the human word responding to it—the "mentioning" of *Allāh*—brings back to God. The Divine Word first creates, then reveals; the human word first transmits, then transforms; it transmits the truth and then, addressing itself to God, transforms and deifies man; to Divine Revelation corresponds human transmission and to Creation, deification. Speech in man has no function but transmission of truth and deification; it is either truthful discourse or else prayer.[33]

Let us here briefly sum up the whole of this doctrine: in order to be able to understand the meaning of the Koran as a sacrament, one must know that it is the uncreated prototype of the gift of speech, that it is the eternal Word of God (*kalāmu 'Llāh*); that man and God meet in the revealed speech, in the *Logos* which has taken on the differentiated form of human language so that, through this language, man may find again the undifferentiated and salvific Word of the Eternal. All this explains the immense saving power of the "theophoric" word, its capacity to convey a divine power and to annihilate a legion of sins.[34]

---

[31] Infinite "Consciousness", free from all objectivation.

[32] Hence the word *kawn*, the "world", "that which exists". *Al-kawn al-kabīr* is the macrocosm: *al-kawn as-saghīr*, the microcosm.

[33] "But let your communication be, Yea, yea; Nay, nay: for whatsoever is more than these cometh of evil" (Matt. 5:37). This is akin to the "sincerity" (*ikhlās*) which is the very essence of *Ihsān*, according to the already mentioned definition: "Virtue in action (spiritual actualization, *al-ihsān*) is to adore God as if thou didst see Him, and if thou seest Him not, He nonetheless seeth thee." Truthful speech is the very symbol of that right intention which in Islam is everything. "Lead us on the straight path" (*as-sirāt al-mustaqīm*), says the *Fātihah*.

[34] "And Adam received words from his Lord" (Koran 2:37). In a certain Trinitarian theology, the "Word" represents the "Knowledge" which "Being" has of itself. "For my Father is greater than I" (John 14:28): Being in itself is greater than the pole "Consciousness", even though the latter is in reality Being, in its intrinsic nature. Moreover, Being also has an aspect of "Consciousness" in relation to Beyond-Being in the sense that it crystallizes the potentialities of Beyond-Being distinctly with a view to their manifestation; but Beyond-Being is nonetheless the supreme "Self", whose infinite Knowledge is undifferentiated by reason of its very infinitude.

The second foundation of the path, as was pointed out at the beginning of this chapter, is contemplative or operative concentration, or prayer in all its forms and at all levels. The support of this concentration—or of quintessential prayer—is in Islam "mentioning" or "remembrance" (*dhikr*),[35] a term whose meaning ranges from the recitation of the whole of the Koran to the mystical exhalation which symbolizes the final *hā* of the Name *Allāh* or the initial *hā* of the Name *Huwa*, "He". Everything that can be said of the Divine Name—for example, that "all things on earth are accursed save the remembrance of *Allāh*", or that "nothing so removes the wrath of *Allāh* as this remembrance"—all this can also be said of the heart and of the Intellect[36] and, by extension, of metaphysical intellection and contemplative concentration. In the heart we are united to pure Being and in the Intellect to total Truth, these two coinciding in the Absolute.[37]

In Islam, concentration appears as the "sincerity" of prayer; prayer is fully valid only on condition of being sincere, and it is this sincerity—and so in fact this concentration—which "opens" the *dhikr*, or enables it to be simple while at the same time having an immense effect.[38] To the objection that jaculatory prayer is an easy and outward thing, that it could neither efface a thousand sins nor have the value of a thousand good works, tradition answers that on the human side the whole merit lies, firstly in the intention that makes us pronounce the prayer—since apart from this intention we would not pronounce it—and secondly in our recollectedness, and thus in our "presence" in

---

[35] "He who mentions Me in himself (*fī nafsihi*), I will mention him in Myself, and he who mentions Me in an assembly, him I will mention in an assembly better than his" (*hadīth qudsī*). The "better assembly" is that of Heaven. According to another *hadīth* belonging to the same category: "I hold company (*Innī jālis*) with him who mentions Me."

[36] "Heaven and earth cannot contain Me, but the heart of My believing servant containeth Me" (*hadīth qudsī*).

[37] "O, happy man", sings Jami, "whose heart has been illuminated by invocation (*dhikr*), in the shade of which the carnal soul has been vanquished, the thought of multiplicity chased away, the invoker (*dhākir*) transmuted into invocation, and the invocation transmuted into the Invoked (*madhkūr*)."

[38] To the "effort of actualization" (*istihdār*) of the servant answers the "presence" (*hudūr*) of the Lord.

face of the Presence of God; but that this human merit is as nothing in comparison with grace.

The "remembrance of God" is at the same time a forgetting of oneself; conversely, the ego is a kind of crystallization of forgetfulness of God. The brain is, as it were, the organ of this forgetfulness;[39] it is like a sponge filled with images of this world of dispersion and heaviness, filled too with the tendencies of the ego toward both dispersal and hardening. As for the heart, it is the latent remembrance of God, hidden deep down in our "I"; in prayer it is as if the heart, risen to the surface, came to take the place of the brain which then sleeps with a holy slumber; this slumber unites and soothes, and its most elementary trace in the soul is peace. "I sleep, but my heart waketh."[40]

If Ibn Arabi and others require—in conformity with the Koran and the *Sunnah*—that a man should "become penetrated by the majesty of *Allāh*" before and during the practice of *dhikr*, they imply not merely a reverential attitude rooted in the imagination and in feeling, but also a conformity of man's whole being to the "Motionless Mover", which means all told a return to our normative archetype, to the pure Adamic substance "made in the image of God"; this is moreover directly connected with dignity, the role of which is clearly to be seen in the sacerdotal and royal functions: priest and king both stand before the Divine Being, over the people, and it might be said that they are at the same time "something of God". In a certain sense the dignity of the *dhākir*—of him who prays—rejoins the "image" that the Divinity takes on in relation to him, or in other words, this dignity—this "holy silence" or this "non-action"—is the very image of the Divine Principle. Buddhism gives us a particularly concrete example of this: the sacramental image of the Buddha is both "divine form" and "human perfection" and marks the meeting point between the earthly and the heavenly. But all this refers to contemplative prayer alone and it is precisely this prayer which is in question where the Sufi *dhikr* is concerned.

---

[39] Fallen man is by definition "forgetfulness"; consequently the path is "remembrance". An Arabic proverb, based on the phonetic connection between the words *nasiya* ("to forget") and *insān* ("man") says that "the first forgetful being (*awwalu nāsin*) was the first man (*awwalu 'n-nās*)".

[40] The Prophet said: "Protect God in thy heart; then God shall protect thee."

The Name *Allāh*, which is the quintessence of all the Koranic formulas, consists of two syllables linked by the double *lam;* this *lam* is like the bodily death which precedes the hereafter and the resurrection, or like the spiritual death which inaugurates enlightenment and sanctity, and this analogy can be extended to the universe, either in an ontological or in a cyclical sense: between two degrees of reality, whether envisaged in relation to their linking or, should such be the case, their succession, there is always a kind of extinction,[41] and this is what is also expressed by the word *illā*[42] ("if it be not") in the *Shahādah*. The first syllable of the Name refers, according to a self-evident interpretation, to the world and to life inasmuch as they are divine manifestations, and the second to God and to the beyond or to immortality. While the Name begins with a sort of hiatus between silence and utterance (the *hamzah*) like a *creatio ex nihilo*, it ends in an unlimited breathing out which symbolically opens into the Infinite—that is, the final *hā* marks the supra-ontological Non-Duality[43]—and this indicates that there is no symmetry between the initial nothingness of things and the transcendent Non-Being. Thus the Name *Allāh* embraces all that "is",[44] from the Absolute down to the tiniest speck of dust, whereas the Name *Huwa*, "He", which "personifies" the final *hā*, indicates the Absolute as such in its ineffable transcendence and its inviolable mystery.

There is necessarily a guarantee of efficacy in the Divine Names themselves. In Amidism[45] the saving certitude of the practice of invo-

---

[41] In the canonical prayer of Islam, which includes phases of abasement and rising up—or more exactly of bowing down and straightening up again, followed by prostration and rest—the former are related to death or "extinction" and the latter to resurrection or immortality, "permanence"; the passage from one phase to the other is marked by the pronouncing of the *takbīr* "God is greater" (*Allāhu akbar*).

[42] This is the strait or narrow gate of the Gospels.

[43] This is what is expressed by the formula: "*Allāh* is neither Himself nor other than Himself" (*Allāhu lā huwa wa lā ghairuhu*). This proposition is also applicable, in a different sense, to the qualities (*sifāt*) of God.

[44] *Al-ulūhiyah*—"Allahness"—is indeed defined as the "sum of the mysteries of Reality" (*jumlatu haqāʾiq al-Wujūd*).

[45] This term, derived from the Japanese, is used because in the West it designates conventionally a Buddhism based on incantation, one which was Chinese before becom-

cation is derived from the "original vow" of Amida; fundamentally this amounts to saying that in every analogous practice in other traditional forms, this certitude is derived from the very meaning comprised in the *mantram* or Divine Name. Thus, if the *Shahādah* comprises the same grace as the "original vow" of Amida,[46] it is by virtue of its very content: because it is the supreme formulation of Truth, and because Truth delivers by its very nature; to identify oneself with Truth, to infuse it into our being and to transfer our being into it is to escape from the grip of error and malice. Now the *Shahādah* is nothing other than an exteriorization in doctrinal form of the Name *Allāh*; it corresponds strictly to the *Ehieh asher Ehieh* of the Burning Bush in the *Torah*. It is by such formulas that God announces "Who He is", and thus what His Name signifies; and it is for this reason that such formulas, or such *mantrams*, are so many Names of God.[47]

We have just pointed out that the meaning of the Name *Allāh* is that *lā ilāha illā 'Llāh*, namely that cosmic manifestation is illusory and that the metacosmic Principle alone is real. In order to make our meaning more clear, we must here repeat a *haqīqah* already touched on in the chapter on the Koran: since from the point of view of manifestation—which is our standpoint given that we exist—the world indisputably possesses a certain reality, it must follow that the truth concerning it in a positive sense is also included in the first *Shahādah*; in fact it is so in the form of the second *Shahādah*—*Muhammadun Rasūlu 'Llāh*—which springs from the word *illā* ("if not") in the first *Shahadah* and means that manifestation has a relative reality which reflects the Principle. This testimony opposes to the total negation of transitory things—or of "accidents"—a relative affirmation, the affirmation of manifestation inasmuch as it reflects the divine, in other words of the world as divine manifestation. *Muhammad* is the world envisaged in respect of perfection; *Rasūl* indicates the relationship of causality and thus connects the world to God. When the Intellect plac-

---

ing Japanese, and Indian before becoming Chinese. Nevertheless it was in Japan that it came to its extraordinary flowering.

[46] We could say as much of the Names of Jesus and Mary and of the jaculatory prayers containing these Names.

[47] The *Shahādah* is in fact considered to be a Divine Name.

es itself at the level of absolute Reality, the relative truth is as it were absorbed by the total truth: from the point of view of verbal symbols, relative truth then finds itself as it were withdrawn into the metaphysical "conditional" which is the word *illā*. As there is nothing outside *Allāh*, the world too must be comprised in Him and cannot be "other than He" (*ghairuhu*); and that is why manifestation "is the Principle" inasmuch as the Principle is "the Outward" (*azh-Zhāhir*), the Principle as such being "the Inward" (*al-Bātin*). Thus the Name *Allāh* includes all that is, and transcends all that is.[48]

In order to make clear the position of the formula of consecration (the *Basmalah*) in all these relationships, let us add the following: just as the second *Shahādah* springs from the first—from the word *illā* which is both the ontological "isthmus" and the axis of the world— so the *Basmalah* springs from the double *lam* in the middle of the Name *Allāh*.[49] But whereas the second *Shahādah* (the Testimony on the Prophet) marks an ascending and liberating movement, the *Basmalah* indicates a descent that is creative, revealing, or merciful; indeed it starts with *Allāh* (*bismi 'Llāhi*) and ends with *Rahīm* whereas the second *Shahādah* starts with *Muhammad* and ends with *Allāh*

---

[48] "I persevered in this exercise until it was revealed to me: 'God has said of Himself that He is the First (*al-Awwal*) and the Last (*al-Ākhir*), the Inward (*al-Bātin*) and the Outward (*azh-Zhāhir*).' I fought against this, concentrating on my exercise, but the more I made efforts to thrust it away, the more it assailed me without respite. At length I answered: 'I understand that God is the First and the Last and the Inner, but that he is equally the Outward I do not understand, since outwardly I see only the universe.' I received this reply: 'If God wished to designate by the word "Outwardness" anything other than visible existence, then this existence would not be outward, but inward; yet I tell you that He (God) is the Outward.' At that very instant, I suddenly realized the truth that there is no existence outside God and that the universe is nothing save He. . ." (the *Rasā'il* of Shaykh Mulay al-Arabi ad-Darqawi).

[49] The four words of the *Basmalah* (*Bismi 'Llāhi 'r-Rahmāni 'r-Rahīm*) are represented as four streams of Paradise springing forth beneath the throne of God, which is *ar-Rūh*. The *lam* in the Supreme Name and the *illā* in the Testimony correspond to the "throne" in the sense that they inaugurate, the former the syllable *Lāh* and the latter the Name *Allāh*, thus the "dimensions of transcendence". This follows from the nature of things and we point it out in order to show, in connection with invocatory practices and sapiential doctrines, how the basic enunciations or symbols serve as vehicles for the whole Divine Message, somewhat as a crystal synthesizes the whole of space.

(*Rasūlu 'Llāh*). The first *Shahādah*—together with the second which it bears within itself—is as it were the content or message of the *Basmalah*; but it is also its principle, for the supreme Name "means" the *Shahādah* once it is envisaged in a distinctive or discursive mode; in this case it can be said that the *Basmalah* springs from the divine *illā*. The *Basmalah* is distinguished from the *Shahādah* by the fact that it marks a "coming forth" as is indicated by the words "in the Name of" (*bismi*), whereas the *Shahādah* is, either the divine "content" or the "message": it is either the sun or the image of the sun, but not the sun's ray, although from another point of view it can also be conceived as a "ladder" linking cosmic "nothingness" to pure Reality.

In the following *hadīth*: "He who invokes God to the point that his eyes overflow from fear and the earth is watered by his tears, him God will not punish on the Day of the Resurrection", it is not solely a question of the gift of tears or of *bhakti*, but above all of the "liquefying" of our post-Edenic hardness, a fusion or dissolving, of which tears—or sometimes melting snow—are traditionally the symbol. But nothing forbids us from pursuing the chain of key images: we may, for instance, pause at the symbolism of the eyes and note that the right eye corresponds to the sun, to activity, to the future, and the left eye to the moon, to the past, to passivity: we have here two dimensions of the ego, the one relating to the future inasmuch as it is the leaven of illusion and the other to the past inasmuch as it is an accumulation of "ego-forming" experiences; in other words, both the past and the future of the ego—what we are and what we want to become or to possess—must be "dissolved" in the instantaneous present luminous with transpersonal contemplation, whence the "fear" (*khashyah*) mentioned in the *hadīth* quoted above. "His eyes overflow" (*fādhat ʿaynāhu*) and "the earth is watered" (*yusību 'l-ardh*): there is both an inward and an outward liquefaction, the latter responding to the former; when the ego is "liquefied", the outward world—from which it is in large measure compounded—seems to be drawn into the same alchemical process, in the sense that it becomes "transparent", so that the contemplative sees God everywhere, or sees all things in God.

Let us now consider prayer in its most general sense: the call to God, if it is to be perfect or "sincere", must be fervent, just as concentration, if it is to be perfect must be pure; now at the level of emotive piety, the key to concentration is fervor. The answer to the question of knowing how one escapes from lukewarmness and realizes fervor or concentration is that zeal depends on our awareness of our goal; a man who is indifferent or lazy certainly knows how to hurry when threatened by danger or when enticed by something agreeable[50] and this is as much as to say that zeal may be motivated either by fear or by love. But this motive may also—and with all the more reason—be knowledge; since knowledge too—to the degree that it is real—supplies us with sufficient reasons for ardor, otherwise it would be necessary to hold that man—every man—is capable of acting only when under the impulsion of threats or promises; this is certainly true of collectivities but not of every individual.

The very fact of our existence is a prayer and compels us to prayer, so that it could be said: "I am, therefore I pray; *sum ergo oro*". Existence is by nature ambiguous and from this it follows that it compels us to prayer in two ways: firstly by its quality of being a divine expression, a coagulated and segmented mystery, and secondly by its inverse aspect of being a bondage and perdition, so that we must indeed "think of God" not merely because, being men, we cannot not take account of the divine basis of existence—insofar as we are faithful to our nature— but also because we are by the same token forced to recognize that we are fundamentally more than existence and that we live like exiles in a house on fire.[51] On the one hand, existence is a wave of creative joy

---

[50] "Blessed are they that have not seen and yet have believed", says the Gospel, and the same meaning is to be found in the *hadīth* about *ihsān*: "And if thou seest Him (God) not, He nonetheless seeth thee". *Gnosis*, far from seeking to abolish these teachings, situates them somewhat differently, for there is not only the difference between earthly ignorance—which requires "faith"—and heavenly knowledge, but also the difference between doctrinal learning and unitive realization; such learning is by no means "blind" in itself, but it is so in relation to realization "in depth".

[51] Like existence, fire is ambiguous, for it is both light and heat, divinity and hell. In *Castes et races*, we made incidental reference to a Hindu theory in which fire, inasmuch as it has a tendency to rise and to illumine, corresponds to *sattva*, whereas water, inasmuch as it spreads out horizontally and fertilizes, is assimilable to *rajas*, while earth then relates to *tamas* through its inertia and its crushing force. But it goes

and every creature praises God: to exist is to praise God whether we be waterfalls, trees, birds, or men; but on the other hand, existence means not to be God and so to be in a certain respect ineluctably in opposition to Him; existence is something which grips us like a shirt of Nessus. Someone who does not know that the house is on fire has no reason to call for help, just as the man who does not know he is drowning will not grasp the rope that could save him; but to know we are perishing means, either to despair or else to pray. Truly to know that we are nothing because the whole world is nothing, means to remember "That which is"[52] and through this remembrance to become free.

If a man has a nightmare and, while still dreaming, starts calling on God for aid, he infallibly awakens; this shows two things: firstly, that the conscious intelligence of the Absolute subsists during sleep like a distinct personality—our spirit thus remaining apart from our states of illusion—and secondly, that when a man calls on God he will end by awakening also from that great dream which is life, the world, the ego. If this call can breach the wall of common dreams, why should it not also breach the wall of that vaster and more tenacious dream that is existence?

There is in this call no egoism, for pure prayer is the most intimate and most precious form of the gift of self.[53] The common man is in the world to receive; even if he gives alms, he steals from God—and steals from himself—insofar as he supposes that his gift is all that God

---

without saying that in another respect fire relates to *rajas* through its devouring and "passional" heat, light alone then corresponding to *sattva*; in this case we have the triad not of the visible elements—fire, water, and earth—but of the sensory functions of "fire-sun": luminosity, heat and negatively, darkness. Pure luminosity is cold through its transcendence; darkness is so through privation. Spiritually speaking, darkness freezes whereas light refreshes.

[52] In expressions such as this we are not taking account of the limitation of "Being": this word is used in an extrinsic sense in relation to the world and without in any way prejudicing the inward limitlessness of the Divine. Theology does exactly the same, just as Sufism, which does not hesitate to speak of the "existence" (*wujūd*) of *Allāh*; it is the intention—clear for the gnostic—and not the literal meaning of the term which establishes the required sense.

[53] A *hadīth* says: "The last hour shall not come until there is no longer any man on earth who says: *Allāh! Allāh!*" Indeed it is sanctity and wisdom—and along with these, universal and quintessential prayer—that sustain the world.

and his neighbor can ask of him; letting "his left hand know what his right hand doeth", he always expects something from his surroundings, either consciously or unconsciously. It is necessary to acquire the habit of the inner gift without which all alms are but half-gifts; and what one gives to God is by that very fact given to all men.

—— .:. ——

If we start from the idea that intellection and concentration, or doctrine and method, are the foundations of the path, it should be added that these two elements are valid and effective only by virtue of a traditional guarantee, a "seal" coming from Heaven. Intellection has need of tradition, of a Revelation fixed in time and adapted to a society, if it is to be awakened in us and not go astray, and prayer identifies itself with the Revelation itself or proceeds from it, as we have already seen. In other words, the point of orthodoxy, of tradition, of Revelation is that the means of realizing the Absolute must come "objectively" from the Absolute; knowledge cannot spring up "subjectively" except within the framework of an "objective" divine formulation of Knowledge.

But this element "tradition", precisely because of its impersonal and formal character, calls for a complement which is essentially personal and free, and this complement is virtue: without virtue, orthodoxy becomes pharisaical, in a subjective sense of course, for its objective incorruptibility is not in question.

If we have defined metaphysics as discernment between the Real and the unreal, then virtue will be defined as the inversion of the relationship between *ego* and *alter*: this relationship being a natural, though illusory inversion of the "real proportions", and so a "fall" and a rupture of equilibrium—for the fact that two people believe themselves to be "I" proves that, on pain of absurdity, neither is right, the "I" being logically unique—virtue will be the inversion of this inversion and so the rectifying of our fall; in a way that is relative although effective, virtue will see the "I myself" in "the other", or the converse. This brings out clearly the sapiential function of virtue: charity, far from being reducible to sentimentality or utilitarianism, brings about a state of consciousness, it aims at the real, not at the illusory; it confers a vision of reality on our personal "being", on our volitive nature, and is not limited to a mode of thought involving no obligation. Likewise, we can say of humility that, when properly conceived, it realizes in us an awareness of our own nothingness before the Absolute and of our imperfection by comparison with other men; like every virtue it is at the same time cause and effect. Just like spiritual exercises, though in a different way, the virtues are fixing agents for what is known by the spirit.[54]

There is an error which all too easily arises in the minds of those who turn to metaphysics in a reaction against a conventional religiosity, namely the error of believing that truth has no need of God—of the personal God who both sees and hears us—nor of our virtues either; that truth has nothing to do with what is human and that consequently it is enough for us to know that the Principle is not manifestation and so forth, as though these notions released us from being men and immunized us against the rigors of natural laws, not to say more. Had destiny not so willed—and destiny does not depend on our doctrinal notions—we would have no knowledge nor even any life; God is in all that we are and He alone can give us life and light and protection. Likewise regarding the virtues: assuredly the truth has no need of our personal qualities and may even lie beyond our destinies, but we have need of truth and must bow to its requirements, which do not concern the mind only;[55] since we exist, our being—whatever the content of our mind—must at every level be in accord with its divine principle. The cataphatic, and thus in some degree "individualistic" virtues are the keys to the apophatic virtues, and these latter are inseparable from *gnosis*; the virtues testify to the beauty of God. It is illogical and pernicious— both for oneself and for others—to think the truth and to forget generosity.

---

[54] The sentimentality with which people surround the virtues leads to their being easily falsified; for many people, humility means despising an intelligence they do not have. The devil has gotten hold of charity and made of it a demagogic and Godless utilitarianism and an argument against contemplation, as though Christ had supported Martha against Mary. Humility becomes servility and charity materialism; in practice, this kind of virtue seeks to furnish the proof that one can get along without God.

[55] "When a man talks of God without having true virtue", says Plotinus, "his words are but hollow". He is referring here, not to simple enunciations that are in accord with orthodoxy, but to spontaneous utterances deemed to spring from a direct knowledge.

Here it may be convenient to explain that the virtues we term "apophatic" are those which are not the "productions" of man but on the contrary radiate from the nature of Being: in relation to us they are pre-existent so that the part played by us in relation to them is that of removing everything in ourselves which opposes their radiation, and not that of producing them "positively"; herein lies the whole difference between individual effort and purifying knowledge. It is in any case absurd to believe that the Sufi who states that he has transcended some particular virtue, or even all virtues, is on that account deprived of the qualities which go to make man's nobility and apart from which there can be no sanctity; the sole difference is that he no longer "experiences" these qualities as his "own", and thus has no awareness of any "personal" merit as is the case with the ordinary virtues.[56] It is a matter of a divergence of principle or of nature, although from another more general and less operative point of view, every virtue or even every cosmic quality can be envisaged apophatically, that is, according to the ontological essence of phenomena; this is what devout people express after their own fashion when they attribute their virtues wholly to the grace of God.

In conformity with the injunctions of the Koran, "remembrance of God" requires the fundamental virtues and, arising from them, the acts of virtue called for by particular circumstances. Now the fundamental and universal virtues, inseparable from human nature, are these: humility or self-effacement; charity or generosity; truthfulness or sincerity and so impartiality; then vigilance or perseverance; contentment or patience; and lastly that "quality of being" which is unitive piety, spiritual plasticity, a disposition to saintliness.[57]

---

[56] In his *Hikam*, Ibn Ataillah says: "If you could attain to Him only after the elimination of all your blemishes and the extinction of your egoism, you would never attain to Him. But if He wishes to lead you to Him, He covers over your qualities with His qualities and your characteristics with His characteristics and unites you to Himself. He makes you reach Him by what comes from Him to you, and not by what comes from you to Him."

[57] This enumeration, of which different versions are to be found in our earlier works, is a synthesis deduced from the very nature of things. Sufism offers various classifications of the virtues and distinguishes among them exceedingly subtle ramifications. Clearly, it also insists on the apophatic nature of the supernatural virtues and sees in these concomitances of the Spirit so many "stations" (*maqāmat*). Nature provides us with many

All that has been said up to this point makes possible an explanation of the meaning of the virtues and of moral laws; the latter are styles of action conforming to particular spiritual perspectives and to particular material and mental conditions, while the virtues on the contrary represent intrinsic beauties fitted into these styles and finding through them their realization. Every virtue and every morality is a mode of equilibrium or, to be more precise, it is a way of participating, even to the detriment of some outward and false equilibrium, in the universal Equilibrium; by remaining at the center, a man escapes from the vicissitudes of the moving periphery; and this is the meaning of Taoist "non-action". Morality is a way of acting, whereas virtue is a way of being—a way of being wholly oneself, beyond the ego, or of being simply That which is.[58] This could also be expressed as follows: the various moralities are at the same time frameworks for the virtues and their application to collectivities; the virtue of the collectivity is its equilibrium determined by Heaven. Moralities are diverse, but virtue as it has been here defined, is everywhere the same, because man is everywhere man. This moral unity of humankind goes hand in hand with its intellectual unity: perspectives and dogmas differ, but truth is one.

Another fundamental element of the Path is symbolism, which is manifested both in sacred art and in virgin nature. No doubt sensory forms do not possess the same importance as verbal or scriptural symbols; however, according to circumstances they fulfill a very precious function either as a "framework" or as "spiritual suggestion", not to mention the ritual importance of the highest order which they can as-

---

images both of the virtues and of the manifestations of the Spirit. The dove, the eagle, the swan, and the peacock reflect respectively purity, strength, contemplative peace, and spiritual generosity or the unfolding of graces.

[58] According to Saint Thomas Aquinas, "truth is the ultimate goal of the whole universe and contemplation of truth is the essential activity of wisdom. . . . By their nature, the virtues do not necessarily form part of contemplation but they are an indispensable condition for it."

sume; furthermore, symbolism has the particular quality of combining the outward and the inward, the sensory and the spiritual, and thus in principle or in fact goes beyond the function of serving merely as a "background".

Sacred art is first of all the visible and audible[59] form of Revelation and then also its indispensable liturgical vesture. The form must be an adequate expression of its content; in no case should it contradict it; it cannot be abandoned to the arbitrary decisions of individuals, to their ignorance and their passions. But we must distinguish different degrees in sacred art, thus different levels of absoluteness or of relativity,[60] and in addition we must take account of the relative character of form as such. The spiritual integrity of the form is a "categorical imperative" but this cannot prevent the formal order from being subject to certain vicissitudes; the fact that the masterpieces of sacred art are sublime expressions of the Spirit must not make us forget that, seen from the standpoint of this same Spirit, these works already appear, in their more ponderous exteriorizations, as concessions to the "world" and re-call the saying in the Gospels: "All they that take the sword shall perish by the sword." Indeed, when the Spirit has need of such a degree of ex-teriorization, it is already well on the way to being lost; exteriorization as such bears within itself the poison of outwardness, and so of exhaus-tion, fragility, and decrepitude; the masterpiece is as it were laden with regrets and is already a "swan song"; one sometimes has the impression that art—through the very surplus of its perfections—is there to make up for the absence of wisdom or of sanctity. The Desert Fathers had no need of colonnades and stained glass windows; but, on the other hand, those who today despise sacred art in the name of "pure spirit" are the

---

[59] For instance, the chanting of the Koran, which can be in various styles, is an art; a choice can be made between one style or another, but nothing can be added to them; one can chant the Koran in certain ways, but not in others. The modes of chanting express different rhythms of the spirit.

[60] First there is sacred art in the strictest sense, as it appears in the Tabernacle of Moses, where God Himself prescribes both the form and the materials; then there is the sacred art which has been developed in conformity with a particular ethnic genius; and finally there are decorative aspects of sacred art in which the ethnic genius is more freely expressed, though always in conformity with a spirit that transcends it. Genius is nothing unless determined by a spiritual perspective.

very people who least understand it and have most need of it.[61] Be this as it may, nothing noble can ever be lost: all the treasures of art and those of nature too are found again, in perfection and infinitely, in the Divine Beatitude; a man who is fully conscious of this truth cannot fail to be detached from sensory crystallizations as such.

But there is also the primordial symbolism of virgin nature, which is an open book, a revelation of the Creator, a sanctuary, and even in certain respects a path. In every epoch, sages and hermits have gone to seek nature; it was near nature that they felt far from the world and close to Heaven; innocent and pious, but nonetheless profound and terrible, nature was ever their refuge. Had we to make a choice between the most magnificent of temples and inviolate nature, we would choose nature; the destruction of all human works would be nothing compared to the destruction of nature.[62] Nature offers both vestiges of the earthly Paradise and foreshadowings of the heavenly Paradise.

All the same, from another point of view, we can ask ourselves which is more precious, the summits of sacred art, inasmuch as they are direct inspirations from God, or the beauties of nature inasmuch as they are divine creations and symbols.[63] The language of nature is doubtless more primordial and more universal, but it is less human and less immediately intelligible than art; for it to be able to deliver its message, more spiritual knowledge is needed, since outward things

---

[61] Art is always a criterion for the "discernment of spirits": real paganism shows up in the style of its art, as for example in the naturalism of Greco-Roman art and, no less strikingly, in the gigantism at once brutal and effeminate of Babylonian sculpture. We may also note the art fraught with nightmarish components of pre-columbian Mexico in its decadence.

[62] In the art of the Far East, which is much less "humanistic" than the arts of the West and of Near-Eastern antiquity, man's work remains profoundly linked with nature to the point of forming with it a sort of organic unity; the art of China and Japan does not include "pagan" elements as do the ancient Mediterranean arts; in its essential manifestations, it is never either sentimental or hollow and crushing.

[63] Should we prefer such works as the hieratic Virgin at Torcello near Venice, the glowing prayer-niches in the mosque of Cordova, the images of divinities of India and the Far East, or the high mountains, the seas, forests, and deserts? Formulated thus, the question is objectively insoluble; for on each side—that of art and that of nature—there are pluses and minuses.

are what we are, not in themselves but as regards their efficacy;[64] the relationship is here the same, or almost the same, as that between traditional mythologies and pure metaphysics. The best answer to this problem is that sacred art, of which a particular saint personally has no "need", nonetheless exteriorizes his sanctity, or precisely that something which can make artistic exteriorization superfluous for that saint himself.[65] Through art, this sanctity or wisdom has become miraculously tangible with all its human *materia* which virgin nature could not provide; in a sense, the "dilating" and "refreshing" virtue of nature is that of being not human but angelic. To say that one prefers the "works of God" to the "works of man" would be to simplify the problem unduly, given that in any art meriting the attribute "sacred" it is God who is the author; man is merely the instrument and what is human is merely the material.[66]

The symbolism of nature is part of our human experience: if the starry vault turns, it is because the heavenly worlds revolve around God; the appearance of turning is due, not only to our position on earth, but also and above all, to a transcendent prototype which is by no means illusory and seems even to have created our position in space in order to enable our spiritual perspective to be what it is. Thus the earthly illusion reflects a real situation, and this relationship is of the highest importance, for it shows that it is the myths—always bound to Ptolemean astronomy—which will have the final say. As we have already pointed out on other occasions, modern science, while it clearly provides exact observations, though ignorant of the meaning and import of symbols, could not *de jure* contradict mythological conceptions in what they contain of the spiritual and thus of value; it changes only the symbolical data, or in other words it destroys the empirical bases of the mythologies without being able to explain the significance of

---

[64] This is also—though to a lesser degree—true of art, precisely because the language of art passes through man.

[65] "Can make", not "must make", since art can have for some saints a function that eludes the ordinary man.

[66] The image of the Buddha combines in the most expressive way the "categories" treated of here: first, knowledge and concentration; then virtue (this being absorbed in the two preceding elements); then tradition and art, represented by the image itself; and finally nature, represented by the lotus.

the new data. From our point of view, this science superimposes a symbolism exceedingly complicated in its language on another that is metaphysically just as true but more human—rather as though some treatise were translated into another more difficult language—but it does not know that it has discovered a language and that implicitly it is putting forward a new metaphysical Ptolemaism.

The wisdom of nature is to be found over and over again affirmed in the Koran, which insists on the "signs" of creation for "those endowed with understanding", and this indicates the relationship between nature and *gnosis*; the vault of heaven is the temple of the eternal *sophia*. The same word "signs" (*āyāt*) also designates the verses of the Book; like the phenomena of nature which are at once virginal and maternal, they reveal God as they spring forth from the "Mother of the Book" and are transmitted by the virgin spirit of the Prophet.[67] Islam, like ancient Judaism, is particularly close to nature from the fact of being grounded in the nomadic spirit; its beauty is that of the desert and of the oasis; sand is a symbol of purity—it is used for the ritual ablutions when water is lacking—while the oasis is a prefiguration of Paradise. The symbolism of sand is analogous to that of snow: it is a great unifying peace—like the *Shahādah* which is peace and light—which in the end dissolves the knots and antinomies of existence, or which by reabsorbing them reduces all ephemeral coagulations to pure and immutable Substance. Islam arose from nature; the Sufis return to it, and this is one of the meanings of the *hadīth*: "Islam began in exile and it will end in exile." Towns, with their tendency to petrifaction and their seeds of corruption, are opposed to nature, which is ever virginal; their sole justification and the sole guarantee of their stability is to be sanctuaries; this guarantee is quite relative, for the Koran says: "And there is no town that We (*Allāh*) will not destroy, or will not severely punish, before the day of Resurrection" (17:58). All this enables us to understand why Islam sought, within the framework of an inevitable sedentarism, to maintain the spirit of nomadism: Muslim cities always retain the imprint of a journeying through space and time; everywhere Islam reflects the sacred sterility and austerity of the desert,

---

[67] In the preceding chapter, this was mentioned in what was said of the blessing on the Prophet.

but also, within this climate of death, the gay and precious overflowing of springs and oases; the fragile grace of the mosques echoes the grace of the palm groves while the whiteness and monotony of the towns reflect the beauty of the desert and so also of sepulchers. Beneath the emptiness of existence and behind its mirages lies the eternal profusion of Divine Life.

But let us return to our starting point, namely metaphysical truth as foundation of the path. Since this truth derives from esoterism—at least in those traditions where there is a polarity of esoterism and exoterism—we must here answer the question of knowing whether or not there exists an "esoteric orthodoxy" or whether this expression is not rather a contradiction in terms or an abuse of language. The whole difficulty, in situations where it arises, lies in too narrow a conception of the term "orthodoxy" on the one hand and of metaphysical knowledge on the other: it is in fact necessary to distinguish between two orthodoxies, the one extrinsic and formal and the other intrinsic and beyond form; the first relates to dogma and thus to "form", the latter to universal truth and thus to "essence". Now in esoterism these two are linked together in the sense that dogma is the key to direct knowledge; once such knowledge is attained we are evidently beyond form, but esoterism is nevertheless necessarily connected to the form which was its point of departure and the symbolism of which always remains valid.[68] For example, Islamic esoterism will never reject the fundamentals of Islam, even if it happens incidentally to contradict some particular exoteric position or interpretation; we can even say that Sufism is orthodox thrice over, firstly because it takes wing from the Islamic form and not from anywhere else, secondly because its realizations and doctrines correspond to truth and not to error, and thirdly because it always remains linked to Islam, since it considers itself to be the "marrow" (*lubb*) of Islam and not of another religion.

---

[68] Herein lies one of the meanings of the Koranic injunction: "Enter houses by their doors" (2:189). There is no *Tarīqah* without the *Sharī'ah*. The latter is the circle and the former the radius; the *Haqīqah* is the center.

Despite his verbal audacity, Ibn Arabi did not become a Buddhist, nor did he reject the dogmas and laws of the *Sharī ah*, and this amounts to saying that he did not depart from orthodoxy, either that of Islam or that of the Truth itself.

If some formulation appears to contradict a particular exoteric point of view, what matters is to know whether it is true or false, not whether it is "conformist" or "free"; in pure intellectuality the concepts of "freedom", "independence", or "originality" are devoid of meaning, as moreover are their contraries. If the purest esoterism comprises total truth—and that is the reason for its existence—the question of "orthodoxy" in the religious sense quite obviously cannot arise; direct knowledge of the mysteries could not be "Muslim" or "Christian", just as the sight of a mountain is the sight of a mountain and not something else. To speak of a "non-orthodox" esoterism is no less absurd for it would amount to holding, firstly that this esoterism was not linked to any form—in which case it would have neither authority nor legitimacy nor even any usefulness—and secondly that it was not the initiatic or "alchemical" outcome of a revealed path, and so did not include a formal and "objective" guarantee of any kind. These considerations should make it clear why the prejudice which attempts to explain everything in terms of "borrowings" or "syncretism" is ill-founded, for the doctrines of wisdom, being true, cannot fail to be concordant; and if the content is identical, the different expressions may be so too. That some particularly felicitous expression may be duplicated by a foreign doctrine is equally in the nature of things—the contrary would be abnormal and inexplicable—but that is no reason for making generalizations based on such an exceptional case or for pressing it to absurdity; this would be like concluding that, because sometimes things influence one another, all analogies in nature arise from unilateral or reciprocal influences.[69]

---

[69] A similar error would have it that everything begins from written texts: this too is a most improper generalization. "The Germanic tribes had a writing of their own, but, as Caesar noted to Lutetius, its use was strictly forbidden: all learning had to be passed on by word of mouth and retained in memory alone. In Peru, down to relatively recent times, only knotted cords were tolerated" (Ernst Fuhrmann, *Reich der Inka* [Hagen, 1922]). Let us add this opinion of Plato's: "All serious men will beware of treating of serious matters in writing"; however, according to the Rabbis, "it is better to profane

The question of the origins of Sufism is resolved by the fundamental discernment (*furqān*) of the Islamic doctrine: God and the world; now there is something provisional about this discernment from the fact that the Divine Unity, followed through to its ultimate consequences, excludes, precisely, the duality formulated by any discernment, and it is in a sense here that we find the starting point of the original and essential metaphysics of Islam. One thing which must be taken into account is that direct knowledge is in itself a state of pure "consciousness" and not a theory; there is thus nothing surprising in the fact that the complex and subtle formulations of *gnosis* were not manifested from the very beginning and at a single stroke, or that on occasion Neoplatonic or Platonic concepts have been borrowed for the purposes of dialectic. Sufism is "sincerity of faith" and this "sincerity"—which has absolutely nothing in common with the modern cult of sincerity—is nothing other, on the level of doctrine, than an intellectual vision that does not halt halfway but on the contrary draws from the idea of Unity its most rigorous consequences. The final term of this is not only the idea of the nothingness of the world but also that of the supreme identity and the corresponding realization: "the unity of Reality" (*wahdat al-Wujūd*).[70]

If perfection or sanctity means, for the Israelite and for the Christian, "to love the Lord thy God with all thy heart, and with all thy soul, and with all thy might" (Deut. 6:5) or "and with all thy mind" (Matt. 22:37)—in the case of the Israelite through the *Torah* and obedience to the Law and in that of the Christian through the vocational sacrifice of "love"—for a Muslim, perfection means to believe with his whole being that "there is no god save God", a total faith whose scriptural expression is the *hadīth* already quoted: "Spiritual virtue (*ihsān*, whose

---

the *Torah* than to forget it" and similarly, ". . . in these days those few old wise men still living among them [the Sioux] say that at the approach of the end of a cycle, when men everywhere have become unfit to understand and still more to realize the truths revealed to them at the origin . . . it is then permissible and even desirable to bring this knowledge out into the light of day, for by its own nature truth protects itself against being profaned and in this way it is possible it may reach those qualified to penetrate it deeply. . ." (J. E. Brown, Foreword to *The Sacred Pipe* [University of Oklahoma Press]).

[70] The realization, through "transforming Virtue" (*ihsān*), of Unity (*Wāhidiyah, Ahadiyah*) is "unification" (*tawhīd*).

function is to render "sincere" both *īmān* and *islām*, faith and practice) consists in adoring God as if thou didst see Him, and if thou dost not see Him, He nonetheless seeth thee."[71] Where Jew and Christian put intensity and thus totality of love, the Muslim puts "sincerity" and so totality of faith, which in becoming realized becomes *gnosis*, union, the mystery of non-otherness.

Viewed from the standpoint of sapiential Islam, Christianity can be considered as the doctrine of the sublime, not as that of the absolute; it is the doctrine of a sublime relativity[72] which saves by its very sublimity—here we have in mind the Divine Sacrifice—but has its root nonetheless and necessarily in the Absolute and can consequently lead to the Absolute. If we set out from the idea that Christianity is "the Absolute become relativity in order that the relative become absolute"[73]—to paraphrase an ancient and well-known formula—we are fully in the realm of *gnosis* and the reservation "felt" by Islam no longer applies. But what must also be said, more generally speaking and apart from *gnosis*, is that Christianity adopts a point of view in which consideration of the Absolute as such need not arise *a priori*; the emphasis is laid on the "means" or the "intermediary", which in a certain sense absorbs the end; or again, the end is as it were guaranteed by the divinity of the means. All this amounts to saying that Christianity is fundamentally a doctrine of Union, and it is clearly through this aspect that it rejoins Islamic and especially Sufi "unitarianism".[74]

---

[71] Since *ihsān* is synonymous with *Tasawwuf* (Sufism), this *hadīth* is the very definition of esoterism and clearly shows that in Islam esoterism is "total belief", given that the conviction *lā ilāha illa 'Llāh* is the pillar of the whole religious edifice. Let us not forget that the Bible says of Abraham that God ascribed his faith to righteousness; now Islam readily refers to Abraham (*Sayyidunā Ibrāhīm*).

[72] This is proven by the doctrine of the Trinitarian "relationships". However, in this respect the Orthodox outlook seems less "closed" than that of Catholicism, or a certain Catholicism.

[73] In the same way: if Christ is an "objectivation" of the divine Intellect, the heart-Intellect of the gnostic is a "subjectivation" of Christ.

[74] The whole Christian perspective and the whole of Christic *gnosis* is summed up in this saying: ". . . as thou, Father, art in me, and I in thee, that they also may be one in us. . . . And the glory which thou gavest me I have given them; that they may be one, even as we are one: I in them, and thou in me. . ." (John 17:21-23). Christ is like the saving Name of God in human form; all that can be said of the one is valid also of the other; or

In the history of Christianity, there is a kind of latent nostalgia for what might be called the "Islamic dimension" if we refer to the analogy between the three perspectives of "fear", "love", and "*gnosis*"—the "reigns" of the "Father", the "Son", and the "Holy Spirit"—and the three forms of monotheism, the Judaic, the Christian, and the Muslim. Islam is in fact, from the point of view of "typology", the religious crystallization of *gnosis*, hence its metaphysical whiteness and its earthly realism. Protestantism, with its insistence on "the Book" and free will and its rejection both of a sacramental priesthood and of the celibacy of priests, is the most massive manifestation of this nostalgia,[75] although in an extra-traditional and modern mode and in a purely "typological" sense.[76] But there were other manifestations of it, more ancient and more subtle, such as the movements of Amalric of Bena or Joachim of Fiore, both of the twelfth century, not forgetting the Montanists of the second century. In the same order of ideas, it is well known that Muslims interpret the foretelling of the Paraclete in Saint John's Gospel as referring to Islam, and clearly without excluding the Christian interpretation, this becomes understandable in light of the ternary already alluded to of "fear-love-*gnosis*". Were it to be pointed out that there is certainly within Islam a converse tendency towards the Christian possibility or "the reign of the Son", we would reply that its traces must be sought in Shiism and in *Bektāshīyah*, that is to say in a Persian and Turkish climate.

In Vedantic terminology, the fundamental enunciation of Christianity is: "*Ātmā* became *Māyā* in order that *Māyā* might become *Ātmā*"; that of Islam then is that "there is no *Ātmā* if not the one *Ātmā*" and for the *Muhammadun Rasūlu 'Llāh*: "*Māyā* is the mani-

---

again, he is not only the Intellect which, as "light of the world", distinguishes between the Real and the unreal, but he is also, in the aspect of the "outward" and "objective" divine manifestation, the Divine Name (the "Word") which by its "redeeming" virtue brings about the reintegration of the non-real into the Real.

[75] It was at the same time a reaction of the German world against the Mediterranean and Judean world. In any case, if Germanic theosophy—insofar as it is valid—could blossom in a Protestant climate, it was thanks to the very indirect analogies already mentioned and not by virtue of the anti-Catholicism of the Lutherans.

[76] Analogously, the Jewish Messianic outlook is dangerously allied to the modern ideology of progress, but this of course outside Judaic orthodoxy.

festation of *Ātmā*." In the Christian formulation there is something equivocal in the sense that *Ātmā* and *Māyā* are juxtaposed; it could be taken to mean that the latter exists in its own full right alongside the former with an identical reality, and it is to this possible misunderstanding that Islam replies in its own way. Or again: all theologies—or theosophies—can, broadly speaking, be summed up in these two types: God-Being and God-Consciousness, or God-Object and God-Subject, or again: objective God, "absolutely other", and subjective God, both immanent and transcendent. Judaism and Christianity belong to the first category; so does Islam, taken as a religion, but at the same time it is as it were the religious and "objectivist" expression of God-Subject, and that is why Islam convinces, not by phenomena or miracles, but by its evidentness, the content or "motor" of which is "unity" and thus absoluteness; and that is also why there is a certain connection between Islam and *gnosis* or "the reign of the Spirit". As for the universal significance of "*Ātmā* became *Māyā* in order that *Māyā* might become *Ātmā*", this is a question of the descent of the Divine, of the *Avatāra*, of the sacred Book, of the Symbol, of the Sacrament, of Grace in every tangible form, and thus also of the Doctrine or of the Name of God, and this brings us to the *Muhammadun Rasūlu 'Llāh*. The emphasis is laid, either on the divine container as in Christianity—in which case this container has necessarily also an aspect of content,[77] and hence of "truth"—or on the content "truth", as in Islam, and still more so in all forms of *gnosis*—and then this content inevitably presents itself in the formal aspect of container, and thus of "divine phenomenon" or of symbol.[78] The container is the "Word made flesh", and the content is the absoluteness of Reality or of the Self, expressed in Christianity by the injunction to love God with the whole of our being and to love our neighbor as ourself, "all things being *Ātmā*".[79]

The diversity of religions and their equivalence in respect of what is essential is due—according to the most intellectual Sufi perspective—to the natural diversity of the collective receptacles: if each in-

---

[77] "I am the Way, the Truth, and the Life. . .".

[78] The Koran is an objective divine "descent", a "sign", and a "mercy", and this coincides with the meaning of the second *Shahādah*.

[79] Or *Allāh* in His aspect of *azh-Zhāhir* ("the Outward"), to use Sufi terminology.

dividual receptacle has its own particular Lord, the same will be true of psychological collectivities.[80] The "Lord" is the Creator-Being inasmuch as He concerns or "looks upon" a particular soul or a particular category of souls and is regarded by them according to their own natures, which in their turn are derived from particular divine possibilities, for God is "the First" (*al-Awwal*) and "the Last" (*al-Ākhir*).

A religion is a form—hence a limit—which "contains" the Limitless, if this paradox is permissible; every form is fragmentary because of its necessary exclusion of other formal possibilities; the fact that these forms—when they are complete, that is to say when they are perfectly "themselves"—represent totality each in its own way, does not prevent them from being fragmentary in respect of their particularization and their reciprocal exclusion. In order to safeguard the axiom—metaphysically unacceptable—of the absolute character of this or that religious phenomenon, people reach the point of denying both principial truth—namely the true Absolute—and the Intellect which becomes conscious of it, transferring to the phenomenon as such the characteristics of absoluteness and certitude proper to the Absolute and the Intellect alone, thus giving rise to philosophical undertakings which, though doubtless clever, thrive chiefly on their own inner contradiction. It is contradictory to base a certitude claiming to be total on the phenomenal order on the one hand and on mystical grace on the other, while at the same time demanding an intellectual acceptance; a certitude belonging to the phenomenal order may be derived from a phenomenon, but the evidentness of something prin-

---

[80] Al-Hallaj says in his *Dīwān*: "I have meditated on the various religions, endeavoring to understand them, and I have found that they arise from a unique principle having numerous ramifications. So do not ask of a man that he should adopt this or that religion, for that would take him away from the fundamental principle; it is this principle itself which must come to seek him; in this principle all heights and all meanings become clear; then he [the man] will understand them." In translating this passage, Massignon speaks of "confessional denominations" (for *adyān*), which is quite right in this context. This universalism—prefigured in Judaism by Enoch, Melchizedek, and Elias, and in Christianity by the two saints John and also, at a lesser level, by the "Christian" exorcist who did not follow Christ ("He that is not against us is for us") and by the centurion of Capernaum—this universalism is personified in Islam by al-Khadir or al-Khidr (Koran 18:60-82), the "immortal" sometimes identified with Elias, and by Uways al-Qarani, a *hanīf* of the Yemen and patron of the gnostics (*'ārifūn*).

cipial can come only from principles, whatever the occasional cause of the intellection may be, in a given case; if certitude can spring from intelligence—and it must be derived from it to the very extent that the truth to be known is profound—this is because it is already to be found therein through its fundamental nature.

On the other hand, if That which is in itself Self-Evidentness *in divinis* becomes sacred Phenomenon in a particular order—in this case the human and historical domain—that is above all because the pre-destined receptacle is a collectivity, and thus a multiple subject differentiated in individuals and extending in time and beyond ephemeral individualities; the divergence of points of view occurs only from the moment the sacred phenomenon becomes separated, in the consciousness of men, from the eternal truth it manifests—a truth no longer "perceived"—and when as a result certitude becomes "belief" based exclusively on the phenomenon, on the objective divine sign, the outward miracle, or—what amounts to the same thing—on the principle as grasped by the reason and reduced in practical terms to the phenomenon. When the sacred phenomenon as such becomes the exclusive factor of certitude, the principial and supra-phenomenal Intellect is brought down to the level of profane phenomena, as though pure intelligence were capable only of grasping relativities and as though the "supernatural" were some arbitrary act of Heaven and not in the very nature of things. When we distinguish between "substance" and "accidents", we conclude that phenomena relate to the latter and Intellect to the former; but of course the religious phenomenon is a direct or central manifestation of the element "substance", whereas the Intellect, in its human actualization and from the point of view of expression alone, necessarily belongs to the accidentality of this world of forms and movements.

The fact that the Intellect is a static and permanent grace makes it merely "natural" in the eyes of some, which amounts to denying it; in the same vein of thought, to deny the Intellect because not everyone has access to it is just as false as to deny grace because not everyone enjoys it. Some would say that *gnosis* is luciferian and tends to void religion of its content and to deny its quality of supernatural gift, but it could just as well be said that the attempt to lend a metaphysical absoluteness to religious concentration on phenomena, or to the exclusivism this implies, is the most clever attempt to invert the normal order of things by denying—in the name of a certitude drawn from the phenomenal order and not from the principial and intellectual order—the self-evidentness the Intellect bears within itself. The Intellect is the criterion of phenomena; if the converse is also true it is so in a more indirect sense and in a much more relative and external manner. At the beginning of a religion, or within a religious world that is still homogeneous, the problem does not in practice arise.

The proof of the cognitive transcendence of the Intellect lies in the fact that, while depending existentially on Being inasmuch as it manifests itself, it can go beyond Being in a certain fashion since it is able to define Being as a limitation—in view of creation—of the Divine Essence, which itself is "Beyond-Being" or "Self". In the same way, to the question of whether or not the Intellect can "place" itself above the religions considered as spiritual and historical phenomena—or whether there exists outside the religions an "objective" point allowing of an escape from a particular religious "subjectivity"—the answer is: yes, certainly, since the Intellect can define religion and ascertain its formal limits; but it is obvious that if by the term "religion" is meant the inner infinitude of Revelation, then the Intellect cannot go beyond it, or rather the question then no longer arises, for the Intellect participates in this infinitude and is even identified with it in respect of its intrinsic nature wherein it is most strictly "itself" and most difficult of access.

In the symbolism of the spider's web, to which we have already had occasion to refer in previous works, the radii represent essential "identity" and the circles existential "analogy", and this demonstrates in a very simple though adequate way the whole difference between the elements "intellection" and "phenomenon", as well as their solidarity with one another; and since because of this solidarity, neither of the two elements shows itself in its pure state, we could also speak—in order not to overlook any important shade of meaning—of "continuous analogy" in the case of the radii and of "discontinuous identity" in the case of the circles. All certainty—and notably that of logical and mathematical proofs—arises from the Divine Intellect, the only one there is; but it arises from it through the existential or phenomenal screen of reason, or, to be more precise, through the screens which separate reason from its ultimate Source; it is the "discontinuous identity" of the sun's light which, even when filtered through a number of panes of colored glass, always remains essentially the same light. As for the "continuous analogy" between phenomena and the Principle which breathes them forth, if it is clear that the phenomenon-symbol is not that which it symbolizes—the sun is not God and that is why it sets—its existence is nonetheless an aspect or mode of Existence as such;[81] this is what allows us to call the analogy "continuous" when we envisage it in relation to its ontological connection to pure Being, although such terminology, here used in a quite provisional way, is logically contradictory and practically useless in fact. Analogy is a discontinuous identity, and identity a continuous analogy;[82] once again, herein lies the whole difference between the sacred or symbolic phenomenon and principial intellection.[83]

Gnosis has been reproached with being an exaltation of the "human intelligence"; in this last expression the error can be caught on the wing for, metaphysically, intelligence is above all intelligence and nothing else; it is only human to the extent that it is no longer altogether itself, that is, when from substance it becomes accident. For man, and indeed for every being, there are two relationships to be envisaged: that of the "concentric circle" and that of the "centripetal radius";[84] according to the first, intelligence is limited by a determinate level of existence, it is then envisaged insofar as it is separated from its source or is only a refraction of it; according to the second, intelligence is all that it is by its intrinsic nature, whatever its contingent situation. The intelligence discernible in plants—to the extent that it is infallible—"is" the intelligence of God, the only intelligence there is; this is even more clearly

---

[81] But not, of course, a "part" of Existence.

[82] Identity presupposes *a priori* two terms, those precisely which show themselves as unilaterally and irreversibly identical; that is to say that at the basis of an apparent diversity there is a single reality, whence the character of analogy.

[83] One could specify by speaking of "continuity accidentally discontinuous" and of "discontinuity essentially continuous", the former referring to Intellect and the latter to phenomena, to the symbol, to objective manifestation.

[84] Herein lies the whole difference between analogy and essential identity, the one being always an aspect of the other.

true of the intelligence of man, inasmuch as it is capable of loftier adequations thanks to its being at once integral and transcendent. There is but one subject, the universal Self, and its existential refractions or ramifications are either itself or not itself according to the relationship envisaged. This truth one either understands or does not understand; it cannot be accommodated to every need for logical explanation, just as it is impossible to "bring within reach of everyone" such ideas as that of the "relatively absolute" or of the "metaphysical transparency" of phenomena. Pantheism would say that "all is God" with the unspoken thought that God is nothing more than the sum of all things; true metaphysics on the contrary says both that "all is God" and that "nothing is God", adding that God is nothing except Himself, and that He is nothing of what is in the world. There are truths expressible only through antinomies, but this does not at all mean that in this case they constitute a philosophical "procedure" which ought to lead to some "conclusion" or other, for direct knowledge stands above the contingencies of reason; vision must not be confused with expression. Moreover, truths are profound, not because they are difficult to express for him who knows them, but because they are difficult to understand for him who does not know them; hence the disproportion between the simplicity of the symbol and the possible complexity of the mental operations.

To claim, as do some, that in *gnosis* intelligence sets itself proudly in the place of God is to ignore the fact that it could not within the framework of its own nature realize what we might call the "being" of the Infinite; pure intelligence does communicate an adequate and efficacious reflection—or system of reflections—of it, but does not directly transmit the divine "being" itself, otherwise intellectual knowledge would immediately identify us with its object. The difference between belief and *gnosis*—between elementary religious faith and metaphysical certitude—is comparable to the difference between a description of a mountain and direct vision of it: the second no more puts us on the mountain top than does the first, but it does inform us about the properties of the mountain and the path to take. Let us not however forget that a blind man who walks without stopping advances more quickly than a normal man who stops at each step. Be this as it may, sight identifies the eye with light, it communicates a correct and homogeneous knowledge[85] and makes possible the taking of shortcuts where the blind would have to feel his way; and this despite those moralistic denigrators of the Intellect who refuse to admit that it too is a grace, though static and "naturally supernatural" in its mode.[86] However, as we have already mentioned, intellection is not the whole of *gnosis*, which includes the mysteries of union and opens out directly onto the Infinite, if one might express it thus; the "uncreated" character of the Sufi in the full sense (*as-Sūfī lam yukhlaq*) concerns *a priori* only the transpersonal essence of the Intellect and not that state of absorption in the Reality which the Intellect makes us "perceive" or of which it makes us "aware". Total *gnosis* goes immensely beyond all that appears in man as "intelligence" precisely because it is an incommensurable mystery of "being"; we have here the whole difference, indescribable in human language, between vision and realization; in the latter, "seeing" becomes "being" and our existence is transmuted into light. But even ordinary intellectual vision—the intellection which reflects, assimilates, and discerns without thereby bringing about ontological transmutation—is already something which goes far beyond mere thought, the discursive and "philosophical" play of the mind.

Metaphysical or esoteric dialectic moves between the simplicity of symbolism and complexity of reflection; now this latter—though modern man has difficulty in understanding the point—can become more and more subtle without for all that getting one inch nearer to truth;

---

[85] To the objection that even fully traditional metaphysicians can contradict one another, we would reply that this may be so in the field of applications where a man may always be ignorant of facts, but never on the plane of pure principles which alone have an absolutely decisive bearing, whatever their level.

[86] The human condition, with all that distinguishes it from animality, is likewise such a grace. If there is here a certain abuse of language, it is metaphysical truth which forces us to it, the reality of things not being subject to the limitations of words.

in other words, a thought may be subdivided into a thousand ramifications and hedge itself with all possible precautions and yet remain outward and "profane", for no virtuosity of the potter will transform clay into gold. It is possible to conceive of a language a hundred times more elaborated than that which is used today, for there is in principle no limit to how far one can go in this domain; every formulation is necessarily "naive" in its way and it is always possible to try to enhance it by a luxuriance of logical or imaginative wordplay. Now, this proves on the one hand that elaboration as such adds no essential quality to an enunciation, and on the other hand, retrospectively, that the relatively simple enunciations of sages of former times were charged with a fullness of meaning which is precisely what people no longer know how to discern *a priori* and the existence of which they readily deny. It is not an elaboration of thought pressed to the point of absurdity which can lead us to the heart of *gnosis*; those who mean to proceed on this plane by investigations and gropings, scrutinizing things and weighing them up, have failed to grasp that we cannot subject all orders of knowledge to the same "system" of logic and experience and that there are realities which are either understood at a glance or else not understood at all.

Not unconnected with what has just been said is the question of the two wisdoms, the one metaphysical and the other mystical; it would be entirely wrong to take certain mystical or "unitive" formulations as authority for denying the legitimacy of intellectual definitions, wrong at least for anyone who is himself outside the special state in question; for in fact it happens that certain contemplatives, speaking in the name of direct experience, reject doctrinal formulations, these having become for them "words", which does not always prevent them from putting forward other formulations of the same type and having possibly the same value.[87] Here we must avoid confusing the strictly intellectual or doctrinal plane, which has all the legitimacy and so all the efficacy conferred on it, at its level, by the nature of things, with the plane of inner experience, the plane of ontological "sensations" or

---

[87] In *De l'Unité transcendante des religions*, we pointed out a characteristic of this kind in connection with the *Risālat al-Ahadiyah* ("Treatise on Unity") attributed rightly or wrongly to Ibn Arabi, but in any case derived directly from his doctrine.

of mystical "perfumes" or "tastes"; it would be as wrong as to dispute the adequacy of a geographical map because one had undertaken an actual journey or, for example, to pretend that because one had traveled from North to South, the Mediterranean is situated "above" and not "below", as shown on the map.

Metaphysics has as it were two great dimensions, the one "ascending" and dealing with universal principles and the distinction between the Real and the illusory, and the other "descending" and dealing on the contrary with the "divine life" in creaturely situations, and thus with the fundamental and secret "divinity" of beings and of things, for "all is *Ātmā*". The first dimension can be called "static" and is related to the first *Shahādah* and to "extinction" (*fanā*), or "annihilation" (*istihlāk*), whereas the second appears as "dynamic", and is related to the second *Shahādah* and to "permanence" (*baqā*). By comparison with the first dimension, the second is mysterious and paradoxical, seeming at certain points to contradict the first, or again, it is like a wine with which the Universe becomes intoxicated; but it must never be lost sight of that this second dimension is already implicitly contained within the first—even as the second *Shahādah* is derived from the first, namely from the "point of intersection" *illā*—so that static, "elementary", or "separative" metaphysics is sufficient unto itself and does not deserve any reproach from those who savor the intoxicating paradoxes of the unitive experience. That which, in the first *Shahādah*, is the word *illā* will be, in the first metaphysics, the concept of universal causality: we start out from the idea that the world is false since the Principle alone is real, but since we are in the world we add the reservation that the world reflects God; and it is from this reservation that the second metaphysics springs forth, from whose point of view the first is like an insufficient dogmatism. Here we see in a sense the confrontation between the perfections of incorruptibility and of life: the one cannot be had without the other, and it would be a pernicious "optical error" to scorn the doctrine in the name of realization, or to deny the latter in the name of the former; however, since the first error is more dangerous than the second—the second moreover hardly arises in pure metaphysics and, if it does, consists in overestimating the "letter" of the doctrine in its formal particularism—we would recall for the glory of the doctrine this saying of Christ: "Heaven and earth shall pass away, but my words shall not pass away." The Hindu, or Hindu-Buddhist, theory of the *upāyas* perfectly takes account of these dimensions of the spiritual realm: concepts are true according to the levels to which they relate; it is possible to transcend them, but they never cease to be true at their own level, and that level is an aspect of absolute Reality.

In the sight of the Absolute, envisaged as pure Self and unthinkable Aseity, metaphysical doctrine is assuredly tainted with relativity, but it nonetheless offers absolutely sure reference points and "adequate approximations" such as the human spirit could not do without; and this is what the simplifiers in pursuit of the "concrete" are incapable of understanding. Doctrine is to the Truth what the circle or the spiral is to the center.

The idea of the "subconscious" is susceptible not only of a psychological and lower interpretation, but also of a spiritual, higher, and consequently purely qualitative interpretation. It is true that in this case one should speak of the "supra-conscious" but the fact is that the supra-conscious has also an aspect that is "subterranean" in relation to our ordinary consciousness, just as the heart resembles a submerged sanctuary which, symbolically speaking, reappears on the surface thanks to unitive realization; it is this subterranean aspect that allows us to speak—in a provisional way—of a "spiritual subconscious", which must never at any time be taken to mean the lower, vital psyche, the passive and chaotic dreaming of individuals and collectivities.

This spiritual subconscious, as here understood, is formed of all that the Intellect contains in a latent and implicit fashion; now the Intellect "knows" through its very substance all that is capable of being known and—like the blood flowing through even the tiniest arteries of the body—it traverses all the egos of which the universe is woven, and opens out "vertically" on the Infinite. In other words: the intellective center of man, which is in practice "subconscious", has knowledge, not only of God, but also of man's nature and his destiny;[88] and this

---

[88] The predictions not only of prophets but also of shamans in a state of trance, are explained by this cosmic homogeneity of the intelligence, and so of "knowing"; the

enables us to present Revelation as a "supernaturally natural" manifestation of that which the human species "knows", in its virtual and
submerged omniscience, both about itself and about God. Thus the
prophetic phenomenon appears as a kind of awakening, on the human
plane, of the universal consciousness that is present everywhere in the
cosmos in varying degrees of unfolding or of slumber. But as humanity is diverse, this springing forth of knowledge is also diverse, not in
respect of its essential content but in respect of its form, and this is
again an aspect of the "instinct of self-preservation" of collectivities or
of their "subconscious" wisdom; for the saving truth must correspond
to its receptacles, it must be intelligible and efficacious for each one of
them. In Revelation, it is always in the last analysis the "Self" which
speaks and, as its Word is eternal, the human receptacles "translate"
it—at their root and by their nature, not consciously or deliberately—
into the language of particular spatial and temporal conditions;[89] individualized consciousnesses are so many veils which filter and adapt the
blinding light of unconditioned Consciousness, of the Self.[90] For Sufi
gnosis, the whole of creation is a play—with infinitely varied and subtle combinations—of cosmic receptacles and divine unveilings.

The interest of these considerations is not to add one speculation
to other speculations, but to give the reader some sense—if not of
demonstrating for every need for logical explanation—that the phenomenon of religion, though wholly "supernatural" by definition, has
also a "natural" side which in its own way guarantees the truthfulness
of the phenomenon. We mean that religion—or wisdom—is connatu-
ral with man and that man would not be man were there not included
in his nature a ground for the flowering of the Absolute; or again that

shaman knows how to put himself in contact with a subconscious that contains facts
past and future, and sometimes penetrates into the regions of the hereafter.

[89] This means that the "translation" is already wrought in God with a view to a given
human receptacle; it is not the receptacle which determines God, but God who pre-
disposes the receptacle. In the case of indirect inspiration (Sanskrit: *smriti*)—the case
of the sacred commentaries—which must not be confused with Revelation (*shruti*),
the part played by the receptacle is not simply existential, but active in the sense that
it "interprets" according to the Spirit instead of "receiving" directly from the Spirit.

[90] They do so in two ways or at two degrees, according to whether it is a case of direct
or indirect, divine or sapiential, inspiration.

he would not be man—"image of God"—if his nature did not allow him to "become conscious", despite his "petrifaction" and through it, of all that "is" and so also of all that is in his ultimate interest. Thus Revelation manifests all the intelligence that virginal things possess; it is by analogy assimilable—though on an eminently higher level—to the infallibility which directs birds on their migration to the South and draws plants towards the light;[91] Revelation is all that we know in the virtual plenitude of our being, and it is also all that we love and all that we are.

Before the loss of the harmony of Eden, primordial man saw things from within, in their substantiality and in the Divine Unity; after the Fall he no longer saw them except outwardly and in their accidentality, and thus outside God. Adam is the Spirit (*rūh*) or the Intellect (*'aql*) and Eve the soul (*nafs*); it is through the soul—"horizontal" complement of the "vertical" spirit and existential pole of pure intelligence—or through the will that the movement towards exteriorization and dispersion came; the tempter serpent, which is the cosmic genius of this movement, cannot act directly on the intelligence and so must seduce the will, Eve. When the wind blows over a perfectly still lake, the sun's reflection is disturbed and broken up, and it is thus that the loss of Eden was brought about, thus that the divine reflection was broken up. The path means return to the vision enjoyed by innocence, to the inward dimension where all things die and are reborn in the Divine Unity—in that Absolute which, with its component dimensions of equilibrium and inviolability, is the whole content of the human condition and the whole reason for its existence.

[91] The allusion here is not simply to the intuition which leads believers to follow the heavenly Message, but to the "natural supernature" of the human species which attracts Revelations in the same way as in nature a given container attracts a corresponding content. As for the "naturally supernatural"—or the converse, which on the whole comes to the same thing—it may be added that the Angels provide a complementary example thereof in relation to the Intellect: the Angels are the "objective" channels for the Holy Spirit just as the Intellect is its "subjective" channel; these two kinds of channels moreover meet in the sense that every intellection passes through *ar-Rūh*, the Spirit.

And this innocence is also the "childhood" which "takes no heed for the morrow". The Sufi is the "son of the moment" (*ibn al-waqt*), which means first of all that he is conscious of eternity and that through his "remembrance of *Allāh*" he remains in the "timeless instant" of "heavenly actuality". But it means also and consequently, that he keeps himself at all times in the Divine Will, that is to say, he realizes that the present moment is what God wants of him; therefore he will not desire to be "before" or "after" or to enjoy that which is in fact outside the divine "now"—that irreplaceable instant in which we belong concretely to God and which is indeed the only instant when we can in fact wish to belong to Him.

At this point we wish to give a concise summary, but one as rigorous as possible, of what fundamentally constitutes "the path" in Islam. At the same time, this conclusion of our book will once more underline the strictly Koranic and Muhammadan character of the Sufi Path.[92]

First let us recall this crucial fact: *Tasawwuf* coincides according to tradition with *ihsān* and *ihsān* is "that thou shouldst adore God as if thou didst see Him, and if thou dost not see Him, yet He seeth thee." *Ihsān*—*Tasawwuf*—is nothing other than the perfectly "sincere" (*mukhlisah*) adoration (*'ibādah*) of God, to bring the intelligence-will into full accord with its "content" and divine prototype.[93]

The quintessence of adoration—and so, in a certain sense, adoration as such—is to believe that *lā ilāha illā 'Llāh* and, as a consequence, that *Muhammadun Rasūlu 'Llāh*. The proof of this is that according to Islamic dogma and within its "radius of jurisdiction", a man is only certainly damned by reason of the absence of this faith. The Muslim is not *ipso facto* damned because he does not pray or does not fast; he may

---

[92] The dialectical borrowings, which were always possible and even inevitable as a result of contact with the wisdom of Greece, add nothing to the intrinsic *haqīqah* of *Tasawwuf*, but simply shed light on it.

[93] The Shaykh al-Alawi, following the current terminology of the Sufis, specifies that the beginning of *ihsān* is "vigilance" (*murāqabah*) whereas its end is "direct contemplation" (*mushāhadah*).

indeed be prevented from doing so and in certain physical conditions women are exempted from these requirements; nor is he necessarily damned because he does not pay the tithe; the poor—and obviously beggars—are exempted from it, which is at least an indication of a certain relativity both in this and in the preceding cases. Still more clearly, a man is not damned through the mere fact of not having accomplished the Pilgrimage; the *muslim* is bound to make the Pilgrimage only if he is able to do so; as for the Holy War, it is not always being waged, and even when it is, the sick, invalids, women, and children are not bound to participate in it. But a man is necessarily damned—still within the framework of Islam or else in a transposed sense—for not believing that *lā ilāha illā 'Llāh* and that *Muhammadun Rasūlu 'Llāh;*[94] this law knows no exception, for it is identified as it were with that which constitutes the very meaning of the human condition. Thus it is indisputably this faith which constitutes the quintessence of Islam; and it is the "sincerity" (*ikhlās*) of this faith or this acceptance which constitutes *ihsān* or *Tasawwuf.* In other words: to take an extreme example, it is conceivable that a *muslim* who, for example, had all his life omitted to pray or to fast, might despite everything be saved and this for reasons that elude us but which would count in the eyes of the Divine Mercy. On the other hand, it is inconceivable that a man who denied that *lā ilāha illā 'Llāh* be saved since this negation would quite clearly deprive him of the very quality of *muslim*, and so of the *conditio sine qua non* of salvation.

Now the sincerity of faith also implies its depth, according to a man's capacity; and to speak of capacity is to speak of vocation.[95] We must understand to the extent that we are intelligent, not to the extent that we are not so and where there is no possible adequation between the knowing subject and the level of the object to be known. The Bible also teaches, in both the Old and the New Testaments, that we must "love" God with all our faculties; thus, intelligence could not be

[94] In the climate of Christianity, it would be said that this was the "sin against the Holy Spirit".

[95] However, God does not require of us on this level that we should reach the goal we conceive of and pursue because we conceive of it and because of its truth; as the *Bhagavad Gītā* clearly teaches, God here requires only effort and does not punish for lack of success.

excluded from this, the more so since it is intelligence which characterizes man and distinguishes him from the animals. Free will would be inconceivable apart from intelligence.

Man is made of integral or transcendent intelligence—therefore capable of abstraction just as well as of supra-sensory intuition—and of free will, and that is why there is a truth and a way, a doctrine and a method, a faith and a submission, an *īmān* and an *islām*. *Ihsān*, being the perfection and the end result of these two, is at the same time in them and above them. It can also be said that there is an *ihsān* because there is in man something which calls for totality, or for something absolute or infinite.

The quintessence of the truth is discernment between the contingent and the Absolute; and the quintessence of the path is permanent consciousness of Absolute Reality. Now to say "quintessence" is to say *ihsān*, in the spiritual context here at issue.

Man, as has just been said, is made of intelligence and will; so he is made of understandings and virtues, of things he knows and things he accomplishes, or in other words of what he knows and what he is. The understandings are prefigured in the first *Shahādah* and the virtues in the second; that is why *Tasawwuf* can be described either by expounding metaphysics or by commenting on the virtues. The second *Shahādah* is in essence identifiable with the first, of which it is but a prolongation, just as the virtues are fundamentally identifiable with truths and are in a sense derived from them. The first *Shahādah*—that of God—enunciates every principial truth; the second *Shahādah*—that of the Prophet—enunciates every fundamental virtue.

The essential truths are as follows: that of the divine and "one" Essence (*Dhāt, Ahadiyah* in the sense of the Vedantic "non-duality"); then the truth of creative Being (*Khāliq*), a Principle that also is "one"— but in the sense of an affirmation and by virtue of a "self-determination" (*Wāhidiyah*, "solitude", "unicity")—and comprising, if not "parts",[96] at least aspects or qualities (*sifāt*).[97] Beneath the principial or divine

---

[96] For that would be contrary to the indivisibility and non-associability of the Principle.

[97] God is not "in existence"—He is beyond Existence—but He can be said to be "not inexistent" if one holds to emphasizing the evident fact that He is "real" without "existing". In no case can it be said of God that He is "inexistent"; He is "non-existent"

realm there is on the one hand the macrocosm—with its "archangelic" and "quasi-divine" center (*Rūh*, "Spirit")—and on the other hand, at the extreme periphery of its unfolding, that coagulation—of universal Substance—which we call "matter" and which is for us the outer shell, at once innocent and deadly, of existence.

As for the essential virtues, of which we have treated elsewhere but which must also figure in this final summary, they are the perfections of "fear", "love", and "knowledge", or in other words, those of "poverty", "generosity", and "sincerity". In a sense they make up *islām* as the truths make up *īmān*, their deepening—or their qualitative conclusion—constituting the nature or the very fruit of *ihsān*. Again, it could be said that the virtues consist fundamentally in fixing oneself in God according to a kind of symmetry or ternary rhythm, in fixing oneself in Him "now", "right here", and "thus"; but these images can also replace one another, each being sufficient in itself. The Sufi remains in the timeless "present" where there are no longer either regrets or fears; he remains at the boundless "center" where the outward and the inward are blended or transcended; or again, his "secret" is the perfect "simplicity"[98] of the ever-virginal Substance. Being only "what he is", he is all "That is".

If man is will, God is Love; if man is intelligence, God is Truth. If man is will fallen and powerless, God is redeeming Love; if man is intelligence darkened and gone astray, God is the illuminating Truth which delivers; for it is in the nature of knowledge—the adequation intelligence-truth—to render pure and free. The Divine Love saves by "making itself what we are", it "descends" in order to "elevate"; the

---

inasmuch as He does not pertain to the existential domain, but "non-inexistent" inasmuch as His transcendence clearly could not involve any privation.

[98] The simplicity of a substance is its indivisibility. The symbolism here evoked perhaps requires clarifying as follows: if the conditions of bodily existence are time, space, substance that is material or that has become such, form, matter, and number, the three last-named—matter, form, and number—are the content of the first two—time and space. Form and number coincide in a sense, on the plane in question, with matter, of which they are respectively the outward determinations of quality and quantity; the corresponding inward determinations are on the one hand the nature of the *materia* envisaged and on the other hand its extent. Like the idea of "substance", the four other concepts of an existential condition can be applied beyond the sensory plane; they are not terrestrial accidents but reflections of universal structures.

Divine Truth delivers by giving back to the Intellect its "supernaturally natural" object and so also its initial purity, that is to say: by "recalling" that the Absolute alone "is", that contingency "is not", or that on the contrary it "is not other than the Absolute" in respect of pure Existence and also, in certain cases, in respect of pure Intelligence or "Consciousness" and in respect of strict analogy.[99]

The *Shahādah*, by which *Allāh* manifests Himself as Truth, addresses itself first of all to the intelligence, but also, as a result, to that extension of intelligence which is the will. When the intelligence grasps the fundamental meaning of the *Shahādah*, it distinguishes the Real from the non-real, or "Substance" from "accidents"; when the will in its turn grasps this same meaning, it becomes attached to the Real, to the Divine "Substance"; it becomes "concentrated" and lends its concentration to the mind. Intelligence enlightened by the *Shahādah* has in the final analysis but one single object or content, *Allāh*, other objects or contents being considered only with respect to Him or in relation to Him, so that the multiple becomes as it were immersed in the One; and the same is true of the will, according to what God may grant the creature. The "remembrance" of God logically depends on the rightness of our idea of God and on the depth of our comprehension: Truth, to the degree that it is essential and that we understand it, takes possession of our whole being and little by little transforms it according to a discontinuous and unforeseeable rhythm. Becoming crystallized in us, it "makes itself what we are in order to make us what it is". The manifestation of Truth is a mystery of Love, just as conversely, the content of Love is a mystery of Truth.

In all these considerations, it has been our aim not to give a picture of Muslim esoterism in its historical unfolding, but to bring it to its most elemental positions by connecting it with the very roots of

---

[99] Analogy or symbolism concerns all manifestation of qualities; Consciousness concerns man inasmuch as he can transcend himself intellectually, his spirit opening out onto the Absolute. As for Existence, it concerns all things—whether qualitative or not and whether conscious or not—by the simple fact they stand out against nothingness, if one may express it thus. Phenomena are "neither God nor other than He": they possess nothing of themselves, neither existence nor positive attributes; they are divine qualities "corroded" in an illusory manner by nothingness—itself non-existent—by reason of the infinitude of universal Possibility.

Islam which of necessity are its own. It was not so much a matter of recapitulating what Sufism may have said as of saying what it is and has never ceased to be through all the complexity of its developments. This way of looking at things has enabled us—perhaps to the detriment of the apparent coherence of this book—to dwell at some length on meeting points with other traditional perspectives and also on the structure of what is—around us as well as within us—both divinely human and humanly divine.

APPENDIX

Selections from Letters and Other Previously Unpublished Writings

1

The enigma of the *Basmalah* is this apparent tautology: the adjunction, after the Name "the Clement" or "the Infinitely Good", of the Name "the Merciful"; is not Mercy contained in Clemency, and would it not be more logical—if one may say so—to add to the Quality of Clemency a Quality of Rigor?

However, this has absolutely nothing to do with the juxtaposition of qualities, but with a doctrine of the Principle in itself, which is the following:

When, in the *Basmalah*, we have pronounced the Name *Allāh*, we have enunciated the one, absolute, and infinite Reality; now it is important to specify its intrinsic nature, which is *Rahmah*: that is to say Goodness, Beauty, Love, Beatitude. *Rahmah* is not therefore one Quality amongst others, it is the inward radiation of the *Dhāt*, of the very Essence. That is why the Koran says: "Call Him (God) *Allāh* or call (Him) *Rahmān*. . .". And that is also why it is written on the Throne of *Allāh*: "In truth, My Clemency (*Rahmah* = Goodness/Beauty) hath preceded My Wrath". And likewise the Koran: "Thy Lord hath prescribed for Himself Clemency".

After having enunciated the nature of the Essence (*Dhāt*), the *Basmalah* intends to mention as well the differentiated degree, that of the Qualities (*Sifāt*) or of Being, and it does so by the Name "the Merciful" (*Rahīm*), in order to indicate clearly that Mercy is the first—or the most fundamental—of the Qualities of Being; that it is in consequence more real, in a way, than the Qualities of Rigor. For: "My Mercy embraceth all things", according to the Koran; Mercy is not only in the Principle, but also in the existential Substance of beings.

Hence, the *Basmalah* teaches us three things: firstly, the Absolute; secondly that the Absolute is, not an unintelligible and somehow anti-human Power, as the omnipotentialist theologians—out of pious ineptitude—would have it, but essentially Goodness, Beauty, Love, Beatitude; thirdly, that the first Quality—at the non-supreme degree of Being—is, therefore, Mercy; for *Allāh* is essentially Communication of His own Good on the one hand and, on the other, Attraction towards Himself. Man is "made in the image of God" and his qualities consequently reflect—and render intelligible—the Divine Qualities, the only ones that are.

2

The most immediate meaning of the Islamic "Benediction of the Prophet" is the homage owed the *Logos*. The necessity of this homage results from the necessity of the worship of God; for the *Logos* is the immediate reflection of God, and there is no possible access to God except through the *Logos*; there is no perfect worship without this homage. It could even be said that the *Logos* is "neither created nor uncreated"; the *Logos* coincides in fact with "the Spirit" (*ar-Rūh*), which certain metaphysical perspectives encompass in the Divinity and thereby in the worship owed God; some even extend this worship to the earthly representative of the *Logos*, that is to say that the Hindus do not hesitate to worship the Guru inasmuch as he is a vehicle or personification of the *Logos*.

If in Islam homage to the *Logos* takes the form of a prayer of benediction, it is because of the particular perspective of Islam, which requires that this homage pass through God; one also wants to offer to the *Logos* what is most precious—for it is necessary to love the *Logos* in virtue of the love of God—and the most precious thing is the divine benediction, the *Rahmah*.

Metaphysically, it could be said that it is impossible to reach God-Being (*Īshvara*) without passing through God-*Logos* (*Buddhi*), as it is impossible to reach God-Essence or Beyond-Being (*Paramātmā*) without passing through God-Being (*Īshvara*). Putting aside for now the distinction between Being and Beyond-Being, and having in view only the Principle as such with respect to Manifestation, we shall say that the formula *lā ilāha illā 'Llāh* concerns the Divine Principle, whereas the formula *Muhammadun Rasūlu 'Llāh* concerns the divine Manifestation; likewise for these two other formulas: *Allāhu akbar* and *wa ladhikru 'Llāhi akbar*.

To love God is to be loved by God; now in order to be loved by God it is necessary to love the *Logos*; and to love the *Logos* is to follow it, that is to say to enter into its mold—the *Sunnah*—the quintessence of which is the Remembrance of God; and it is for this reason that one of the names of the Prophet is *Dhikru 'Llāh*. The Prophet personifies both *Dhikr* and *Faqr*, as is indicated by the qualities *Rasūl* and *ʿAbd*, and as is expressed by the designation *an-Nabī al-Ummī*. The *Logos* comprises secondary manifestations, and these are firstly the "Family" (*ālihi*) and the "Companions" (*sahbihi*).

In the *Logos* there is a descending *Dhikr* and an ascending *Dhikr*: the first, which corresponds to the *Laylat al-Qadr*, is Revelation; the second, which corresponds to the *Laylat al-Miʿrāj* is the Invocation.

If the sun were God, who would not render homage to the moon which illuminates the night with light lent by the sun? And if the moon were God, who would not render homage to the reflection of the moon in a pond? It is thus that homage to the *Logos* imposes itself as a result of our worship of God.

3

The meaning of the blessing on the Prophet (*salāt ʿalā 'n-nabī*) is actually this: "Lead me back to the primordial state"; this means; to the *Fitrah*, the primordial intention of the human state, the primordial perfection; to the perfection of the *hanīf*, of him who has remained faithful to the primordial state and has preserved the intuition of the nature of things. The name of this perfection in Islam is *Muhammad*, and its two complementary extensions are *Salāt* and *Salām*, "blessing" and "peace"; the lotus and the jewel.

All greetings addressed to the *Logos*—be it manifested in masculine or feminine form—have essentially the same meaning.

4

The Prophet said: "The key to Paradise is prayer, and the key to prayer is the ablution."

The term "ablution" has both a literal meaning and a symbolic one. In the first sense, the ablution refers to the canonical prayer; in the second sense, it signifies a disposition of the soul and refers to all prayer. The first meaning is particular and the second universal.

It is this universal meaning that Christ expressed when he said: "But thou, when thou prayest, enter into thy closet, and when thou hast shut thy door, pray to thy Father in secret." In other words, the "ablution", in the universal sense which is its essence and its reason for being, is to separate oneself from the world in virtue of the consciousness of God; indeed, prayer is valid only on condition that we know Whom we are addressing.

To be qualified for prayer, man must realize in his heart that "there is no divinity except the sole Divinity" (*lā ilāha illā 'Llāh*). And likewise: "The Supreme Principle is Reality, the world is merely appearance" (*Brahma satyam, jagan mithyā*). And "there is no lustral water like unto Knowledge."

5

Tradition teaches us that the gestures of the canonical prayer—whether they are Hanafite, Shafite, Malikite, or Hanbalite—go back to gestures of the Prophet who prayed in different ways; but tradition does not teach us why these gestures differ from one another, nor what their respective symbolism is. In order to know it—insofar as our need for logical understanding requires this—we cannot appeal to anything other than to the objective symbolism of the forms and to the subjective experiences of the acts. Western Africa, if I am not mistaken, is Malikite; consequently, the arms are left hanging alongside the body during the *Fātihah*; this is the natural and primordial position of the man who stands before *Allāh*, without thinking of anything other than his own existence or his ontological innocence. Other gestures—in other ritual schools—symbolize diverse modes of concentration, or rather, they symbolize concentration in diverse ways or according to diverse aspects. There is no need to ask oneself what manner must be chosen; it is the *madhhab* that has made this choice for us. One must not mix the practices of the four ritual schools, as some do; the norm is to follow the *madhhab* of the country in which one lives; or of our country of origin.

6

Regarding the Pilgrimage, in broad outline, I would say this, from the perspective of *Tasawwuf*: the visit to Mount Arafat enables the pilgrim to partake of the *barakah* of the Prophet; it is as if one took part in his contemplation, or as if one were listening to his most recent sermon; it is a meeting with his spiritual presence. The stoning of the *jamarāt* means, mystically speaking, the rejection of what is evil in our own soul (*an-nafs al-ammārah*); it is our own evil that we are stoning, which indicates, precisely, that it is not truly ourselves. The sacrifice of the animal requires no special explanation; it is sacrifice as such; which is an act of gratitude toward *Allāh*. The Kaaba is our own heart, receptacle of the Divine Presence (*hudūr*); the *tawāf* is the *tawbah*, it is to withdraw from the world or from outwardness, in order to remain within the Center (*maqām ilāhī*); consequently, the *tawāf* is the centripetal movement, the "inward life". To kiss the Black Stone is to kiss the Divine Presence; it is a fragment of Paradise. As for the ritual race between the hills of Safa and Marwah, it refers to trust in God (*tawakkul*), since it repeats Hajar's race in the desert; analogously, to drink the water of Zamzam is to drink of Mercy (*rahmah*). The inside of the Kaaba is the spiritual secret (*as-sirr*); here one is beyond all forms.

7

The Name *Allāh*, which contains all the Names, has in a certain sense something too lofty for the state of habitual dissipation in which modern man finds himself. The name *Allāh* is like an abyss of light, it has something unfathomable, inaccessible, solitary; the *Shahādah* is that abyss of light arranged in view of the human receptacle, namely the mind; it as if a white surface became transformed into snowflakes; I am thinking here of the geometric form of crystals. The Name *Rahmān*, which the Koran expressly advises one to invoke, represents Beauty, Divine Beatitude which, symbolically speaking, "unfolds" above us, like the sky, but without touching us; the Name *Rahīm*, for its part, is like a ray of warmth which touches, embraces, and warms us up. The Name *Rahmān* is like the view, from atop a mountain, over a boundless landscape; the happiness of such a view requires somehow that it not touch us, that is to say that it be disinterested: if such a view refreshes the soul and makes us happy, it is not because it gives us bread, but on the contrary because it invites us to forget ourselves. This is the virtue of the Name *Rahmān*, which "dilates the bosom" (*alam nashrah laka sadrak*). The twofold invocation "*yā Rahmān yā Rahīm*" is in some way the equivalent of a Hindu Divine Name with its *Shakti* (*Sita-Ram*, *Radha-Krishna*), or the Christian invocation "*Jesu-Maria*"; I would also say that the invocation of the Names *Rahmān* and *Rahīm*— or of *Rahīm* alone—is equivalent to that of Christ, with his "personal" presence. The Name *Rahmān*, I repeat, is like an unfolding "upwards", a "dilation", whereas the Name *Rahīm* is like a merciful and reviving ray that descends on us.

8

Allāh is the Name of Unity, of Union, of Transcendence, and of the Self.

Lā ilāha illā 'Llāh is the formula—or the Name—of metaphysical discernment between the Real and the unreal.

Muhammadun Rasūlu 'Llāh is the formula—or the Name—of strength and of generosity, hence of human nobleness or human perfection.

Bismi 'Llāhi 'r-Rahmāni 'r-Rahīm is the formula—or the Name— of Mercy and of Revelation. This corresponds to "*Jesu-Maria*", or to "*Sita-Ram*".

Huwa is the Name of the Self, but in an exclusive sense, in opposition to the distinction of "self and God", whereas *Allāh* is the Name of the Self in an inclusive sense: Principle-Totality.

Huwa 'Llāh combines both meanings, and means: the Divine Self is (also) the Divine Totality, for nothing can remain outside of Him.

9

Each religion has its perfume; each religious collectivity has its own mentality; authentic Muslims have an Islamic mentality and no other, and this mentality is that of the Caliph Umar, of Saladin, of the Emir Abd al-Qadir, of Shamil, to mention only a few particularly outstanding names; it is composed, not only of piety and courage, but also—and essentially—of nobility and generosity; it excludes all moral ugliness. I mentioned Saladin: he had facing him the Crusaders, which was no trivial matter; the Crusaders, who had massacred without pity the whole population of Jerusalem; nevertheless he was always chivalrous, impartial, and generous; he never stooped to a systematic and mean hatred. One certainly cannot say as much of certain present-day Muslim leaders who, while meticulously practicing the prescriptions of the *Sunnah*, no longer have the Islamic mentality, and this is a sign of our time. There is also, together with the disappearance of nobility of character, a strange diminishing of the intelligence, even in people who arrogate to themselves the right to speak in the name of God.

10

The Maghrebi garb—like other non-worldly Muslim garbs—suggests resignation to the Will of God, and more profoundly the mystery of Peace, *dār as-Salām*. And this calls for another comment: if it is true that Maghrebi garb, or any other analogous Muslim garb, manifests *de facto* a religious perspective, exclusivist by definition, along with the specific *barakah* it contains, it is no less true—and necessarily so—that this garb manifests at the same time attitudes and mysteries appertaining to esoterism, and that in this sense it suggests no confessional limitation. Each civilization produces, by heavenly inspiration, several paragon phenomena; the representative dress of Islam is an example of this, as are the arabesques, the *mihrāb*, and the call to prayer.

The Plains Indians' dress represents a *jalwah*—an "exteriorization" or a "radiation"—the content of which derives from the concept of the "Holy War"; that of the Muslims indicates a *khalwah*, an "interiorization" made of holy poverty and divine Peace. I will note in this context that the partial nudity combined with a profusion of precious stones, found among the ancient maharajas, is not gaudy luxury, it is a quasi-celestial splendor befitting their status as demigods. Altogether different is the sumptuousness, part-bigot, part-worldly, of many a Turkish sultan, which can hardly be admired, except for the ceremonial robes when taken on their own, the inspiration for which is fundamentally Mongol.

11

Since she alluded to trials, I shall remind her that there are four great arguments that help us to overcome them, which are: firstly, the *Shahādah*, that enounces the absolute primacy of Divine Reality; secondly, holy resignation to the will of God (*mā shā'a 'Llāh*); thirdly, trust in Divine Mercy (*Allāhu karīm*); and fourthly, gratitude, which prevents us from losing sight of all of the good things God has given us and that He continues to give us (*al-hamdu li 'Llāhi wa'l-shukru li 'Llāhi*). Truth, resignation, trust, gratitude: this is a viaticum that we cannot do without and that no one can ravish from us. Our spiritual relationship with the Supreme Truth presupposes or requires our human relationship with God.

12

An individual is damned not because of a mortal sin, nor because this mortal sin was accomplished in the last moment of life, but he is damned uniquely because of the fundamental tendency of his nature, a tendency of which mortal sin, and the destiny preventing this sin from being redeemed before death, are but the culminating manifestations; given that these manifestations have the character of a criterion, the religious point of view, placing itself as it does always and by definition at the standpoint of the individual, considers them as causes. In other words, an individual is not damned because he has committed a mortal sin, but because he has demonstrated through this mortal sin that he is damned; to think otherwise is to think that God is limited by time.

Some object that a temporal fact cannot lead to a perpetual outcome; but precisely, if sin is indeed a temporal fact, namely the fundamental tendency of a being, a tendency that is either in conformity or contrary to the pure Essence of Divine Reality, then this tendency cannot be more limited than perpetuity; if the soul is perpetual, then so too is its fundamental tendency, and sin will simply be its signature. However, it is difficult to determine, for the human state, in contrast to what takes place with spirits (that is to say angels and demons) and also with animals, what the fundamental tendency of an individual is so long as it has not been manifested by means of a touchstone of a spiritual order. Such a touchstone is always the contact the individual has with Divine Reality, by means of a spiritual reality; it is then the individual's reaction that betrays his fundamental tendency; yet even then, it is usually difficult or even impossible to determine what this tendency is as long as the person is still alive; all that can be said is that a given individual, if he dies without a repentance accepted by God, is damned. That he may die without this repentance and without grace is not certain; but that he will be damned if he dies without this repent-ance and without grace, that is absolutely certain.

Another objection formulated against hell adduces Divine Good-ness and human misery (that is to say irresponsibility). This is a very feeble objection and hardly deserves to be taken into account, since Divine Goodness, though it is unconditional in itself, is conditional in manifestation, and that, on the other hand, human responsibility exists given that man is, metaphysically, necessarily free by his ontological participation in Divine Freedom; this is the fundamental character of the human species; the existence of heaven and hell proves this, pre-cisely. One likes to blame hell for its *atrocious* aspect and its *definitive* aspect; but what is forgotten is that the atrocious and the definitive are cosmic possibilities. A secondary cycle always reflects a total cycle; now earthly life is a secondary cycle, and the existence of the soul is a total cycle. There are atrocities that, for an earthly life, are definitive; this indicates that they can be so also for a total cycle. Imagine a child who, while playing, has an accident that results in the loss of his sight or of a hand; no supplication can bring back life to his blinded eyes, or make an amputated hand to grow back; this is therefore definitive, in spite of Divine Goodness, which proves there are things whose defini-tive character results from their own nature; the same applies to hell and paradise.

13

The great religious happiness of a Muslim as such is Islam in all of its extension; it is not *a priori* the Prophet or the Koran, but Islam; it is the happiness of plunging the individual will deeply into all the ramifications of the Law—*Sharī'ah* and *Sunnah*—for the Law is the crystallization of the Divine Will, and to accumulate supererogatory practices and merits. In an analogous way, the happiness of a Christian is Christ; the Church with the sacraments is the extension of Christ, who is everything. For a Muslim, it is Islam, with all that it comprises, that is everything—and not the Prophet—for here what matters is to-tality, not the center; the Prophet is the personification of totality just as Christ is the center of the cosmos; the totality—the Koran—comes "before" the Prophet, just as Christ comes "before" the cosmos.

14

There is between Jesus and Muhammad something of a compensation: for the first, it is the mode of manifestation which is superior; with the second, it is the message, in the sense that this message is more directly metaphysical and universal and that because of this it is complete, having a *Sharī'ah* and a *Haqīqah*. But even when formulated in this manner, the question is not made completely clear, for on the one hand the Muhammadan message contains an underlying quality—or a substance—that transcends its formal mode, and on the other hand the Christic message expresses in its way all essential truth and indicates all of its earthly applications. Strictly speaking, an *Avatāra* should always be envisaged according to his own mode and not according to other avataric modes; but in the case of the Semitic religions, such comparisons cannot always be completely avoided, unfortunately, all the more as certain misunderstandings and different types of lack of imagination oblige us to make them.

15

The Prophet is at once *'abd* and *ummī*, therefore he personifies *faqr*, but he is also *Dhikru 'Llāh*, that is to say he personifies the complementarity in question. Nonetheless, the mention of other Prophets in the Koran allows traditionally for the mystical or devotional reference to one or another of them from the point of view of a specific element of contemplative alchemy. Even though each *Rasūl* realizes all the spiritual excellences, he appears at the same time more particularly as the "genius" of a specific excellence or of a specific element; and this is true not only for the Prophets, but also for the Saints. The actualization of such a reference is, for the Sufi, a question of experience or of grace.

16

I know from experience that one of the hardest things to bear is human absurdity; to accept it on the basis of its ontological necessity is part of Islam. There are people who think it is virtuous not to see evil and to pretend that black is white, which is the very negation of intelligence; in reality, one has to discern exactly between good and evil while resigning oneself, not to evil as such, but to the metaphysically unavoidable existence of evil. All of this is obvious, but I write it because the sight of evil makes one suffer and it is already a degree of holiness to know how to combine an implacable discernment with an unalterable serenity; however, I might add, this serenity does not exclude holy wrath.

17

If one wished to give to the word "sin" a universal meaning—but it would be an improper usage of the word, strictly speaking—one could say that the universal sin is "outwardness": that is, the fact of living "on the outside", in the world, and neglecting—indeed, forgetting—the inward dimension.

This outwardness comprises two modes, one passive and the other active: it consists, either in letting oneself be carried along by the waves of the phenomenal world, with heedlessness and apathy, or on the contrary in being dispersed and restless; it is the vice of heaviness on the one hand and the vice of superficiality on the other, but always the same vice of outwardness.

The norm is not total inwardness, which is possible only in a state of concentration or of ecstasy; the norm is the equilibrium between the inward and the outward. For God wills that we be in the outward, otherwise He would not have created us; this being the case, He likewise wills that we be in the inward, otherwise He would not have created us men. "I was a hidden treasure and I wished to be known, hence I created the world." There are two positive modes of outwardness: the first is passive and consists in "seeing God everywhere"; it is the sense of the archetypes or essences, or living symbolism; the second is active and consists in manifesting God, spiritual things, the sacred; it is the heavenly message that resides in the very nature of man.

There is inevitably a false inwardness: this is narcissism, which is passive and static; as also egotism, which is active and dynamic.

Outwardness is also "horizontality", and inwardness is "verticality", each of these dimensions comprising an active and a passive mode. Verticality can be either discriminating or contemplative, which two modes ought evidently to be combined; horizontality, for its part, can consist on the one hand of confusion, non-discernment, or blindness, and on the other hand of passionality or concupiscence.

The equilibrium between verticality and horizontality, or between inwardness and outwardness, cannot be maintained in a stable fashion and without the slightest fluctuation—as is indicated, moreover, in the word "equilibrium" itself; the righteous man therefore submits to rites—or formulas—of purification, even if he has committed no sin properly speaking, that is to say no intrinsic violation of a norm. It is said that "the righteous man sins seven times a day", and this means that he too is subject to the ineluctable laws of duration and movement; time, as well as space, is there in order to manifest possibilities, and these possibilities must be of various kinds and uneven worth.

The universal norm is inwardness, and with it equilibrium; inwardness takes precedence over equilibrium, just as the Principle takes precedence over Manifestation. All the virtues, beginning with humility and charity, derive from spiritual inwardness and the equilibrium between it and the outward life; all the vices derive from a forgetfulness of these two great imperatives of the human condition.

To speak of inwardness is to speak of equilibrium between the heart and the world; and the key to inwardness is the "Remembrance of God".

18

To understand a religion in depth, one must understand religion as such: now the religious phenomenon is identified, in its essence, with the one and universal wisdom, hence with esoterism or with the "primordial tradition", or if one prefers with the *philosophia perennis*. In other words, esoteric wisdom is based, doctrinally and methodically, on what is common to all religions, or on what underlies each one of them. If I am repeating here something that is obvious, it is to emphasize that one must never lose sight of this fact—for experience proves that the temptation to do so is great—when engaged in the practice of an orthodox spirituality, that is to say when one is surrounded by a framework of formalism or a mythology.

19

A true metaphysician could not identify himself with a religious *upāya* without reservations, and plunge himself into it with a kind of nationalism; but obviously he must identify with what is essential—hence both universal and primordial—in the *upāya*, and this is "Islam" *a fortiori*. It is unnecessary to add that what is essential transcends the *upāya*.

I shall give two examples here of confessional limitation. For Christianity, man is a "sinner"; this is the definition of man, and it entails the idea that the entire world is bad and that there exists only the alternative between the "flesh" and the "spirit"; it goes without saying that this perspective has a certain relative justification, but its disadvantage is that it deems itself absolute. For Islam, man is not totally corrupted by the fall—a total corruption would be contrary to the very definition of man—but he is totally a "servant" or a "slave", which metaphysically is in fact an aspect of his nature, but which could not be a summary of human nature as such; to believe the contrary is to deny the specifically human intelligence and dignity, and it is thus to deny what constitutes the very reason for the existence of *homo sapiens*. In the case of Islam as in that of Christianity, theology tends to push the respective dogmatic image to the point of absurdity, and most mystics identify *de facto* with these pious excesses, something which could never be done by a thorough metaphysician, who is aware of the nature of things.

If in Muslim thought, the axiom "He hath no associate" gives rise to the most abusive of conclusions in various domains, in Christian thought, on the contrary, it is hypostatic diversity—the Trinity—that takes the place of absoluteness, and the absence of the idea of *Māyā* is particularly noticeable; now a true metaphysician could not possibly identify himself with such positions, hence he could not commit himself to what I term a "religious nationalism". With good reason, Guénon defined the "religious point of view"—the word "religious" having for him the meaning of "exoteric"—as a "sentimental attachment to an idea". And one should not forget all the secondary excesses—sometimes very troublesome—to which confessional sentimentalism gives rise.

Personally, I am very sensitive to the following argument: when you say that you are a "Muslim" or a "Christian", you exclude an immense part of humanity; you separate yourself from it and reproach it with not being what you are; you proclaim, before the entire world, that only you are in the truth, unless you speak with tacit Guénonian understandings that no one can presuppose *a priori*. Nothing of the kind is to be found with the Red Indians; "the Great Spirit has given you your way of praying, and has given us our way of praying"; and that is all.

The Three Dimensions of Sufism

"Fear" (*makhāfah*), "Love" (*mahabbah*), "Knowledge" (*maʿrifah*): these are, in Sufism (*Tasawwuf*), the three dimensions or stations of the Way (*Tarīqah*); "dimensions" from the point of view of their vocational separateness or from the point of view of their coincidence in every spiritual vocation, and "stations" from the point of view of their succession in spiritual development.

By "Fear" must be understood our consciousness of the Divine Rigor and all the volitional consequences that this consciousness entails, whether by way of actions or abstentions: we must accomplish those things that bring us closer to God, in principle or in fact, and we must abstain from those things that separate us or take us away from God. "In principle or in fact": for it sometimes happens that a thing is forbidden notwithstanding that it may not separate such and such a man from the intrinsic Divine Will, and thereby from Grace, or it may happen, on the contrary, that a thing may separate such and such a man from God notwithstanding that it is not forbidden; thus, poetry, music, and dance are to all intents and purposes forbidden in Islam, but the Sufis practice them in their own way; inversely, many apparently inoffensive occupations or pastimes are permitted exoterically, but the Sufis abstain from them so as not to be distracted from intimacy with God, or so as not to poison themselves spiritually, as the case may be. On this ambiguous plane, everything depends on circumstances and intangible factors, both subjectively and objectively.

Be that as it may, the fact that Christ stressed the love of God at the expense of formal precepts, or the inward at the expense of the outward, proves the relativity of the rule of "Fear"; and consciousness of this relativity is already an element of esoterism, without being esoterism as such, for esoterism, while encompassing "Love", pertains essentially to the domain of "Knowledge".

If we were asked where exoterism (*Sharīʿah*) ends and esoterism (*Haqīqah*) begins, our answer would be that the boundary line passes through love, which amounts to saying that love is at the same time both exoteric and esoteric, and that it thus constitutes the link between the two domains. And yet, exoterism necessarily comprises—albeit indirectly—an element of Knowledge, namely speculative theology, just as, inversely, esoterism comprises an element of Fear, namely discipline, including first and foremost the exoteric framework which is obligatory for everyone.

If there are three spiritual categories, namely "Fear", "Love", and "Knowledge"—in place of "Fear" one could also say "Action" or "Merit", and in place of "Love" one could also say "Grace"—it follows that there are men who are more particularly qualified for one or other of these ways. Strictly speaking, the man who is limited by the perspective of "Fear" has no place in esoterism, except *de facto* and through indirect participation; but esoterism welcomes the man of "Love", all things being equal, and *a fortiori* the man of "Knowledge", that is to say those who prefer the "Gardener" to the "Garden" or, in other words, who aspire to a mode of Union rather than a pure and simple reward.

If this be so, what is it that distinguishes the man who is naturally destined for the perspective of Love from the man who possesses the qualifications for Knowledge? Or to put it differently—to make use of well-known Hindu terms—how is one to know whether a man is by nature a *bhakta* or a *jnānin*? The following is a decisive criterion: notwithstanding that a man may have understood the doctrines of *jnāna*, if these doctrines do not extirpate the defects in his character he is by nature "bhaktic", assuming of course that he is a spiritual and not a worldly man, and that *bhakti* is therefore capable of curing him of his defects. The born *jnānin* is a man who perfects himself morally through arguments that are intellectual and refer therefore to the nature of things, while the born *bhakta* is a man who perfects himself through arguments that are moral, whence referring to a particular conception of the good; the *bhakta*'s will is *de facto* indifferent to metaphysical arguments, whereas the will of the *jnānin* is indifferent to the sentimental pressures of morality. A *bhakta* may well have understood the doctrines of *jnāna*, as we said, but in fact, if these doctrines do not improve his character, this means that he does not understand them perfectly; his understanding may be complete in the dimension of concepts, but the concrete, imaginative, or existential dimension is missing, one might say. When theologians rail against Platonists, they are subjectively right, for the doctrines of Plato and Plotinus could not in their case give rise to a moral regeneration; but they forget that there are men for whom the doctrines in question possess this virtue, men whose moral nobility—or the full flowering of this nobility—results in fact from their Knowledge, directly or indirectly.

It is important not to lose sight of the fact that if there are men whose nature is "bhaktic" and others whose nature is "jnanic", elements of both *bhakti* and *jnāna* are to be found in every man, not to mention that spiritual temperaments are sometimes mixed, in which case the Way will be a question of destiny rather than of choice. Be that as it may, the true *jnānin* is so detached that, under the pressure of his environment, it sometimes happens he takes himself *a priori* for a *bhakta*, only recognizing his true nature later when it becomes unmistakable; conversely, many of those who without hesitation take themselves for *jnānin*s are not so, their conviction arising from their readings, self-esteem doing the rest. The true *jnānin*, out of concern for "objectivity", is neither glacial and arrogant through rationality, nor soft and indifferent; he is essentially receptive to the truth while remaining fully human in the positive meaning of the word, that is while practicing the virtues, for the virtues are intrinsically linked to the truth whether we are conscious of this or not; and to be a *jnānin*, precisely, is to be conscious of this. For he who possesses a sense of the true or the real possesses thereby a sense of beauty; one might be tempted to say, somewhat schematically, that the *jnānin* is an aesthete before being a moralist, or that he is a moralist in being an aesthete, in short, that a sense of the moral good amounts, in his case, to a sense of beauty at every level, to the extent aesthetic intuition or musicality is a necessary component of knowledge of the Real. It enters into this knowledge owing to the fact that Beauty, which in God coincides with Beatitude and Generosity, is a dimension of the Divine Essence itself, as is indicated by the Vedantic ternary *Sat-Chit-Ānanda,* and as is indicated in Islam by the Name *Rahmān* inasmuch as it is a Name of the Essence; this is what the Gospel means when it teaches that "God is Love". And since it is above all with Sufism that we are concerned here, it may be recalled that for Ibn Arabi the complementarity Beauty-Love constitutes in the final analysis the very substance of universal Reality.

It is on this complementarity that the soul of the *jnānin* lives, and he glimpses the traces of it on every plane, for he possesses naturally a sense of the metaphysical transparency of phenomena; no *gnosis* is possible without beauty of soul, and for the *jnānin*—the *'ārif bi 'Llāh* ("knowing by *Allāh*") of Sufism—this beauty is a function of the perception of the Divine Beauty, the only Beauty there is. God is essentially "Majesty" (*Jalāl*) and "Beauty" (*Jamāl*), or "Majesty" and "Benevolence" (*Ikrām*) according to the Koran; being Absolute, He is Infinite, and His Infinitude is nothing else but His Radiation and His Beauty.

—— ·⁙· ——

An allusion was made above to the opposition between the celestial "Garden" and the Divine "Gardener", which allows or even compels a digression, since we find it difficult to approve of this way of speaking. The opposition or alternative in question is an example, not simply of an intention directed at the Essence and unwilling to stop at phenomena—be they celestial—but also an example of a certain dialectical carelessness. Logically, it is not plausible that the gardener is more than the garden, for the garden is the reason for the existence of the gardener and not the other way round; on the other hand, the reason for the existence of the palace is the king, who is not the servant of the palace but its end or its content. Instead of speaking metaphorically of the Garden of Paradise and the Divine Gardener, one might have said: the wine is to be preferred to the cup, or the bride to the bridal robe; for the thirsty man cares little for the cup, were it of gold, and the bridegroom desires the woman and not the dress, were it studded with pearls. One ought to have rested content with the Koranic image of the Garden, and developed the distinction sought within this image and on the basis of it, for the celestial phenomena are one thing and our ways of perceiving and enjoying them are another; or else, one ought to have adhered to the notion of "creation" and "Creator", for no one is in any doubt that the Creator takes precedence over creation; the Koran says nothing other than this, while it never speaks of the "Gardener" nor permits the Garden to be scorned. In the same order of ideas, to speak with disdain of the houris on the pretext of wanting only God has the grave disadvantage not only of being disobliging to God who promises the houris, but also of giving the impression that the human individual as such can have a motive for this disdain; here again one should transpose the symbolism and return to the Divine Prototypes of phenomena. Be that as it may, we shall doubtless be told that the "Gardener" of the Sufis is perfectly intelligible since everyone knows that it refers to God; in that case, there was no point in veiling the clear idea of God with the questionable image of the gardener. And this is precisely what has been avoided by those Sufis who established the metaphor on the basis of the Garden: instead of the "Gardener" they spoke of the "Garden of the Essence" which they oppose to the different phenomenal Gardens; now the Garden of the Essence is none other than God Himself. This image possesses the immense advantage, not only of being logical in itself, but also of not contradicting the Koran, be it only indirectly.

A Koranic notion which allows the relationship in question to be harmoniously expressed is that of *Ridwān*, Divine "Contentment".[1] One might say in fact that the Beatitude of the Sufis is centered upon this "Contentment" or "Acceptance", whereas the Beatitude of the men of "Fear" is sustained by various phenomena rather than by the unitive Presence. A simple manner of speaking, perhaps, but one that nevertheless has its value in a mystical language mindful of Scriptural imagery.

After this digression, which is not without some relevance in this general context, let us return to the question of the three dimensions of spirituality.

"Fear", "Love", and "Knowledge": this ternary, as we have seen, is divergent as well as convergent, successive as well as simultaneous; the three dimensions constitute distinct ways as well as being aspects of one and the same way, and they are stages or stations as well as being virtues. All these situations or functions result from the fact that the

---

[1] While this word has a rather general meaning in the majority of passages, it refers to a more particular reality in the three following verses: "For those who fear (God), there are beside their Lord gardens in which rivers flow, wherein they will abide eternally, and there are pure spouses, and Acceptance (*Ridwān*) from God. . ." (3:15); "Their Lord giveth them good tidings of Mercy from Him, and Acceptance, and gardens where enduring pleasure will be theirs" (9:21); "God promiseth to the believers, men and women, gardens in which rivers flow, wherein they will abide—excellent dwellings in gardens of Eden. And Acceptance from God is greater still; it is the supreme Beatitude" (9:72).

three dimensions reside in the very nature of man, of which the three elements *corpus, anima, spiritus*, bear witness above all, along with the corresponding human characteristics.[2]

That the ternary, *makhāfah-mahabbah-maʿrifah* belongs to *Tasawwuf*—aside from the fact that it results from the nature of things—is proved by two principal factors, one extrinsic and the other intrinsic: on the one hand, the historical or cyclical unfolding of Sufism was accomplished in three stages, *grosso modo*, namely by the succession of the rule of Fear, that of Love, and that of Knowledge; on the other hand, the Sufi Rosary, the *wird*, which constitutes the basic practice of the *Tarīqah*, essentially comprises three formulas relating respectively to *makhāfah, mahabbah*, and *maʿrifah*. Regarding the cyclical unfolding, it should be noted that it obviously does not imply any sort of progress, for everything essential was present from the beginning; but it does indicate, all told, an order of spiritual aptness, if one may so put it, from the point of view of the doctrinal and accentuated manifestation of the mysteries.

The three formulas of the *wird* are the *Istighfār*, the *Salāt ʿalā ʾn-Nabī*, and the *Shahādah*; that is to say, the "Asking for forgiveness", the "Blessing of the Prophet", and the "Attestation of faith". This signifies that "Fear" essentially calls forth regret and forgiveness; that "Love" of necessity passes through the Prophet or the *Logos*; that "Knowledge" is above all that of the unique God, and that it is therefore in substance discernment between the Real and the illusory, or between the Absolute and the contingent.

——— ·|· ———

"I ask forgiveness of God": this is the literal content of the *Istighfār*, and it is the formula of ascesis and thus of purification or of the reestablishment of equilibrium. This concerns every man, for every man finds himself by definition subject to ambiguity and wavering; "the righteous man sins seven times a day", that is to say there is always

---

[2] In Gnostic terminology: *hylikos* or *somatikos, psychikos, pneumatikos*. The hylic and the somatic—the material type and the corporeal type—are synonymous.

in contingency a margin of imperfection, even if there is no transgression strictly speaking. According to Islamic doctrine the Prophets are exempt from sinning, but not from this margin, which is the price paid for our ontological separation from God; without this margin, the "servant" (*'abd*) would be the Lord (*Rabb*); and if Muhammad himself sought forgiveness of God every day, it was not for his sins that he did so, but uniquely on account of the traces of human contingency. For the most perfect man undergoes a kind of obscuration or disequilibrium owing to the uneven quality in the ambience of his surroundings and to the reactions this ambience inevitably provokes; now reactions to an imperfect environment cannot always be absolutely perfect, and there is not always a strict dividing line between the different qualities of a situation. It is to be noted that the Prophet, who is *'abd*, and who is even the synthesis and summit of the "servants" since he realizes their prototype, had to manifest to perfection all the attitudes implied in the existential state of "servitude" (*'ubūdīyah*); he was therefore the first to "ask forgiveness of God", and he did so, in effect, in the name of the whole of humanity, which his community in fact represented.

"Fear" has a negative aspect, and this is ascesis or abstention, including fasting, vigils, silence, and solitude; it also comprises a positive or affirmative aspect, and this consists in activity and works, *karma-yoga* as Hindus would say. This point of view could not on its own constitute an esoterism, yet no man can wholly escape its demands.

As for the dimension of "Love", it is expressed in the *wird* in the following form: "O my God,[3] bestow thine illuminative Blessing upon our Lord Muhammad, Thy Servant and Messenger, the unlettered Prophet, and upon his Family and his Companions, and bestow upon them Thy peace-giving Blessing".[4] According to the Koranic doctrine, love of God depends, practically speaking, on the love of the Messenger, and love of the Messenger implies the imitation of his example; whosoever wishes to love God must enter into the mold of the Prophet and love God through participation in the Muhammadan

---

[3] *Allāhumma* is an almost untranslatable vocative of the Name *Allāh*; it can be rendered "O my God", though this has the disadvantage of putting into the singular prayers whose subject is in the plural.

[4] See our book *Comprendre l'Islam*, chapter on the Prophet.

perfection; God loves the Prophet and He will love man to the extent that he is integrated in the spiritual form of the Prophet. It is in this way that Islam approaches the mystery of *mahabbah*; it is not *a priori* a movement of the servant toward the Lord, it is a reciprocity which lays down its conditions. To love God is to be loved by God; God loves the *Sunnah*, therefore one must enter into the *Sunnah* in order to become, through its framework, the object of the Divine Love. There is a formal and historical *Sunnah*, and this is the example (*uswah*) of the Arab Prophet; but there is also a *Sunnah* according to the *Fitrah*—the primordial, supra-formal, intrinsic Norm—of which the Muhammadan *Sunnah* is a particular application, and which is the inward and universal condition of all love of God; in this sense we may say that to love God is to realize the beauty of the soul, for "*Allāh* is beautiful and He loves beauty".

The practical primacy of an objective *Sunnah* over the subjective experience of Love has the aim of allowing every man access to Love, and hence to the grace of being loved by God. This aim and this perspective cannot prevent the love of God from being a pure gift, and thus an *a priori* unconditional favor; it is in this sense that Saint Augustine was able to say: "Love God, and do what thou wilt". This is a possibility that Islam could not deny; if it admits it necessarily as a quasi-charismatic gift, it is by referring to the innate *Sunnah*, to the "secret" (*sirr*) of the Heart, which brings us back to the doctrine of the primordial Norm, the *Fitrah*.[5]

"Love" as a spiritual principle—whether we look upon it as a gift or as a form of zeal, the two being moreover interdependent—presupposes and brings into operation an active quality, and this is goodness, generosity, fervor; generosity which gives itself to God and which, in giving itself to God, gives itself also to men. "Love" also comprises a passive perfection, and this is the sense of beauty, of peace, of harmony; it is this quality, at once contemplative and moral, that is referred to in the Koran in these terms: "There (in Paradise) they will hear no vain talk and no sinful word; only the words: Peace, Peace!" (56:25-

---

[5] The *Torah* stresses the primacy of Love inasmuch as it coincides with observance of the Law. Christ stresses this primacy inasmuch as Love coincides with the inward Law, and hence with virtues that are both "horizontal" and "ascending". Islam, concerned as always with equilibrium and synthesis, combines both points of view.

26).[6] The following verse is completely similar: "Say: *Allāh!* Then leave them to their vain discourse" (6:91). For the Name *Allāh* is as it were the Substance that reabsorbs the accidents; the existential foundation of things is Goodness, Beauty, and Peace; privative accidentality superimposes itself thereon while allowing the message of Love to show through.

As for the dimension of "Knowledge", it is enunciated in the *wird* by the *Shahādah*, with the addition of the following words from the Koran: "He is without associate; to Him belongeth the Kingdom, and to Him returneth praise; and He hath power over all things" (64:1). This is to say that secondary causes—such as the natural laws—are only reverberations of the First Cause; it is the Absolute which determines every phenomenon, and nothing escapes it, even in the realm of infinitesimal contingencies.

Knowledge comprises essentially two perspectives, one objective regarding transcendence, and the other subjective regarding immanence; but there is also an objective immanence, namely the Omnipresence of God, just as there is also a subjective transcendence, namely pure Intellect—*increatus et increabilis* according to Eckhart—which is in fact transcendent in relation to the ego. The first of the two perspectives just mentioned gives rise to metaphysical doctrine in its mental adequation, while the second concerns mystical realization determined by the "Unity of the Real" (*wahdat al-wujūd*); in other words *maʿrifah* is metaphysical discernment in the objective dimension, that of the Principle, and mystical enlightenment in the subjective dimension, that of the immanent Essence; this is tantamount to saying that it includes everything.

With respect to the Absolute in itself, considered independently of the polarization just discussed, we must call attention once again to the following point which is of capital importance. Metaphysical doctrine, as one knows, essentially involves discernment between the Absolute and the relative; and this implies that one must take into consideration the root of relativity in the Absolute, and, conversely, the manifestation of the Absolute within relativity. The first of these two *hypostases*, if one may so put it, is the creative Principle or the

---

[6] The word "Peace" (*Salām*) is also a Divine Name.

Divine Intellect as the locus of the archetypes; the second *hypostasis* is the created *Logos* in all its aspects: Prophet, Revelation, Archangelic Spirit (*Rūh*), spiritual Authority, sacramental Symbol.

From the standpoint of the microcosm or of subjectivity, or from the mystical standpoint if one wishes, the position is analogous: one must discern in the immanent Absolute—which is pure Consciousness, pure Spirit, pure Ipseity—the uncreated anticipation of relative and hence individual consciousness, just as, conversely, one must discern the manifestation of absolute Consciousness within this subjective relativity. This is to say that within the Supreme Self—considered as residing in ourselves—one must discern the affirmation of the differentiated and differentiating Intellect, which corresponds to the creative Principle conceived objectively, just as, within the individual soul, one must discern a faculty of impersonal knowledge, namely reason, which would be inconceivable without the presence of the pure and quasi-divine Intellect in the depths of the heart.

Now *ma'rifah* or *gnosis* is the reintegration of the immortal soul in this immanent Intellect, and correlatively, the penetration of the Intellect into the soul; this is the miracle, to speak in Christian terms, of the coincidence of "true man and true God", and this is the whole mystery of the personification of the incommensurable, without opposition or admixture. This mystery enables us to grasp the intention behind this esoteric maxim which is at once paradoxical, elliptical, and profoundly true: "The Sufi is not created" (*as-Sūfī lam yukhlaq*).

EDITOR'S NOTES

Numbers in bold indicate pages in the text for which the following citations and explanations are provided.

Islam

1: *Theomorphic being:* "And God said, Let us make man in our image, after our likeness" (Gen. 1:26). "Indeed we created man in the most beautiful form (*Sūrah* "The Fig" [95]:4).

3: *The triad traditional in Islam, that of* al-īmān (*the "Faith"*), al-islām (*the "Law", literally "submission"*), *and* al-ihsān (*the "Path", literally, "virtue"*): "One day when we were sitting with the Messenger of God there came unto us a man whose clothes were of exceeding whiteness and whose hair was of exceeding blackness; nor were there any signs of travel upon him, although none of us knew him. He sat down knee unto knee opposite the Prophet, upon whose thighs he placed the palms of his hands saying: 'O Muhammad, tell me what is the surrender (*islām*).' The Messenger answered him saying: 'The surrender is to testify that there is no god but God and that Muhammad is God's Messenger, to perform the prayer, bestow the alms, fast Ramadan, and make if thou canst, the pilgrimage to the Holy House.' He said: 'Thou hast spoken truly', and we were amazed that, having questioned him, he should corroborate him. Then he said: 'Tell me what is faith (*īmān*).' He answered: 'To believe in God and His Angels and His Books and His Messengers and the Last Day, and to believe that no good or evil cometh but by His Providence.' 'Thou hast spoken truly', he said, and then: 'Tell me what is excellence (*ihsān*).' He answered: 'To worship God as if thou sawest him, for if thou seest Him not, yet seeth He thee.' 'Thou hast spoken truly', he said, and then: 'Tell me of the Hour.' He answered: 'The questioned thereof knoweth no better than the questioner.' He said: 'Then tell me of its signs.' He answered: 'That the slave-girl shall give birth to her mistress; and that those who were but barefoot naked needy herdsmen shall build buildings ever higher and higher.' Then the stranger went away, and I stayed a while after he had gone; and the Prophet said to me: 'O Umar, knowest though the questioner, who was he?' I said: 'God and His Messenger know best.' He said: 'It was Gabriel. He came unto you to teach you your religion'" (*hadīth*).

4: *Of "God"—or of the "Godhead" in the Eckhartian sense of this* distinguo: Meister Eckhart (c. 1260-1327), a German Dominican mystic and writer, distinguished between *Gott* or "God", that is, the Divine insofar as it manifests itself as a person (*Being*), and *Gottheit* or "*Godhead*", which is the transpersonal divinity of the Absolute as such (*Beyond-Being*). The latter is to be identified with the Divine Essence that transcends the polarity servant-Lord. See the author's chapter "The Servant and Union" in *Logic and Transcendence: A New Translation with Selected Letters*, ed. James S. Cutsinger (Bloomington, IN: World Wisdom, 2009), pp. 181-88.

6: Note 8: Muhyi ad-Din *Ibn Arabi* (1165-1240), author of numerous works including *Meccan Revelations* and *Bezels of Wisdom*, was a prolific and profoundly influential Sufi mystic, known in tradition as the *Shaykh al-akbar*, that is, "the great master".

The *Spanish scholar* Miguel Asín Palacios' (1871-1944) book, *El Islam cristianizado* (1931), or "Islam Christianized", is a study of Ibn Arabi that presents Sufi spirituality as deeply indebted to Christian mysticism.

"*All things are* Ātmā": "*Ātmā* was indeed *Brahma* in the beginning. It knew only that 'I am *Brahma*'. Therefore it became all. And whoever among the gods knew it also became That; and the same with sages and men. . . . And to this day whoever in like manner knows 'I am *Brahma*' becomes all this universe. Even the gods cannot prevail against him, for he becomes their *Ātmā*" (*Brihadāranyaka Upanishad*, 1.4.10).

"An invisible and subtle essence is the Spirit that pervades the whole universe. That is Reality. That is Truth. *That art thou*" (*Chāndogya Upanishad*, 6.14.3).

7: Mansur *al-Hallaj* (858-922), a Sufi from Baghdad, was dismembered and crucified for his mystical pronouncement, "I am the Truth (*anā 'l-Haqq*)".

8: *The Muslim rejection of the cross*: "And because of their saying: We slew the Messiah, Jesus son of Mary, God's messenger—they slew him not nor crucified him, but it appeared so unto them; and lo! those who disagree concerning it are in doubt thereof; they have no knowledge thereof save pursuit of a conjecture; they slew him not for certain, but God took him up unto Himself" (*Sūrah* "Women" [4]:157-58).

"*Will lead many astray by his wonders*": "For there shall arise false Christs, and false prophets, and shall shew great signs and wonders; insomuch that, if it were possible, they shall deceive the very elect" (Matt. 24:24).

Note 10: *Abu Hatim* Razi (874-934) was a prominent Ismaili philosopher whose views on the crucifixion influenced al-Ghazzali (see editor's note for "The Koran and the *Sunnah*", p. 58, Note 49).

The French Islamicist and Melkite Catholic priest Louis *Massignon* (1883-1962), best known for his magisterial study of the Sufi Mansur al-Hallaj, published an article in 1932 entitled "*Le Christ dans les Evangiles selon al-Ghazzali*", or "Christ in the Gospels according to al-Ghazzali". On the subject of the crucifixion in Islam, the author writes elsewhere: "As for the apparent denial of the crucifixion by the Koran, we have always held that this is a question of theology rather than history, and we have encountered the same point of view in a work of Massignon ('Le Christ dans les Evangiles selon al-Ghazzali'): 'Abu Hatim, basing himself on the opinion of one of his masters (who is not named), declares that the beginning of the Koranic verse (4:157) in no way denies the crucifixion and that it must be interpreted after taking account of its ending, "and they did not kill him truly (*yaqīnā*). God raised him to Himself", and, since Jesus died a martyr, remembering the verses (2:154; cf. 3:169) on the death of martyrs: "Do not say of those who have been killed on the way of God that they are dead: but that they are living; although you are not aware of it""" (*Gnosis: Divine Wisdom: A New Translation with Selected Letters*, ed. James S. Cutsinger [Bloomington, IN: World Wisdom, 2009], p. 7n).

9: The Sufi doctrine of the renewing of creation at each instant, or *continual creation*, is, among others, Ibn Arabi's interpretation of "a new creation" (*al-khalq al-jadīd*) in the verse, "When we are dust, are we then forsooth (to be raised) in a new creation?" (*Sūrah* "Thunder" [13]:5).

10: "And when I [God] have fashioned him and breathed into him *of My Spirit* (*min Rūhī*), then fall down before him prostrate" (*Sūrah* "Sad" [38]:72).

Note 12: *The metaphysical level specific to all* bhakti refers to the level of Being, whereas Beyond-Being is by definition independent from *relationships*.

11: *The Koran affirms that the Messiah is not God*: "They indeed have disbelieved who say: Lo! God is the Messiah, son of Mary" (*Sūrah* "The Table Spread" [5]:17). "The Messiah, son of Mary, was no other than a messenger, messengers (the like of whom) had passed away before him. And his mother was a saintly woman. And they both used to eat (earthly) food" (*Sūrah* "The Table Spread" [5]:75), *passim.*

The Koran rejects the dogma of the Trinity: "So believe in God and His messengers, and say not 'Three'. Cease! (it is) better for you! God is only One God" (*Sūrah* "Women" [4]:171). "They surely disbelieve who say: Lo! God is the third of three" (*Sūrah* "The Table Spread" [5]:73). "Say: He is God, the One! God, the eternally Besought of all! He begetteth not nor was begotten. And there is none comparable unto Him" (*Sūrah* "The Unity" [112]:1-4), *passim.*

The Koran appears to deny the death of Christ: "They slew him not nor cruci-fied, but it appeared so unto them; . . . they slew him not for certain, But God took him up unto Himself" (*Sūrah* "Women" [4]:157-158).

12: Note 16: *Christ appeared between Moses and Elias in the light of the Trans-figuration:* "And after six days Jesus taketh Peter, James, and John his brother, and bringeth them up into an high mountain apart, and was transfigured before them: and his face did shine as the sun, and his raiment was white as the light. And, behold, there appeared unto them Moses and Elias talking with him" (Matt. 17:1; cf. Mark 9:2-5; Luke 9:28-31).

"*Bosom of Abraham*": "And it came to pass, that the beggar died, and was carried by the angels into Abraham's bosom" (Luke 16:22).

The seeming contradiction between Saint John the Baptist denying that he was Elias and Christ affirming the contrary: "And they asked him [John the Baptist], What then? Art thou Elias? And he saith, I am not. Art thou that prophet? And he answered, No" (John 1:21). "But I say unto you, That Elias is come already, and they knew him not, but have done unto him whatsoever they listed. Likewise shall also the Son of man suffer of them. Then the dis-ciples understood that he spake unto them of John the Baptist" (Matt. 17:12).

13: *Islam distinguishes between man as such and collective man:* for the author this means the respective domains of "the human person and society" (see author's note 19), and by extension the Path (*Tarīqah*) and the Law (*Sharī'ah*).

Note 17: Alchemy distinguishes between four cosmic regions: dry, moist, warm, and cold, which combine, *in an alchemical sense*, to form the four elements.

14: Note 18: The "*Word from which all things were made and without which nothing was made*": "All things were made by him; and without him was not any thing made that was made" (John 1:3).

Note 20: Ahmad *Ibn Hanbal* (780-855) was a Muslim jurist whose branch of Islamic law, one of the four Sunni schools of jurisprudence, accentuated a literal interpretation of the Koran. Anthropomorphic descriptions of God were not open to *meditation* but accepted *bi-lā kayf*, that is, "without asking any questions" or "without asking how" they apply to God.

15: The *corpus mysticum* or "*Mystical Body*" is one of the traditional epithets for the Christian Church, understood as the Body of Christ (cf. Eph. 4:4-13) and nourished by the Eucharist. The term is used here in a more general sense to refer to the spiritual community of believers within a given religion as epitomized in the saint, who embodies its principles and perspective.

Note 20 (cont.): *Jalal ad-Din Rumi* (1207-73), author of the monumental *Mathnawī* and founder of the Mevlevi Sufi order, is well known for his insistence on spiritual love as the proper basis for the seeker's relation to God.

Abu al-Qasim *al-Junayd* (830-910) was an influential Persian Sufi known for his emphasis upon spiritual sobriety.

Note 21: *"Do not go to the prayer in a state of drunkenness"*: "O ye who believe! Draw not near unto prayer when ye are drunken till ye know that which ye utter. . ." (*Sūrah* "Women" [4]:43).

16: *The metaphysical transparency of things*: elsewhere the author writes: "The sense of the Sacred likewise implies a sense of the metaphysical transparency of things, the capacity to grasp the uncreated in the created; or to perceive the vertical ray—a messenger from the Archetype—independently of the horizontal plane of refraction, the latter determining the existential degree but not the divine content" (*Esoterism as Principle and as Way* [Bedfont, Middlesex: Perennial Books, 1981], p. 239).

In a well-known hadīth, *the Prophet said he* "*loved women*": "Made beloved to me from your world are women and perfume, and the coolness of my eyes is in prayer."

Note 22: *"Not to resist evil"*: "Ye have heard that it hath been said, An eye for an eye, and a tooth for a tooth: But I say unto you, That ye resist not evil: but whosoever shall smite thee on thy right cheek, turn to him the other also. And if any man will sue thee at the law, and take away thy coat, let him have [thy] cloak also. And whosoever shall compel thee to go a mile, go with him twain. Give to him that asketh thee, and from him that would borrow of thee turn not thou away. Ye have heard that it hath been said, Thou shalt love thy neighbor, and hate thine enemy. But I say unto you, Love your enemies, bless them that curse you, do good to them that hate you, and pray for them which despitefully use you, and persecute you; That ye may be the children of your Father which is in heaven: for he maketh his sun to rise on the evil and on the good, and sendeth rain on the just and on the unjust. For if ye love them which love you, what reward have ye? do not even the publicans the same? And if ye salute your brethren only, what do ye more [than others?] do not even the publicans so? Be ye therefore perfect, even as your Father which is in heaven is perfect" (Matt. 5:38-48; cf. Luke 6:27-36).

Note 23: In Mughal India, Emperor Akbar's (1542-1605) tolerant policies towards *Hindus* meant that they *were then considered to be the same as the* "*people of the Book*".

16-17: *The God of the Old Testament is no less a warrior than the God of the Koran, quite the opposite*: "Thus saith the Lord of hosts, I remember that which Amalek did to Israel, how he laid wait for him in the way, when he came up from Egypt. Now go and smite Amalek, and utterly destroy all that they have, and spare them not; but slay both man and woman, infant and suckling, ox and sheep, camel and ass" (1 Sam. 15:2), *passim.*

17: *Constantine* the Great (d. 337) was the first Christian emperor whose patronage and defense of the religion by the *sword* facilitated its expansion in Europe and surrounding regions.

Note 24: "And Jesus went into the *temple* of God, and cast out all them that sold and bought in the temple, and overthrew the tables of the *money changers*, and the seats of them that sold doves" (Matt. 21:12).

Note 25: Abu Amir Muhammad Ibn Abdallah Ibn Abi Amir al-Hajib *al-Mansur* ruled Islamic Andalusia in the late tenth and early eleventh century.

The Cathedral of Santiago de Compostela in Spain contains the *tomb of the Apostle* James, son of Zebedee.

18: Note 25 (cont.): *Ernst Kühnel* (1882-1964) was the curator of the Islamic collections at the State Museum in Berlin and a widely acknowledged expert on Islamic art.

Note 26: "*Think not that I am come to send peace on earth*: I came not to send peace, but a sword" (Matt. 10:34).

19: Note 28: *Pythagoreans* were followers of the ancient Greek philosopher Pythagoras of Samos (c. 569-c. 475), whose teaching was at once mathematical, astronomical, and musical; Pythagoras' teachings influenced *Plato* (427-347 B.C.), the most renowned of the ancient Greek philosophers.

Fernand Brunner (1920-91) was a Swiss philosopher who criticized the foundations of modern science in light of traditional wisdom.

21: Note 30: Pierre *Teilhard de Chardin* (1881-1955), a Jesuit paleontologist and heterodox theological writer, claimed that traditional Christian theology, especially its teachings concerning the creation and fall of man, had been rendered outmoded by modern evolutionary biology and that Christ should be reconceived as the "Omega Point", the culmination of a universal development beginning with matter.

24: Note 35: The *ablution before prayer* or *wudhū* consists of a washing of the hands, face, forearms, and feet in view of ritual purity before performing the canonical prayers.

25: *The* dāllūn, *the "strayers", of the* Fātihah: "Show us the straight path (*as-sirāt al-mustaqīm*), the path of those whom Thou hast favored; Not the (path) of those who earn Thine anger nor of those who go astray" (*Sūrah* "The Opening" [1]:6).

Note 37: *Vincent de Paul* (1581-1660) was a Catholic priest who founded the *Sisters of Charity* to serve the poor.

27: The *Kaaba* (literally "cube") is the most sacred sanctuary of Islam, dating back to the patriarch Abraham, who was instructed by God to build it nearby the miraculous well of Zamzam in the valley of Mecca (see *Sūrah* "Pilgrimage" [22]:26-27). The cube-like structure is the point of orientation for Muslim prayer and is ritually circumambulated during the pilgrimage.

29: *"Stones from which streams spring forth", whereas there are hearts which are "harder than stones"*: "Then, even after that, your hearts were hardened and became as rocks, or worse than rocks, for hardness. For indeed there are rocks from out which rivers gush, and indeed there are rocks which split asunder so that water floweth from them. And indeed there are rocks which fall down for the fear of God" (*Sūrah* "The Cow" [2]:74).

"Living water" of Christ: "There cometh a woman of Samaria to draw water: Jesus saith unto her, Give me to drink. (For his disciples were gone away unto the city to buy meat.) Then saith the woman of Samaria unto him, How is it that thou, being a Jew, askest drink of me, which am a woman of Samaria? for the Jews have no dealings with the Samaritans. Jesus answered and said unto her, If thou knewest the gift of God, and who it is that saith to thee, Give me to drink, thou wouldest have asked of him, and he would have given thee living water. The woman saith unto him, Sir, thou hast nothing to draw with, and the well is deep: from whence then hast thou that living water? Art thou greater than our father Jacob, which gave us the well, and drank thereof himself, and his children, and his cattle? Jesus answered and said unto her, Whosoever drinketh of this water shall thirst again: But whosoever drinketh of the water that I shall give him shall never thirst; but the water that I shall give him shall be in him a well of water springing up into everlasting life" (John 4:7-14).

29-30: *"Rivers of living water" which according to the Gospel, "flow from the hearts of saints"*: "He that believeth on me, as the scripture hath said, out of his belly shall flow rivers of living water" (John 7:38; cf. Ezek. 47:1; Zech. 14:8).

30: Note 47: "*The letter killeth*, but the spirit maketh alive" (2 Cor. 3:6).

31: *Tarjumān al-ashwāq*, literally "the interpreter of loving desires", is a collection of mystical odes by Ibn Arabi.

The Koran and the *Sunnah*

33: *The traditional thesis of Islam* is that the Koran has a miraculous incomparability (*ihjāz*) making it superior to all other books.

34: Note 4: Johann Wolfgang von *Goethe* (1749-1832) was a German poet, novelist, and playwright, of whom the author has said: "[Goethe] was the victim of his epoch owing to the fact that humanism in general and Kantianism in particular had vitiated his tendency toward a vast and finely shaded wisdom; he thus became, quite paradoxically, the spokesman of a perfectly bourgeois 'horizontality'" (*To Have a Center* [Bloomington, IN: World Wisdom, 1990], p. 16). His *Westöstlicher Diwan* (1819), a collection of lyric poetry, incorporates Eastern components inspired by the Persian poet Hafiz.

35: *Christ called his body "the Temple"*: "Jesus answered and said unto them, Destroy this temple, and in three days I will raise it up. Then said the Jews, Forty and six years was this temple in building, and wilt thou rear it up in three days? But he spake of the temple of his body" (John 2:19-21).

The Temple of *Solomon* was the first Israelite temple built in Jerusalem by the prophet-king Solomon in the tenth century B.C.; it was destroyed by the Babylonians in the fifth century B.C. The Second Temple, also known as *Herod*'s Temple, was rebuilt by the Jewish king Herod the Great (74-4 B.C.); it was destroyed by the Romans in 70 A.D.

Note 5: The *Kitāb fīhi mā fīhi*, literally "in it what is in it", is a collection of discourses given by the Sufi *Jalal ad-Din Rumi* (see editor's note for "Islam", p. 15, Note 20) to his disciples.

Augustine (354-430), Bishop of the North African city of Hippo, was the greatest of the Western Church Fathers.

Pope *Pius XII* (1876-1958) wrote the *encyclical Divino Afflante* or *Divino Afflante Spiritu*, "Inspired by the Divine Spirit", in 1943.

Note 6: The *Bhagavad Gītā*, the best known and arguably the most important of all Hindu sacred texts and part of the much longer epic *Mahābhārata*, consists of a dialogue between the prince Arjuna and his charioteer, the *avatāra*

Krishna, concerning the different paths to God.

36: *A sacred text with its seeming contradictions and obscurities is in some ways like a mosaic, or even an anagram*: the author offers these complementary remarks in the chapter "Keys to the Bible": "When approaching Scripture, one should always pay the greatest attention to rabbinical and kabbalistic commentaries and in Christianity to the patristic and mystical commentaries; then will it be seen how the word-for-word meaning practically never suffices by itself and how apparent naiveties, inconsistencies, and contradictions resolve themselves in a dimension of profundity for which one must possess the key. The literal meaning is frequently a cryptic language that more often veils than reveals and that is only meant to furnish clues to truths of a cosmological, metaphysical, and mystical order; the Oriental traditions are unanimous concerning this complex and multidimensional interpretation of sacred texts" (*Light on the Ancient Worlds: A New Translation with Selected Letters*, ed. Deborah Casey [Bloomington, IN: World Wisdom, 2006], p. 115).

37: The *Torah* is the written law of God, as revealed to Moses on Sinai and embodied in the Pentateuch or the first five books of the Old Testament (Genesis, Exodus, Leviticus, Numbers, Deuteronomy).

The *Mishnah* is a collection of Jewish oral tradition received by Moses on Sinai and transmitted to the Sanhedrin by Moses' successor, Joshua. It includes both commentary on the *Torah* and an application of its principles to a wide array of themes such as sacrificial rites, dietary obligations, and criminal laws.

The Jewish *Tabernacle* was a portable, tent-like sanctuary which served as the dwelling place for the divine presence during the period of the Jewish exodus from Egypt until the entry of the Israelites into the Promised Land; it was later installed in the First Temple at Jerusalem.

The prophet *Joshua* succeeded Moses as the religious leader of the Jews and led them in the conquest of Canaan.

The *Sanhedrin* was the supreme legal assembly of ancient Israel.

Note 9: *Nicodemus came to find Christ by night*: "There was a man of the Pharisees, named Nicodemus, a ruler of the Jews. The same came to Jesus by night, and said unto him, Rabbi, we know that thou art a teacher come from God: for no man can do these miracles that thou doest, except God be with him. Jesus answered and said unto him, Verily, verily, I say unto thee, Except a man be born again, he cannot see the kingdom of God" (John 3:1-3).

38: *Abu Hanifah* (699-765) was the founder of the Hanafi school of jurisprudence, one of the four Sunni schools of Islamic law.

At-Tahawi (843-935) was a follower of the Hanafi school of Islamic law and wrote several treatises on jurisprudence and *hadīth*.

Note 10: *Risālat al-Quds*, or "Epistle on Sanctity", is a major work by *Ibn Arabi* (see editor's note for "Islam", p. 6, Note 8) in which he describes his encounters with various Sufi saints during the first part of his life in Andalusia.

39: Note 11: The *Talmud* (literally, "learning, study") is a body of Jewish rabbinical writings and traditional commentaries based on the oral law given to Moses on Sinai; it is the foundation of Jewish civil and religious law, second in authority only to the *Torah*.

Daniel is a biblical figure whose exploits—particularly his ordeal in the lion's den—are recounted in the Book of Daniel in the Old Testament; in Christianity he is considered to be a prophet.

Esdras is the Greek form of Ezra, a priestly scribe who led the return of the Jews to Jerusalem in 459 B.C., following their exile in Babylon. He is referred to in the Book of Ezra and the Book of Nehemiah in the Old Testament.

40: Note 13: Sikhism, or the *Sikh brotherhood*, is an *esoterism* that bases itself on the teachings of Guru Nanak (1469-1539) and his successors; its adherents are to be found primarily in the Punjab region of India.

Kabir (1440-1518) was an Indian mystic and poet, revered alike by Hindus, Muslims, and Sikhs, who emphasized the path of *bhakti*, or love of God, rather than outward religious observances.

41: Note 16: For *Meister Eckhart*, see editor's note for "Islam", p. 4.

44: *John of the Cross* (1542-91) was a Spanish priest and mystic and co-founder, with Teresa of Avila, of the reformed or Discalced Carmelites.

For *the negation of the Christian Trinity in the Koran*, see editor's note for "Islam", p. 11.

46: Note 24: *According to the Koran, the* kāfir *is in effect characterized by his "worldliness"*: "(On that day) neither the riches not the progeny of those who disbelieve (*alladhīna kafarū*) will aught avail them with God" (*Sūrah* "Family of Imran" [3]:10), *passim.*

Note 25: *According to the Gospels, the pagans imagine they will be answered "for their much speaking"*: "But when ye pray, use not vain repetitions, as the heathen do: for they think that they shall be heard for their much speaking" (Matt. 6:7).

Note 26: *Of "hyperborean" or "Atlantean" affiliation:* according to certain esoteric doctrines, Hyperborea is the Northern polar origin of human civilization; the mythic continent of Atlantis is mentioned by Plato (see editor's note for "Islam", p. 19, Note 28) in his dialogues *Timaeus* and *Critias*.

47: Christianity is a *"bhaktic" esoterism* in that it lays emphasis on inwardness while being a perspective of love (*bhakti*).

Brahmanism is the doctrine of Hindu brahmins or priests.

49: "And *the Spirit of God* moved upon the face of *the waters*" (Gen. 1:2).

"The wind bloweth where it listeth, and *thou hearest the sound thereof, but canst not tell whence it cometh, and whither it goeth:* so is every one that is born of the Spirit" (John 3:8).

"Hath expanded our breast for Islam": "And whomsoever it is God's will to guide, He expandeth his bosom unto Islam" (*Sūrah* "Cattle" [6]:125).

50: *"The next world is better for you than the here below"* (*Sūrah* "The Early Hours" [93]:4).

"Earthly life is but a play" (*Sūrah* "Iron" [57]:20).

"In your wives and your children ye have an enemy" (*Sūrah* "Mutual Disillusion" [64]:14).

"Say: Allāh! *then leave them to their vain talk"* (*Sūrah* "Cattle" [6]:91).

When it [the Koran] *promises Paradise to "him who has feared the station of his Lord and refused desire to his soul"*: "But as for him who feared to stand before his Lord and restrained his soul from lust, Lo! the Garden will be his home" (*Sūrah* "Those Who Pull Out" [79]:40).

"Made in the image of God": "And God said, Let us make man in our image, after our likeness" (Gen. 1:26).

Note 33: For *Louis Massignon*, see editor's note for "Islam", p. 8, Note 10.

51: Note 36: *It was the objectivity of human intelligence which enabled Adam to "name" all things and all creatures:* "And Adam gave names to all cattle, and to the fowl of the air, and to every beast of the field" (Gen. 2:20). "And He (God) taught Adam all the names, then showed them to the angels, saying: Inform Me of the names of these, if ye are truthful" (*Sūrah* "The Cow" [2]:31).

Note 37: Ahmad *al-Alawi* (1869-1934), a famous Algerian Sufi, was the author's spiritual master.

52: Shaivite, or *Shivaite*, Hinduism is a path of knowledge (*jnāna*) or *intellectual "ascent"* connected with the God Shiva, the transformer; Vishnuite, or *Vaishnavite*, Hinduism is a path of love (*bhakti*) characterized by devotion to the God Vishnu, the preserver, and his incarnations or *divine "descents"*.

"The world is false, Brahma *is true"*: this summation of *Advaita Vedānta* is traditionally ascribed to Shankara (788-820), the pre-eminent spokesman of non-dualism, whom the author regarded as the greatest of Hindu metaphysicians.

"All is Ātmā": "*Ātmā* was indeed *Brahma* in the beginning. It knew only that 'I am *Brahma*'. Therefore It became all. And whoever among the gods knew It also became That; and the same with sages and men. . . . And to this day whoever in like manner knows 'I am *Brahma*' becomes all this universe. Even the gods cannot prevail against him, for he becomes their *Ātmā*" (*Brihadāranyaka Upanishad*, 1.4.10).

Note 41: Abu Bakr *ash-Shibli* (861-946) was a Persian *Sufi* of ecstatic leaning and a friend of al-Hallāj.

55: The *mystery of ipseity* refers to the infinite Selfhood of the Divine Essence.

57: Note 47: O *son of Kunti* refers to Arjuna, the protagonist of the *Bhagavad Gītā*.

58: *A superficial formalism or even Pharisaism,* in the sense of the Gospel's description of the Pharisees, a powerful religious school at the time of Jesus that laid emphasis on outer actions and legal conformity in a spirit of self-righteous formalism.

Note 48: *The "indulgences" attached in Catholicism to certain formulas or prayers* refer to the remission of sins granted by the Catholic Church under certain designated conditions.

Note 49: Abu Hamid Muhammad *al-Ghazzali* (1058-1111), an Islamic jurist and theologian, entered upon the Sufi path in search of a direct confirmation of God, which he described in his *Mishkāt al-Anwār*, "The Niche of Lights". He is credited with revitalizing exoteric Islam by integrating aspects of Sufism into the fold of the religion.

59: *Omnipotence, being something definite, cannot pertain to the Absolute in* *the strictly metaphysical sense of that term*: on this question see the chapters "The Question of Theodicies" in *Form and Substance in the Religions* (Bloomington, IN: World Wisdom, 2002), pp. 151-64, and "On the Divine Will" in *Christianity/Islam: Perspectives on Esoteric Ecumenism: A New Translation with Selected Letters*, ed. James S. Cutsinger (Bloomington, IN: World Wisdom, 2008), pp. 181-86.

62: Note 55: *Mazdeism* or Mazdaism is an ancient Persian religion, also referred to as Zoroastrianism, which is based on the teachings of the prophet Zoroaster.

63: Note 56: "*He who draws the sword shall perish by the sword*": "Then said Jesus unto him (Peter), Put up again thy sword into his place: for all they that take the sword shall perish with the sword" (Matt. 26:52).

"*Every house divided against itself shall fall*": "Every kingdom divided against itself is brought to desolation; and a house divided against a house falleth" (Luke 11:17).

"*Made in the image of God*": "And God said, Let us make man in our image, after our likeness" (Gen. 1:26).

64: *According to the Koran, it is his bodily members themselves which accuse him*: "On the day when their tongues and their hands and their feet testify against them as to what they used to do" (*Sūrah* "Light" [24]:24), *passim*.

65: *A shirt of Nessus* refers to the poisoned shirt of the centaur Nessus, which burned Heracles (Hercules) to death. Symbolically, it refers to an ineluctable, fatal destiny.

66-67: Note 61: The *Durrat al-Fākhirah* ("The Precious Pearl") is an eschatological treatise attributed to *al-Ghazzali*.

67: Abd al-Karim al-*Jili* (c. 1365-c. 1412) systematized the teachings of Ibn Arabi (see editor's note for "Islam", p. 6, Note 8), notably in his most important work, *The Universal Man*, which is concerned with both cosmological and metaphysical questions.

Abu Ali Husayn ibn Sina (980-1037), known in the West as *Avicenna*, was a prodigious and highly influential authority on a wide array of subjects, including theology, philosophy, medicine, and natural science.

Note 61: The *Bodhisattva Kshitigarbha* made a vow to postpone Buddhahood until all the hells are emptied of human souls.

Note 63: *Vishnu* is the second god of the Hindu *Trimūrti*, or trinity—Brahmā being the first and Shiva the third—and is the preserver of creation, incarnating himself as an *avatāra*, or divine descent, in such forms as Rama and Krishna (see editor's note for "The Prophet", p. 85, p. 93, Note 17).

Amida (Japanese) or Amitabha (Sanskrit) is the name of the Buddha of "infinite light", who as a *Bodhisattva* named Dharmakara vowed not to enter *Nirvāna* until he had brought all who invoked his Name into the paradise of his Pure Land, also known as *Sukhāvatī* ("place of bliss") or the Western Paradise.

67-68: For further elucidations on *the point of intersection between the Semitic conception of perpetual hell and the Hindu and Buddhist conception of transmigration*, see the author's chapter "Cosmological and Eschatological Viewpoints" in *Treasures of Buddhism* (Bloomington, IN: World Wisdom, 1993), pp. 49-65.

68: Note 63 (cont.): In Hindu cosmology the "*lives of* Brahmā" are immense cycles of time comprising thousands of *kalpa*s or "days of *Brahmā*".

The "reign of a thousand years": "And I saw an angel come down from heaven, having the key of the bottomless pit and a great chain in his hand. And he laid hold on the dragon, that old serpent, which is the Devil, and Satan, and bound him a thousand years, And cast him into the bottomless pit, and shut him up, and set a seal upon him, that he should deceive the nations no more, till the thousand years should be fulfilled: and after that he must be loosed a little season" (Rev. 20:2-3).

Note 64: The *Mānava Dharma Shastra*, also known as the "Laws of Manu", is a traditional Hindu scripture consisting of discourses given by the sage Manu concerning the principles of the social order.

The *Markendeya Purāna* is a Hindu religious text consisting of a dialogue between the two *rishi*s Markandeya and Jaimini.

69: Note 65: *René Guénon* (1886-1951), a French metaphysician, scholar of traditional symbolism, critic of the modern world, and one of the formative authorities of the traditionalist or perennialist school, published *L'Homme et son devenir selon le Vedānta* (*Man and His Becoming According to the Vedānta*) in 1925.

Note 66: *Ihya 'Ulūm ad-Dīn*, or "The Revivification of Religious Sciences", is one of the major works of *al-Ghazzali.*

70: Note 67: O *Partha* refers to Arjuna, the protagonist of the *Bhagavad Gītā*.

72: *The meeting between Moses and al-Khidr* is recounted in the *Sūrah* "The Cave" [18]:65-82. The Koran refers to "one of Our slaves, unto whom We had given mercy from Us, and had taught him knowledge from Our presence", which the tradition considers to be al-Khidr ("the Green One"), a mysterious prophetic figure whose teaching transcends the Law, which is here represented by the prophet Moses.

"The *wind* bloweth where it listeth, and thou hearest the sound thereof, but *canst not tell whence it cometh, and whither it goeth*: so is every one that is born of the Spirit" (John 3:8).

Note 74: "*Heaven and earth shall pass away, but my words shall not pass away*" (Matt. 24:35; Mark 13:31; Luke 21:33).

"*All things are ephemeral save the Face of* Allāh" (*Sūrah* "The Story" [28]:88).

73: "*The resurrection of the body*": "I believe in the Holy Spirit, the holy Catholic Church, the communion of saints, the forgiveness of sins, the resurrection of the body, and the life everlasting" (Apostles' Creed, Art. 3; cf. 1 Cor. 15:35-50). "And We send down from the sky blessed water whereby We give growth unto gardens and the grain of crops, and lofty date palms with ranged clusters, provision (made) for men; and therewith We quicken a dead land. Even so will be the resurrection of the dead" (*Sūrah* "Qaf" [50]:9-11), *passim*.

74: Note 78: *According to the Koran, all earthly ills "come from yourselves"* (min anfusikum), *which does not mean that "everything" does not "come from God"* (kullun min 'indi 'Llāhi): "So We took each one in his sin; of them was he on whom We sent a hurricane, and of them was he who was overtaken by the (Awful) Cry, and of them was he whom We caused the earth to swallow, and of them was he whom We drowned. It was not for God to wrong them, but they wronged themselves" (*Sūrah* "Spider" [29]:40). "Wheresoever ye may be, death will overtake you, even though ye were in lofty towers. Yet if a happy thing befalleth them they say: This is from God; and if an evil thing befalleth them they say: This is of thy doing (O Muhammad). Say (unto them): All is from God. What is amiss with these people that they come not nigh to understand a happening?" (*Sūrah* "Women" [4]:78).

75: *Hindu cosmology teaches that the souls of the dead go first of all to the Moon*: "When people depart from this world, it is to the moon that they all go. By means of their lifebreaths the moon swells up in the fortnight of waxing, and through the fortnight of waning, it propels them to new birth. Now the moon is the door to the heavenly world" (*Kausitaki Upanishad* 1.2).

76: For *Mazdean-Gnostic dualism*, see above p. 62, Note 55 and editor's note for "The Path", p. 114.

Semitic monism refers to Jewish, Christian, and Islamic monotheism.

"God alone is good": "Why callest thou me good? There is none good but one, that is, God" (Matt. 19:17; Mark 10:18).

77: *The higher cannot be merely defined in terms of the lower*: this principle and its consequences are also developed in the author's chapter, "Consequences Flowing from the Mystery of Subjectivity": "And yet, starting from the recognition of the immediately tangible mystery that is subjectivity or intelligence, it is easy to understand that the origin of the Universe is, not inert and unconscious matter, but a spiritual Substance which, from coagulation to coagulation and from segmentation to segmentation—and other projections both manifesting and limiting—finally produces matter by causing it to emerge from a more subtle substance, but one which is already remote from principial Substance. It will be objected that there is no proof of this, to which we reply—aside from the phenomenon of subjectivity which precisely comprises this proof, leaving aside other possible intellectual proofs, not needed by Intellection—to which we reply then, that there are infinitely fewer proofs for this inconceivable absurdity, evolutionism, which has the miracle of consciousness springing from a heap of earth or pebbles, metaphorically speaking" (*From the Divine to the Human: Survey of Metaphysics and Epistemology* [Bloomington, IN: World Wisdom, 1982], p. 6).

The Intellect, in its essence, conceives of God because it "is" itself increatus et increabile: Meister Eckhart (see editor's note for "Islam", p. 4) taught that *aliquid est in anima quod est increatum et increabile . . . et hoc est Intellectus*: "There is something in the soul that is uncreated and uncreatable . . . and this is the Intellect" (The Bull *In agro dominico* [1329]).

78: *The Koran itself speaks of the* Sunnah *of* Allāh: "There is no reproach for the Prophet in that which God maketh his due. That was God's way (*Sunnat Allāh*) with those who passed away of old—and the commandment of God is certain destiny" (*Sūrah* "The Confederates" [33]:38).

81: Muhammad Ibn Abd al-Jabbar al-*Niffari* (d. c. 970), one of the earliest Sufi writers, was the author of "The Book of Spiritual Stations" and "The Book of Spiritual Addresses", works well known for the density and obscurity of their style and the spiritual depth of their insights.

82: Abu Abdullah Muhammad al-Arabi ad-*Darqawi* (1760-1823) was a Moroccan Sufi master of the Shadhiliyyah lineage.

83: Ahmad *ibn Ajiba* (1747-1809) was a Moroccan Sufi of the Darqāwiyyah lineage.

Amidism, or Pure Land Buddhism, is based on the practice of the invocation of the Buddha Amida, especially through the formula *Namu Amida Butsu*, "I trust in the Buddha of Immeasurable Light".

The Prophet

85: *Rama* and *Krishna* are the seventh and eighth *avatāra*s, or incarnations, of the Hindu God Vishnu.

86: *In the case of the Prophet marriage had a spiritualized or "tantric" character.* this dimension of the Prophet's personality relates—in a phenomenological, but not historical, way—to the general principle of Tantrism, a cluster of Asian spiritual schools and disciplines emphasizing the immanent energy of the Divine within manifestation, effecting a spiritual transmutation of human experiences and pleasures. Elsewhere, the author writes as follows on this subject: "The Divine Beauty manifested through earthly beauties never ceases to be itself, in spite of the limitations of relativity. It is within this context that one must situate that feature of the Muhammadan Substance which could be called 'Solomonian' or 'Krishnaite', namely its spiritual capacity to find concretely in woman all the aspects of the Divine Femininity, from immanent Mercy to the infinitude of universal Possibility" ("The Mystery of the Prophetic Substance", in *In the Face of the Absolute* [Bloomington, IN: World Wisdom, 1989], p. 221).

Note 3: *On our first visits to Arab towns, we were impressed by the austere and even sepulchral atmosphere*: the author's German poem "Mostaghanem" (translated by Seyyed Hossein Nasr in *The Essential Frithjof Schuon*, ed. S. H. Nasr [Bloomington, IN: World Wisdom, 2005], p. 525), written in Algeria in 1933, amplifies this point further:

> . . . White domes and ever-weeping sea
> And stones upon golden sand.
> The voice of the muezzin falls lone and heavy
> Like the howl of wolves his lamenting cry
> Strays through infinite space.
> Houses like graves are standing nearby
> And a swaying, meditative tree.

Note 4: "The Ringstones of Wisdom" (*Fusūs al-Hikam*), or the *Wisdom of the Prophets by Ibn Arabi* (see editor's note for "Islam", p. 6, Note 8), is a major work of the Andalusian Sufi comprising twenty-seven chapters, each devoted to the wisdom of a particular prophet, beginning with Adam and ending with Muhammad. The partial translation of this work by the author's lifelong *friend, Titus Burckhardt* (1908-1984), the author of several major works on Islam, Sufism, arts, and cosmology, first appeared in French under the title *La Sagesse des Prophètes* (Paris: Albin Michel, 1955); it was translated into English as *The Wisdom of the Prophets* by A. Culme-Seymour (Sherbourne: Beshara, 1975).

87: *At the beginning of the Prophet's career there were painful obscurities and uncertainties* which were gradually put to rest by the Prophet's wife, Khadijah, her cousin Waraqah, and subsequent divine revelations: "He [the Prophet] fled from the cave, and when he was half-way down the slope of the mountain he heard a voice above him saying: 'O Muhammad, thou art the Messenger of God, and I am Gabriel.' The Prophet stood gazing at the Angel; then he turned away from him, but whichever way he looked the Angel was always there, astride the horizon, whether it was to the north, to the south, to the east, or to the west. Finally the Angel turned away, and the Prophet descended the slope and went to his house. 'Cover me! Cover me!' he said to Khadijah as with still quaking heart he laid himself on his couch. Alarmed, yet not daring to question him, she quickly brought a cloak and spread it over him. But when the intensity of his awe had abated he told her what he had seen and heard; and having spoken to him words of reassurance, she went to tell her cousin Waraqah, who was now an old man, and blind. 'Holy! Holy!', he said. 'By Him in whose hand is the soul of Waraqah, there hath come unto Muhammad the greatest Nāmūs [the Greek *Nomos*, in the sense of Divine Law or Scripture, here identified with the Angel of Revelation], even he that would come unto Moses. Verily Muhammad is the Prophet of this people. Bid him rest assured'" (Martin Lings, *Muhammad: His Life Based on the Earliest Sources* [Rochester, VT: Inner Traditions, 1983], p. 44).

Note 7: *In the case of Moses, his difficulty in speaking indicated the divine prohibition to divulge the mysteries:* "(Moses) said: My Lord! relieve my mind and ease my task for me; And loose a knot from my tongue, that they may understand my saying. Appoint for me a henchman from my folk, Aaron, my brother. Confirm my strength with him and let him share my task, that we may glorify Thee much and much remember Thee" (*Sūrah* "Ta Ha" [20]:25-34).

89: "Jesus saith unto him (Thomas), I am the way, the truth, and the life: *no man cometh unto the Father, but by me*" (John 14:6).

90: Note 12: Arguably the two most famous works of Islamic architecture are the *Alhambra*, a palace located in Granada, Spain, which was built by the Moorish rulers of Andalusia in the fourteenth century, and the *Taj Mahal*, located in Agra in Northern India, which was built as a mausoleum by the Mughal Emperor Shah Jahan for his wife Mumtaz in the seventeenth century.

93: Note 17: *The cult of Rama or of Krishna* refers to the Hindu devotion (*bhakti*) to the seventh and eighth *avatāra*s of Vishnu. Rama is the main protagonist of the ancient Sanskrit epic the *Rāmāyana* ("Rama's Journey") by Valmiki, as well as the addressee of the sage Vasistha's teachings in the *Yoga Vasishta*, one of the major texts of Hindu metaphysics. Krishna is the teacher of the warrior Arjuna in the *Bhagavad Gītā*, included in the epic *Mahābhārata*, while the *Srīmad Bhāgavatam* includes narrations of the life of Krishna, among other *avatāra*s of Vishnu.

93-94: *The two categories of corruptible beings:* "We shall dispose of you, O ye two dependents (man and jinn)" (*Sūrah* "The Beneficent" [55]:31).

94: Note 19: The Pali phrase, *Sabbe sattā sukhi hontu*, or *"May all beings be blissful"*, is chanted as a *mantra* in Buddhism.

Note 21: *Our regular readers are familiar with the following Vedantic classification, also found in the writings of René Guénon* (see editor's note for "The Koran and the *Sunnah*", p. 69, Note 65): "The personality, indeed, is unmanifested, even insofar as it is regarded more especially as the principle of the manifested states, just as Being, although it is properly the principle of universal manifestation, remains outside of and beyond that manifestation. . . ; on the other hand, formless manifestation is also, in a relative sense, principial in relation to formal manifestation, and thus it establishes a link between the latter and its higher unmanifested principle, which is, moreover, the common principle of these two orders of manifestation. Similarly, if we distinguish, in formal or individual manifestation, between the subtle and the gross state, the first is, more relatively still, principial in relation to the second, and hence placed hierarchically between it and formless manifestation. We have, therefore, through a series of principles becoming progressively more relative and determined, a chain at once logical and ontological . . . extending from the unmanifested downward to gross manifestation, passing through the intermediary of formless manifestation and then of subtle manifestation" (*Man and His Becoming According to the Vedānta*, trans. Richard C. Nicholson [Hillsdale, NY: Sophia Perennis, 2001], pp. 53-54; see also pp. 27-30).

95: *The Koran says: "And give him greeting" or "salutation"*: "Lo! God and His angels shower blessings on the Prophet. O ye who believe! Ask blessings on him and salute him with a worthy salutation" (*Sūrah* "The Clans" [33]:56).

Note 23: *The Koran mentions it [the Spirit] separately from the angels:* "The angels and the Spirit descend therein [on the Night of Revelation], by the permission of their Lord, with all decrees" (*Sūrah* "The Destiny" [97]:4).

96: For *Ahmad al-Alawi*, see editor's note for "The Koran and the *Sunnah*", p. 51, Note 37.

According to Meister Eckhart (see editor's note for "Islam", p. 4), "there is something in the soul which is uncreated and uncreatable (*increatus et increabile*); if the whole soul were such, it would be uncreated and uncreatable, and this is the Intellect [*Intellectus*]" (The Bull *In agro dominico* [1329]).

97: "*And God saw that it was good*": "And God saw every thing that he had made, and, behold, it was very good" (Gen. 1:31).

Note 27: For *De l'Homme Universel by Abd al-Karim Jili*, see editor's note for "The Koran and the *Sunnah*", p. 67. The French translation and commentary by *Titus Burckhardt* (Lyon: Derain, 1953) was translated into English as *Universal Man* by A. Culme-Seymour (Roberton: Beshara, 1983).

98: *These symbols are the signs* (āyāt) *spoken of in the Koran, the proofs of God which the Sacred Book recommends for meditation by those "endowed with understanding"*: "And of His signs is this: He created you of dust, and behold you human beings, ranging widely! And of His signs is this: He created for you helpmeets from yourselves that ye might find rest in them, and He ordained between you love and mercy. Lo, herein indeed are portents for folk who reflect. And of His signs is the creation of the heavens and the earth, and the difference of your languages and colors. Lo! herein indeed are portents for men of knowledge. And of His signs is your slumber by night and by day, and your seeking of His bounty. Lo! herein indeed are portents for folk who heed. And of His signs is this: He showeth you the lightning for a fear and for a hope, and sendeth down water from the sky, and thereby quickeneth the earth after her death. Lo! herein indeed are portents for folk who understand. And of His signs is this: The heavens and the earth stand fast by His command, and afterward, when He calleth you, lo! from the earth ye will emerge" (*Sūrah* "The Romans" [30]:20-25), *passim*.

Note 30: The Japanese *Shinto* tradition makes use of the term *kami* to designate a mysterious sacred power, at once singular and plural, pervading the world and embodied in mountains, seas, rivers, rocks, trees, birds, and animals.

The *North American Indians* of the Plains base their spiritual perspective on Nature as the symbolic repository of spiritual realities; according to the author, "it is through the animal species and the phenomena of Nature that the Indian contemplates the angelic Essences and the Divine Qualities" (*The Feathered Sun: Plains Indians in Art and Philosophy* [Bloomington, IN: World Wisdom, 1990], p. 47).

The *tradition of the Sacred Pipe*, central to the religion of the Plains and revealed to them through the celestial Buffalo Cow Woman, is described by the author as the central expression of the "polysynthetic" view according to which "the Universe is considered only as it relates to God" (*The Feathered Sun*, p. 51).

99: Muhammad ibn Ali al-*Tirmidhi* (d. c. 932), surnamed al-Hakim, "the sage", was the first Sufi authority to connect the degrees of spiritual knowledge with a hierarchy of sanctity, headed by the *qutb*, the spiritual "pole" or "pivot" for a given age.

100: Note 35: "Jesus saith unto him, I am the way, the truth, and the life: *no man cometh unto the Father, but by me*" (John 14:6).

Note 36: *The four archangels* in Islam are Gabriel (Arabic: Jibrail), Michael (Mikhail), Raphael (Israfil), and Azrael (Izrail).

The first four Caliphs in Islam were Abu Bakr as-Siddiq (573-634), Umar ibn al-Khattab (c. 586-90-644), Uthman ibn Affan (c. 579-656), and Ali ibn Abi Talib (c. 599-661).

Note 38: *Bernard* of Clairvaux (1090-1153) was a Cistercian monk and author of numerous homilies on the Song of Songs.

103: The Prophet is a *Platonic idea* inasmuch as he is envisaged as a prototype of all perfections *in divinis*, in conformity with Plato's (see editor's note for "Islam", p. 19, Note 28) metaphysics of the Ideas or Forms. These Ideas are the essential realities of which phenomena are but "shadows".

Note 45: *Al-Burdah* by *al-Busiri* (608-96) is one of the most celebrated poems in praise of the Prophet. Two of its most famous verses are: "Muhammad, Lord of the two worlds, and of the two weighty kinds, and of the two branches, Arabs and non-Arabs. Our Prophet who commands and forbids, none is more truthful in saying yes and no."

104: The *Prajnā Pāramitā Hridaya Sūtra*, "the Heart of Perfect Wisdom", is a celebrated *Mahāyāna* Buddhist *sūtra* or manual of aphorisms.

The Path

105: "*The world is false*, Brahma *is true*": this summation of *Advaita Vedānta* is traditionally ascribed to Shankara (see editor's note for "The Koran and the *Sunnah*", p. 52).

"*All things are* Ātmā": "*Ātmā* was indeed *Brahma* in the beginning. It knew only that 'I am *Brahma*'. Therefore It became all. And whoever among the gods knew It also became That; and the same with sages and men. . . . And to this day whoever in like manner knows 'I am *Brahma*' becomes all this universe. Even the gods cannot prevail against him, for he becomes their *Ātmā*" (*Brihadāranyaka Upanishad*, 1.4.10).

106: "*All things are ephemeral save the Face of* Allāh" (*Sūrah* "The Story" [28]:88).

Note 4: *We believe the attribution to Heraclitus of the modern "actualism"* (*Aktualitäts-Theorie*) *to be mistaken*: the thought of the pre-Socratic philosopher Heraclitus of Ephesus (c. 535-475 BC) is extant in the form of fragments, some of which express *the cosmic play of the All-Possibility* in terms of a "war" between possibilities and a constant, epitomized by the proverbial fragment "All things flow" (*panta rhei*). These views have been associated with the modern "actualist" theories that deny the reality of any substance and affirm the exclusive reality of "acts" in constant becoming. Heraclitus' references to the *Logos* clearly indicate that his philosophy is not to be reduced to a *materialistic pantheism* of the kind that is implied by most "actualist" theories.

107: *The Divine Name azh-Zhāhir* ("*the Outward*") is often correlated with the Divine Name *al-Bātin* ("the Inward").

Note 5: The theology of the Jesuit paleontologist *Teilhard de Chardin* (see editor's note for "Islam", p. 21, Note 30) envisages reality as an evolutionary continuum between matter and the supreme consciousness (the "Omega point"); it is therefore unable to conceive of *the overriding discontinuity between matter and the soul*.

108: "Brahma *is not in the world*": elsewhere the author writes: "It is useless to seek to realize that 'I am *Brahma*' before understanding that 'I am not *Brahma*'; it is useless to seek to realize that '*Brahma* is my true Self' before understanding that '*Brahma* is outside me'; it is useless to seek to realize that '*Brahma* is pure Consciousness' before understanding that '*Brahma* is the almighty Creator'. It is not possible to understand that the statement 'I am not *Brahma*' is false before having understood that it is true. Likewise it is not possible to understand that the statement '*Brahma* is outside me' is not precise before having understood that it is; and likewise again it is not possible to understand that the statement '*Brahma* is the almighty Creator' contains an error before having understood that it expresses a truth" (*Spiritual Perspectives and Human Facts: A New Translation with Selected Letters*, ed. James S. Cutsinger [Bloomington, IN: World Wisdom, 2007], p. 116).

"*He* (*the delivered one, the* mukta) *is* Brahma": the Hindu *mahāvākyas*, or "great sayings", "*Ayam ātmā Brahma*" ("This Self is *Brahma*") from the *Māndūkya Upanishad* (4.4.5) and "*Aham Brahmāsmi*" ("I am *Brahma*") from the *Brihadāranyaka Upanishad* (1.4.10), enunciate the identification of the "liberated soul" (*jīvan-mukta*) with the Divine Self (*Brahma*).

According to Plato (see editor's note for "Islam", p. 19, Note 28) and other sources of *Greek gnosis*, the saying *Gnothi seauton*, or "*know thyself*", was inscribed on the Temple of Apollo in Delphi.

"*The kingdom of heaven is within you*": "And when he was demanded of the Pharisees, when the kingdom of God should come, he answered them and said, The kingdom of God cometh not with observation: Neither shall they say, Lo here! or, lo there! for, behold, the kingdom of God is within you" (Luke 17:20-21).

"*Whoso knoweth himself knoweth his Lord*" (*hadīth*).

Note 7: *Light of the world*: "I am come a light into the world, that whosoever believeth on me should not abide in darkness" (John 12:46).

If elementary belief cannot consciously and explicitly attain to total truth that is because in its own way it too limits the intelligence; it is moreover inevitably and paradoxically allied to a certain rationalism—Vishnuism shows in this respect the same phenomenon as the West: the author characterizes this convergence of monotheistic theology and Vishnuism (see editor's note for "The Koran and the *Sunnah*", p. 52) as follows: "It is precisely this spirit of alternatives, this inability to reconcile apparent antinomies on a higher plane . . . , which are common to Semitic exoterism and Hindu bhaktism" ("Dilemmas of Muslim Scholasticism" in *Christianity/Islam: Perspectives on Esoteric Ecumenism*, ed. James S. Cutsinger [Bloomington, IN: World Wisdom, 2008], p. 155). For the author, the perspective of exclusive devotional faith gives rise to rationalistic tendencies because it does not take into account the divine root of human intelligence, which it opposes to faith in *an apparent antinomy*.

Note 8: *Cartesianism* refers to the philosophy of René Descartes (1596-1650), who propounded a method based upon a systematic doubting of everything except one's own self-consciousness, as summed up in the phrase *cogito ergo sum* ("I think; therefore I am"). The French philosopher is considered one of the major figures of seventeenth-century rationalism and one of the founders of modern philosophy. In the author's view he is "the mere 'thinker' who 'gropes alone through the darkness' (Descartes) and whose pride it is to deny that there could be any knowledge which does not proceed in the same fashion" ("Orthodoxy and Intellectuality" in *Language of the Self: Essays on the Perennial Philosophy* [Bloomington, IN: World Wisdom, 1999], p. 9).

111: Note 12: *"My name is Legion", said a devil in the story of the Gadarene swine in the Gospel*: "For Jesus had commanded the evil spirit to come out of the man. Many times it had seized him, and though he was chained hand and foot and kept under guard, he had broken his chains and had been driven by the demon into solitary places. Jesus asked him, 'What is your name?' 'Legion', he replied, because many demons had gone into him" (Luke 8:30-31). This miracle occurred in the region of the Gadarene at Gadara (or Gerasa or Gergesa).

112: Note 16: *As we pointed out in* Stations of Wisdom, *in the chapter "Orthodoxy and Intellectuality"*: "Unintelligence and vice may be merely superficial, that is, to some extent accidental and so curable, just as they may be relatively 'essential' and in practice incurable; an essential lack of virtue however is incompatible with transcendent intelligence, just as a very high degree of virtue is scarcely to be found in a fundamentally unintelligent being" (*Stations of Wisdom* [Bloomington, IN: World Wisdom, 1995],

113: *"Die before* ye *die"* (*hadīth*).

114: *This knowledge cannot be reduced to the Gnosticism of history, otherwise it would be necessary to say that Ibn Arabi or Shankara were Alexandrine "gnostics"*: the author clearly distinguishes *gnosis*, or "heart-knowledge" of spiritual realities—as found in the most diverse traditions such as the Sufism of Ibn Arabi (see editor's note for "Islam", p. 6, Note 8) and the *Advaita Vedānta* of Shankara—from ancient Gnosticism, a syncretistic religion with a broadly dualistic set of doctrines particularly associated with the Egyptian city of Alexandria in the early centuries of the Christian era, hence the reference to *Alexandrine "gnostics"* and *the Greco-Oriental syncretism of later classical times.*

The term "theosophy" has *unfortunate associations* with the Theosophical Society, a syncretistic school of occultism founded by Helena Petrovna Blavatsky (1831-91) in the late nineteenth century.

115: "*God became what we are, in order that we might become what He is*": the essential teaching expressed by this Patristic formula is common to many Church Fathers, including *Irenaeus* (c. 130-c. 200), according to whom "the Son of God became the Son of man so that man, by entering into communion with the Word and thus receiving divine sonship, might become a son of God" (*Against Heresies*, 3:19).

"*God became man*", *says Saint Irenaeus*, "*because of the immensity of His love*": "The Word of God, our Lord Jesus Christ . . . did, through His immense love, become what we are, that He might bring us to be even what He is Himself" (*Against Heresies*, 5, Preface).

"*God is Love*" (1 John 4:8).

Note 22: According to *Dante* Alighieri (1265-1321), author of the *Divine Comedy*, "We have come to where I said you would see the miserable sinners *who have lost the good of the Intellect (il ben de l'intelletto)*" (*Inferno* 3:16-18).

116: "And the King shall answer and say unto them, Verily I say unto you, Inasmuch as ye have done it unto one of *the least of these* my brethren, ye *have done it unto me*" (Matt. 25:39-40).

"And *the light shineth in darkness; and the darkness comprehended it not*" (John 1:5).

Note 23: For *Shaivite Vedantists* and *Vaishnavite dualism* see editor's note for "The Koran and the *Sunnah*", p. 52.

Note 24: *A passage in the recently discovered Gospel of Thomas*: "Jesus said to his disciples: 'Compare me, and tell me whom I am like.' Simon Peter said to him: 'You are like a just messenger.' Matthew said to him: 'You are like an (especially) wise philosopher.' Thomas said to him: 'Teacher my mouth will not bear at all to say whom you are like.' Jesus said: 'I am not your teacher. For you have drunk, you have become intoxicated at the bubbling spring that I have measured out.' And he took him, (and) withdrew, (and) he said three words to him. But when Thomas came back to his companions, they asked him: 'What did Jesus say to you?' Thomas said to them: 'If I tell you one of the words he said to me, you will pick up stones and throw them at me and fire will come out of the stones (and) burn you up" (*Gospel of Thomas* 13:1-8).

117: *Wisdom after the flesh*: "In simplicity and godly sincerity, not with fleshly wisdom, but by the grace of God, we have had our conversation in the world" (2 Cor. 1:12).

For the *Pauline* doctrine of *charity*, see 1 Cor. 13.

Note 25: *The "recollection" of Plato* refers to the doctrine, notably presented in the dialogues *Phaedo* and *Meno*, according to which real knowledge is inscribed in human intelligence from eternity and needs merely to be "recollected" (*anamnesis*) though intellectual intuition.

118: For *al-īmān*, *al-islām*, and *al-ihsān*, see editor's note for "Islam", p. 3.

119: "(*Al-ihsān* is) to *worship* Allāh *as though thou didst see Him,* for *if thou dost not see Him, He nonetheless seeth thee*" (*hadīth*).

In following the example of Mary in the Gospels and not that of Martha: "Now it came to pass, as they went, that he entered into a certain village: and a certain woman named Martha received him into her house. And she had a sister called Mary, which also sat at Jesus' feet, and heard his word. But Martha was cumbered about much serving, and came to him, and said, Lord, dost thou not care that my sister hath left me to serve alone? bid her therefore that she help me. And Jesus answered and said unto her, Martha, Martha, thou art careful and troubled about many things: But one thing is needful: and Mary hath chosen that good part, which shall not be taken away from her" (Luke 10:38-42).

Note 28: For *the* hadīth *just cited*, especially as *it defines* al-islām, see editor's note for "Islam", p. 3.

122: Note 37: Nur ad-Din Abd ar-Rahman *Jami* (1414-92) is one of the most celebrated Persian Sufi poets. He is the author of several works of poetry, Sufi biographies, and a treatise of Sufism entitled *Lawā'ih* ("Flashes of Light").

123: "*I sleep, but my heart waketh*: it is the voice of my beloved that knocketh, saying, Open to me, my sister, my love, my dove, my undefiled: for my head is filled with dew, and my locks with the drops of the night" (Song of Sol. 5:2).

The *Motionless Mover*, or Unmoved Mover, is the classic expression of Aristotle (384-322 B.C.) for the divine Principle, as in the *Metaphysics*, 1072b.

"*Made in the image of God*": "God created man in His own image, in the image of God created He him; male and female created He them" (Gen. 1:27).

The author recounts the spiritual impression left upon him by *the sacramental image of the Buddha* in the following passage: "Our first encounter—intense and unforgettable—with Buddhism and the Far East took place in our child-hood before a great Japanese Buddha of gilded wood, flanked by two images of Kwannon. Suddenly faced with this vision of majesty and mystery, we might well have paraphrased Caesar by exclaiming *veni, vidi, victus sum.* We mention the above reminiscence because of the light it throws on this over-whelming embodiment of an infinite victory of the Spirit—on this amazing condensation of the Message in the image of the Messenger—represented by the sacramental statue of the Buddha" (*Treasures of Buddhism* [Bloomington, IN: World Wisdom, 1993], pp. 88-89). The author paraphrases the words of Julius Caesar on the occasion of an expeditious battle victory (*Veni, vidi, vici* ["I came, I saw, I conquered"]), while using the latter verb in the passive form, *victus sum* ("I was conquered").

124: For *Amidism*, see editor's note for "The Koran and the *Sunnah*", p. 83.

Note 42: "Enter ye in at the *strait gate*: for wide is the gate, and broad is the way, that leadeth to destruction, and many there be which go in thereat" (Matt. 7:13).

125: In a previous life as a *Bodhisattva* named Dharmakara, the future *Amida* Buddha (see editor's note for "The Koran and the *Sunnah*", p. 67, Note 63) made his *"original vow"* not to enter *Nirvāna* until he had brought all who invoked his Name into the paradise of his Pure Land.

The Ehieh asher Ehieh *of the Burning Bush in the* Torah is the Hebrew phrase for "I am that I am": "Now Moses kept the flock of Jethro his father in law, the priest of Midian: and he led the flock to the backside of the desert, and came to the mountain of God, even to Horeb. And the angel of the Lord appeared unto him in a flame of fire out of the midst of a bush: and he looked, and, behold, the bush burned with fire, and the bush was not con-sumed. And Moses said, I will now turn aside, and see this great sight, why the bush is not burnt. . . . And Moses said unto God, Behold, when I come unto the children of Israel, and shall say unto them, The God of your fathers hath sent me unto you; and they shall say to me, What is his name? what shall I say unto them? And God said unto Moses, I AM THAT I AM: and he said, Thus shalt thou say unto the children of Israel, I AM hath sent me unto you" (Exod. 3:1-3, 13-14).

Note 46: *The Names of Jesus and Mary* are among the principal *jacula-tory prayers*, or invocatory formulae, used in the Roman Catholic Church. Elsewhere the author states: "The most important practice is ejaculatory prayer—for instance, the Prayer of Jesus: *Domine Jesu Christe miserere nobis.* Or the beginning of the Lord's Prayer: *Pater noster qui es in Caelis.* Or just

Jesu-Maria" (*Prayer Fashions Man: Frithjof Schuon on the Spiritual Life*, ed. James S. Cutsinger [Bloomington, IN: World Wisdom, 2005], Appendix, No. 36, p. 207).

126: Note 48: The *Rasā'il*, or "Letters", of *Mulay al-Arabi ad-Darqawi* (see editor's note for "The Koran and the *Sunnah*", p. 82) are a collection of writings to his Sufi disciples containing practical spiritual advice.

128: Note 50: "*Blessed are they that have not seen and yet have believed*" (John 20:29).

Note 51: In *Castes et races*, the author *made incidental reference to a Hindu theory* of the *guna*s or cosmic qualities: "The Hindus attribute fire, which rises and gives light, to the ascending tendency, *sattva*; water, which is transparent and spreads horizontally, to the expansive tendency, *rajas*; and earth, which is heavy and opaque, to the descending or solidifying tendency, *tamas*" (*Castes and Races* [Pates Manor, Bedfont: Perennial Books, 1982], p. 51).

129: For *a shirt of Nessus*, see editor's note for "The Koran and the *Sunnah*", p. 65.

130: "But when thou doest alms, let not thy *left hand know what* thy *right hand doeth*" (Matt. 6:3).

131: Note 55: *Plotinus* (c. 205-270), founder of the Neoplatonic school, endeavored to synthesize the teachings of Plato and Aristotle in his monumental *Enneads*, a collection of discourses compiled by his disciple Porphyry. The second Tractate of the first *Ennead* is entitled "On Virtue" and discusses the likeness of virtues with God's nature.

132: Note 56: The *Hikam* (literally "wisdoms") of the Egyptian Sufi Ibn Ataillah al-Iskandari (1250-1309) is a well-known collection of spiritual aphorisms.

133: *Taoist "non-action"* (Chinese *wu wei*) refers to activity that stems from the Tao or Being, and does not involve individualistic motivations.

Note 58: *Thomas Aquinas* (c. 1225-74), a giant among the medieval scholastics and author of the monumental *Summa Theologica*, is considered by the Roman Catholic Church to be the greatest Christian theologian in history. He refers to the relationship between the virtues and contemplation as follows: "A thing may belong to the contemplative life in two ways, essentially or dispositively. The moral virtues do not belong to the contemplative life essentially, because the end of the contemplative life is the consideration of truth: and as the Philosopher [Aristotle] states (Ethic. ii, 4), 'knowledge', which pertains to the consideration of truth, 'has little influence on the moral virtues': wherefore he declares (Ethic. x, 8) that the moral virtues pertain to active but not to contemplative happiness. On the other hand, the moral virtues belong to the contemplative life dispositively. For the act of contemplation, wherein the contemplative life essentially consists, is hindered both by the impetuosity of the passions which withdraw the soul's intention from intelligible to sensible things, and by outward disturbances. Now the moral virtues curb the impetuosity of the passions, and quell the disturbance of outward occupations. Hence moral virtues belong dispositively to the contemplative life" (*Summa Theologica*, 179, "Of the Division of Life into Active and Contemplative", Second Article [II-II, Q. 180, Art. 2]).

134: "And, behold, one of them which were with Jesus stretched out his hand, and drew his sword, and struck a servant of the high priest's, and smote off his ear. Then said Jesus unto him, Put up again thy sword into his place: for *all they that take the sword shall perish by the sword*" (Matt. 26:51-52).

The Desert Fathers were Christian ascetics and hermits of the third, fourth, and fifth centuries who withdrew to the wilderness in Egypt, Syria, Palestine, and Arabia to lead lives of interior prayer.

Note 60: For the *Tabernacle*, see editor's note for "The Koran and the *Sunnah*", p. 37.

135: Note 63: *The hieratic Virgin at Torcello near Venice* is a mosaic of the Virgin and the Child in the Cathedral of Santa Maria Assunta ("Holy Mary of the Assumption") on the island of Torcello.

The mosque of Cordova is one of the major works of Islamic architecture in southern Spain. Originally a church built in the seventh century, it was reconstructed as a mosque by the Caliph Abd ar-Rahman, founder of the Umayyad Emirate of Cordova.

136: *Ptolemean astronomy* was based on geocentric models developed by the ancient astronomer Ptolemaeus, or Ptolemy (c. 90-c. 168). These astronomical models remained authoritative until the time of the scientific revolution of the late Renaissance.

137: *The wisdom of nature is to be found over and over again affirmed in the Koran, which insists on the "signs" of creation for "those endowed with understanding"*: "Lo! In the creation of the heavens and the earth, and the difference of night and day, and the ships which run upon the sea with that which is of use to men, and the water which God sendeth down from the sky, thereby reviving the earth after its death, and dispersing all kinds of beasts therein, and (in) the ordinance of the winds, and the clouds obedient between heaven and earth: are signs (of God's Sovereignty) for people who have sense" (*Sūrah* "The Cow" [2]:164), *passim.*

"We have made it a Koran in Arabic, that ye may be able to understand (and learn wisdom). And verily, it is in the *Mother of the Book* [*Umm al-Kitāb*], in Our Presence, high (in dignity), full of wisdom" (*Sūrah* "Gold Adornments" [43]:4). The "Mother of the Book" is often identified with the "Guarded Tablet" mentioned in the *Sūrah* "The Constellations" ([85]:22), and refers to the celestial Prototype of the Koran.

139: Note 69: *Ernst Fuhrmann* (1886-1956) was a German poet, philosopher, and photographer.

"All serious men will beware of treating of serious matters in writing": "He who thinks, then, that he has left behind him any art in writing, and he who receives it in the belief that anything in writing will be clear and certain, would be an utterly simple person, and in truth ignorant of the prophecy of Ammon, if he thinks written words are of any use except to remind him who knows the matter about which they are written. . . . Writing, Phaedrus, has this strange quality, and is very like painting; for the creatures of painting stand like living beings, but if one asks them a question, they preserve a solemn silence. And so it is with written words; you might think they spoke as if they had intelligence, but if you question them, wishing to know about their sayings, they always say only one and the same thing" (*Phaedrus* 275c-d).

140: *Sufism is "sincerity of faith" and this sincerity . . . has absolutely nothing in common with the modern cult of sincerity*: for a further development of this distinction, see the author's chapter "Sincerity: What it Is and what it Is Not" in *Esoterism as Principle and as Way* (Bedfont, Middlesex: Perennial Books, 1981), pp. 123-28.

Note 69: Joseph Epes *Brown* (1920-2000) was an expert on the religion of the North American Indians, particularly those of the Plains. In 1947 he spent a year with the Lakota holy man, Black Elk (Hehaka Sapa), and recorded the medicine man's account of the Lakota beliefs and practices, which were later published as *The Sacred Pipe: Black Elk's Account of the Seven Rites of the Oglala Sioux* (Norman: University of Oklahoma Press, 1953).

141: *An ancient and well-known formula* could refer, among others, to Irenaeus, who taught that "the Son of God became the Son of man so that man, by entering into communion with the Word and thus receiving divine sonship, might become a son of God" (*Against Heresies*, 3:19); or to Athanasius (c. 296-373), who wrote, "The Son of God became man in order that we might become God" (*On the Incarnation*, 54:3); the essential teaching is common to many Church Fathers.

Note 71: *The Bible says of Abraham that God ascribed his faith to righteousness*: "And he brought him forth abroad, and said, Look now toward heaven, and tell the stars, if thou be able to number them: and he said unto him, So shall thy seed be. And he believed in the Lord; and he counted it to him for righteousness" (Gen. 15:5-6).

Note 72: *The doctrine of the Trinitarian "relationships"* could refer, among others, to Gregory Nazianzus (c. 329-c. 389), a Byzantine archbishop and theologian who spoke of the three Persons of the Trinity as "substantial relationships": "Father is not a name either of an essence or of an action . . . it is the name of the relation in which the Father stands to the Son, and the Son to the Father. For as with us these names make known a genuine and intimate relation, so, in the case before us too, they denote an identity of nature between Him that is begotten and Him that begets" (*Oration*, 29:16).

142: *Protestantism, with its insistence on "the Book" and free will and its rejection both of a sacramental priesthood and of the celibacy of priests, is the most massive manifestation of this nostalgia, although in an extra-traditional and modern mode and in a purely "typological" sense*: some of the positive aspirations expressed by Protestantism have been expanded upon and reinforced in the author's later writings, particularly in such chapters as "The Question of Protestantism" in *Christianity/Islam: Perspectives on Esoteric Ecumenism* (Bloomington, IN: World Wisdom, 1985, 2008) and "Christian Divergences" in *In the Face of the Absolute* (Bloomington, IN: World Wisdom, 1989, 1994). In these later works the author acknowledges more fully the spiritual legitimacy of Protestantism as a Christian possibility carrying profound Biblical and spiritual values, albeit not on the same level as Catholicism and Orthodoxy. The "modern" character assigned by the author to Protestantism stems from a consideration of Catholicism and Orthodoxy as the ancient repositories of the Christian tradition, given that the crystallization of their dogmatic and spiritual forms preceded modern history. In other words, sixteenth century Protestantism is "modern" in relation to the Patristic and Scholastic periods. Consequently, the characterization of Protestantism in this passage, although less positive than some of the author's reflections in later works, is neither pejorative nor exclusive of a seminal recognition of the genuine spiritual possibilities of the Lutheran Reformation. This point is reinforced by the author's distinction, in Note 75, between the positive "typology" of Protestantism and its extrinsically anti-Catholic aspect, the latter allowing for a characterization of Protestantism as "extra-traditional" in so far as it relies solely on scripture and rejects the ecclesial and theological "tradition" of Christianity. This is Luther's rallying call of *sola Scriptura* or "Scripture alone" ("The Question of Protestantism", pp. 50-51). Finally it is important to note that the author clearly differentiates between "Lutheranism, Calvinism, and 'High Church' Anglicanism" ("Christian Divergences", p. 135), on the one hand, and "liberal Protestantism or just any sect", on the other hand, in asserting that the former "incontestably manifests a Christian possibility—a limited one, no doubt, and excessive through certain of its features, but not intrinsically illegitimate, and therefore representative of certain theological, moral, and even mystical values" ("The Question of Protestantism", p. 23).

Certain of the doctrinal statements of the French theologian *Amalric of Bena* (d. c. 1204-1207), such as the idea that everything is essentially God, and the *Apocatastasis* or ultimate reintegration of all things in God, were declared heretical by Pope Innocent III.

Joachim of Fiore (c. 1135-1202), an Italian theologian and mystic, taught a theory of three reigns or ages, corresponding to the three Persons of the Trinity; these are characterized respectively by obedience to the Law ("the age of the Father"), the Incarnation ("the age of the Son"), and the inspiration by the Holy Spirit ("the age of the Spirit").

The Montanists, originally called Phrygians, were a Christian movement *of the second century* founded by Montanus and the two prophetesses, Maximilla and Priscilla; their most famous adherent was Tertullian. The ecstatic and prophetic nature of the movement represented a challenge to the fledgling magisterium Church, whence the eventual excommunication of Montanus and his followers.

The foretelling of the Paraclete in Saint John's Gospel: "And I will pray the Father, and he shall give you another Comforter, that he may abide with you for ever; . . . But the Comforter, which is the Holy Ghost, whom the Father will send in my name, he shall teach you all things, and bring all things to your remembrance, whatsoever I have said unto you" (John 14:16, 26).

The *Bektāshīyah* is an Islamic mystical movement that issued from Shiite Islam in the thirteenth century. It incorporated various Sufi and Shiite ideas and practices, and spread throughout Turkey and the Balkans. In the twentieth century the *Bektāshī* movement has tended to become more distinct from mainstream Islam and Sufism.

Note 74: "I am the *light of the world*; he that followeth me shall not walk in darkness, but shall have the light of life" (John 8:12).

143: "And *the Word* was *made flesh,* and dwelt among us" (John 1:14).

The injunction to love God with the whole of our being and to love our neighbor as ourself. "Thou shalt love the Lord thy God with all thy heart, and with all thy soul, and with all thy mind. This is the first and great commandment. And the second is like unto it: Thou shalt love thy neighbor as thyself. On these two commandments hang all the law and the prophets" (Matt. 22:37-40), *passim.*

Note 77: "Jesus saith unto him, *I am the Way, the Truth, and the Life:* no man cometh unto the Father, but by me" (John 14:6).

144: Note 80: The passage from the *Dīwān* of *al-Hallaj* (see editor's note for "Islam", p. 7) has been rendered into verse (in Martin Lings, *Sufi Poems: A Mediaeval Anthology* [Cambridge, UK: The Islamic Texts Society, 2004], p. 34) as follows:

> Earnest for Truth, I thought on the religions:
> They are, I found, one root with many a branch.
> Therefore impose on no man a religion,
> Lest it should bar him from the firm-set root.
> Let the root claim him, a root wherein all heights
> And meanings are made clear, for him to grasp.

For Louis *Massignon*, see editor's note for "Islam", p. 8, Note 10.

Enoch, Melchizedek, and Elias are three major figures from the Old Testament. Enoch (Idris in Islam), the son of Seth and the great grandson of Adam, was taken directly to Heaven by God: "And Enoch walked with God, and he was not, for God took him" (Gen. 5:24; cf. Heb. 11:5); Melchizedek was a king and priest who blessed Abraham: "For this Melchizedek, king of Salem, priest of the most high God . . . to whom also Abraham gave a tenth part of all; first being by interpretation King of righteousness, and after that also King of Salem, which is, King of peace; without father, without mother, without descent, having neither beginning of days, nor end of life; but made like unto the Son of God; abideth a priest continually" (Heb. 7:1-3); Elias, or Elijah (Ilyas in Islam), was a biblical prophet of the ninth century B.C. who ascended to heaven in a chariot: "And it came to pass, as they still went on, and talked, that, behold, there appeared a chariot of fire, and horses of fire, and parted them both asunder; and Elijah went up by a whirlwind into heaven" (2 Kings 2:11). According to certain Jewish traditions, he is prophesied to return before the end of times to reconcile divergent religious opinions (Mal. 4:5; cf. Matt. 16:14, Mark 6:15, Luke 9:8).

"And John answered him, saying, Master, we saw one casting out devils in thy name, and he followeth not us: and we forbad him, because he followeth not us. But Jesus said, Forbid him not: for there is no man which shall do a miracle in my name, that can lightly speak evil of me. For *he that is not against us* is on our part" (Mark 9:38-40).

"And when Jesus was entered into *Capernaum*, there came unto him a *centurion*, beseeching him, and saying, Lord, my servant lieth at home sick of the palsy, grievously tormented. And Jesus saith unto him, I will come and heal him. The centurion answered and said, Lord, I am not worthy that thou shouldest come under my roof: but speak the word only, and my servant shall be healed. For I am a man under authority, having soldiers under me: and I say to this man, Go, and he goeth; and to another, Come, and he cometh; and to my servant, Do this, and he doeth it. When Jesus heard it, he marveled, and said to them that followed, Verily I say unto you, I have not found so great faith, no, not in Israel" (Matt. 8:5-10).

For *al-Khidr*, see editor's note for "The Koran and the *Sunnah*", p. 72.

148: *Such ideas as that of the "relatively absolute" or of the "metaphysical transparency" of phenomena*: elsewhere the author defines the crucial concept of the *"relatively absolute"* as follows: "[The personal God] is the Absolute reflected in the limiting and diversifying mirror of *Māyā*; He is *Īshvara*, the creating, destroying, saving, and punishing Principle and 'relatively absolute' prototype of all perfections. This personal and all-powerful God is perfectly real in Himself, and even more so in relation to the world and man; but He nonetheless pertains to *Māyā* compared with the Absolute properly so called" (*Esoterism as Principle and as Way* [Bedfont, Middlesex: Perennial Books, 1981], p. 21). For the *"metaphysical transparency" of phenomena*, see editor's note for "Islam", p. 16.

150: Note 87: *In* De l'Unité transcendante des religions *, we pointed out a characteristic of this kind in connection with the* Risālat al-Ahadīyah (*"Treatise on Unity"*) *attributed rightly or wrongly to Ibn Arabi*: "To return, however, to the purely principial consideration of the relationship between form and spirit, we cannot do better than quote, by way of example, the following passage from the *Treatise on Unity* (*Risālat al-Ahadīyah*) by Muhyi ad-Din Ibn Arabi, which clearly illustrates the esoteric function of 'shattering the form in the name of the spirit': 'Most initiates say that the knowledge of *Allāh* follows upon the extinction of existence (*fanā' al-wujūd*) and the extinction of this extinction (*fanā' al-fanā'*); but this opinion is entirely false. . . . Knowledge does not demand the extinction of existence [of the ego] or the extinction of this extinction; for things have no existence, and that which does not exist cannot cease to exist.' Now the fundamental ideas which Ibn Arabi rejects, moreover with a purely speculative or 'methodic' intention, are still accepted even by those who consider Ibn Arabi as the greatest of spiritual masters; and in an analogous manner all exoteric forms are 'transcended' or 'shattered', and therefore in a certain sense 'denied' by esoterism, which is nevertheless the first to recognize the perfect legitimacy of every form of Revelation, being indeed alone competent to recognize this legitimacy" (*The Transcendent Unity of Religions* [Wheaton, IL: Quest Books, 1984], pp. 31-32).

151: "*Heaven and earth shall pass away, but my words shall not pass away*" (Matt. 24:35).

154: Man—"*image of God*": "And God said, Let us make man in our image, after our likeness" (Gen. 1:26).

155: "Take therefore no thought *for the morrow*: for the morrow shall take thought for the things of itself. Sufficient unto the day is the evil thereof" (Matt. 6:34).

Note 93: For Ahmad *al-Alawi*, see editor's note for "The Koran and the *Sunnah*", p. 51, Note 37.

156: *The Bible also teaches, in both the Old and the New Testaments, that we must "love" God with all our faculties*: "And thou shalt love the Lord thy God with all thine heart, and with all thy soul, and with all thy might" (Deut. 6:5). "And now, Israel, what doth the Lord thy God require of thee, but to fear the Lord thy God, to walk in all His ways, and to love Him, and to serve the Lord thy God with all thy heart and with all thy soul" (Deut. 10:12). "Jesus said unto him, Thou shalt love the Lord thy God with all thy heart, and with all thy soul, and with all thy mind" (Matt. 22:37). "And thou shalt love the Lord thy God with all thy heart, and with all thy soul, and with all thy mind, and with all thy strength: this is the first commandment" (Mark 12:30). "And he answering said, Thou shalt love the Lord thy God with all thy heart, and with all thy soul, and with all thy strength, and with all thy mind; and thy neighbor as thyself" (Luke 10:27).

Note 94: "*Sin against the Holy Spirit*": "All manner of sin and blasphemy shall be forgiven unto men: but the blasphemy against the Holy Ghost shall not be forgiven unto men" (Matt. 12:31; cf. Mark 3:29, Luke 12:10).

Note 95: *As the* Bhagavad Gītā *clearly teaches, God here requires only effort and does not punish for lack of success*: "Arjuna spoke: one who is uncontrolled though he has faith, whose mind has fallen away from yoga, who does not attain perfection in yoga, which way, Krishna, does he go? Is he not lost like a disappearing cloud, having fallen from both worlds, having no solid ground, O Krishna, confused on the path of *Brahman?* . . . The Blessed Lord spoke: Arjuna, neither here on earth nor in heaven above is there found destruction of him; none who does good goes to misfortune, my son" (6:37-40).

159: "*Makes itself what we are in order to make us what it is*": Irenaeus taught that "the Son of God became the Son of man so that man, by entering into communion with the Word and thus receiving divine sonship, might become a son of God" (*Against Heresies*, 3:19); and Athanasius (c. 296-373) wrote, "The Son of God became man in order that we might become God" (*On the Incarnation*, 54:3); the essential teaching is common to many Church Fathers.

Appendix

163: Selection 1: "The Book of Keys", No. 576, "The Enigma of the *Basmalah*".

"*Call Him (God) Allāh or call (Him) Rahmān.* . .": "Call upon *Allāh* or call upon *ar-Rahmān*; to Him belong the most beautiful Names" (*Sūrah* "The Cave" [18]:110).

"When God finished the creation, He wrote in His presence above His Throne, '*My Clemency hath preceded My Wrath*'" (*hadīth*).

"And when those who believe in Our revelations come unto thee, say: Peace be unto you! *Your Lord hath prescribed for Himself clemency*, that whoso of you doeth evil through ignorance and repenteth afterward thereof and doeth right, (for him) lo! He is Forgiving, Merciful" (*Sūrah* "The Cattle" [6]:54).

"And ordain for us in this world that which is good, and in the Hereafter (that which is good), Lo! We [Moses and seventy men of his people] have turned unto Thee. He (God) said: I smite with My punishment whom I will, and *My Mercy embraceth all things*, therefore I shall ordain it for those who ward off (evil) and pay the poor-due, and those who believe Our revelations" (*Sūrah* "The Elevated Places" [7]:156).

"*Made in the image of God*": "God created man in His own image, in the image of God created He him; male and female created He them" (Gen. 1:27).

164: Selection 2: "The Book of Keys", No. 626, "Homage to the *Logos*".

"Recite that which hath been inspired in thee of the Scripture, and establish worship. Lo! worship preserveth from lewdness and iniquity, but verily remembrance of God is greatest (*wa ladhikru 'Llāhi akbar*)" (*Sūrah* "The Spider" [29]:45).

165: Selection 3: Letter of January 17, 1981.

Selection 4: "The Book of Keys", No. 1071, "Meaning of Ablution".

165-66: *"But thou, when thou prayest, enter into thy closet, and when thou hast shut thy door, pray to thy Father which is in secret; and thy Father which seeth in secret shall reward thee openly"* (Matt. 6:6).

166: *"The Supreme Principle is Reality, the world is merely appearance"* (Brahma satyam, jagan mithyā) is a summation of *Advaita Vedānta* traditionally ascribed to Shankara (see editor's note for "The Koran and the *Sunnah*", p. 52).

"There is no lustral water like unto Knowledge" is a traditional Hindu teaching often quoted by the author, based in one of its formulations on the *Bhagavad Gītā*, 4:38.

Selection 5: Letter of March 10, 1973.

The *Hanafite, Shafite, Malikite, or Hanbalite* schools of Islamic jurisprudence are named after their respective founders: Abu Hanifah (see editor's note for "The Koran and the *Sunnah*", p. 38), Muhammad Ibn Idris ash-Shafii (767-820), Malik Ibn Anas (c. 711-795), and Ahmad Ibn Hanbal (see editor's note for "Islam", p. 14, Note 20).

Selection 6: Letter of March 10, 1973.

Mount Arafat is a hill situated east of Mecca where the Prophet gave his farewell sermon.

167: During the pilgrimage, the act of *stoning* the three "pillars" (*jamarāt*) at the city of Mina is intended as a symbolic stoning of the devil.

The hills of Safa and Marwah are two hills in Mecca between which pilgrims must run back and forth seven times, repeating Hagar's desperate search for water.

The well of *Zamzam* is the miraculous spring discovered by Hagar and her son Ishmael while they were in search of water.

Selection 7: Letter of March 18, 1954.

The Koranic phrase *Alam nashrah laka sadrak* means, "Have We not caused thy bosom to dilate?" (*Sūrah* "The Expansion" [94]:1).

168: *A Hindu divine Name with its Shakti (Sita-Ram, Radha-Krishna)*: Sita is the wife, or *shakti*, of Rama (see editor's note for "The Prophet", p. 85, p. 93, Note 17), or Ram, while Radha is the main female devotee of Krishna (see editor's note for "The Prophet", p. 85, p. 93, Note 17). The story of Sita and Rama is told in the epic *Rāmāyana*, while that of Krishna and Radha is recounted in the *Srīmad Bhāgavatam*.

Selection 8: Letter of 5 January, 1957.

Selection 9: Letter of 17 January, 1980.

The *Caliph Umar* ibn al-Khattab (see editor's note for "The Prophet", p. 100, Note 36) reigned from 634-644 and was known for his justice toward Muslims and non-Muslims alike.

Saladin, or Salah ad-Din Yusuf ibn Ayyub (c. 1138-93) was a Kurdish sultan and military general who gained control of Jerusalem from the Crusaders in 1187, among whom he gained a reputation for chivalry and magnanimity.

Emir Abd al-Qadir al-Jazairi (1808-83) was a Muslim leader, scholar, and mystic who led the Algerian rebellion against the French colonizers. After being taken prisoner by the French, he befriended French military leaders and churchmen, and became renowned for his courage and generosity. In 1860, while residing in Damascus after his liberation in 1852, he saved a large group of Christians from massacre during an attack by the Druze.

Imam *Shamil* (1797-1871) was a political, military, and religious leader from Dagestan and Chechnya who led the anti-Russian resistance during the Caucasian War. His bravery and magnanimity earned him the respect of Tsar Alexander II and his generals.

169: Selection 10: Letter of September 3, 1983.

Selection 11: Letter of November 8, 1985.

170: Selection 12: Letter of May 8, 1942.

In this instance the author uses the phrase "*the religious point of view*" to refer to the exoteric point of view in general.

171: Selection 13: Letter of April 4, 1956.

172: Selection 14: Letter of September 9, 1970.

Selection 15: Letter of October 31, 1972.

Selection 16: Letter of February 7, 1980.

173: Selection 17: "The Book of Keys", No. 1036, "Inwardness and Equilibrium".

"I was a hidden treasure and I wished to be known, hence I created the world" (*hadīth qudsī*).

174: *"The righteous man sins seven times a day"*: "For a just man falleth seven times, and riseth up again: but the wicked shall fall into mischief" (Prov. 24:16).

Selection 18: Letter of November 21, 1975.

175: Selection 19: Letter of November 18, 1984.

"For when we were in the *flesh*, the motions of sin, which were by the law, did work in our members to bring forth fruit unto death. But now we are delivered from the law, that being dead wherein we were held; that we should serve in newness of *spirit*, and not in the oldness of the letter" (Rom. 7:5-6). "There is therefore now no condemnation to them which are in Christ Jesus, who walk not after the *flesh*, but after the *Spirit*" (Rom. 8:1).

"He hath no associate" (*Sūrah* "Cattle" [6]:164), *passim.*

In the writings of René *Guénon* (see editor's note for "The Koran and the Sunnah", p. 69, Note 65) the term "religion" is reserved for the exoterism of the Abrahamic traditions, where salvation is understood to consist in the preservation or perpetuation of the human individual rather than in final deliverance from individuality as such.

The Three Dimensions of Sufism

177: "Les Trois Dimensions Du Soufisme", unpublished in French, first appeared in English in *Studies in Comparative Religion*, Winter 1976, Vol. 10, No. 1, pp. 5-13.

178: For *Plato*, see editor's note for "Islam", p. 19, Note 28.

For *Plotinus*, see editor's note for "The Path", p. 131, Note 55.

179: *"God is love"* (1 John 4:8).

For *Ibn Arabi*, see editor's note for "Islam", p. 6, Note 8.

179-80: *God is essentially "Majesty"* (Jalāl) *and "Beauty"* (Jamāl), *or "Majesty" and "Benevolence"* (Ikrām) *according to the Koran:* "Blessed be the name of thy Lord, majestic and benevolent (*dhī'l jalāli wa'l ikrām*)!" (*Sūrah* "The Merciful" [55]:78), *passim*.

180: *The Koranic image of the Garden:* "But for him who feareth the standing before his Lord there are two gardens. . . . Of spreading branches. . . . Wherein are two fountains flowing. . . . Wherein is every kind of fruit in pairs. . . . Reclining upon couches lined with silk brocade, the fruit of both the gardens near to hand. . . . Therein are those of modest gaze, whom neither man nor jinn will have touched before them. . . . (In beauty) like the jacinth and the coral-stone. . . . And beside them are two other gardens, . . . Dark green with foliage. . . . Wherein are two abundant springs. . . . Wherein is fruit, the date-palm and pomegranate. . . . Wherein (are found) the good and beautiful—. . . . Fair ones, close-guarded in pavilions. . . . Whom neither man nor jinn will have touched before them. . . . Reclining on green cushions and fair carpets" (*Sūrah* "The Merciful" [55]:46-68), *passim*.

182: *"The righteous man sins seven times a day"*: "For a just man falleth seven times, and riseth up again: but the wicked shall fall into mischief" (Prov. 24:16).

Note 2: Ancient *Gnostic terminology* distinguishes between three types of human beings: the hylic (*hylikos*) or somatic (*somatikos*), who is centered upon matter (*hyle*) or the body (*soma*); the psychic (*psychikos*), who is centered upon the soul (*psyche*); and the pneumatic (*pneumatikos*), who is centered upon the spirit (*pneuma*).

183: *According to the Koranic doctrine, love of God depends, practically speaking, on the love of the Messenger.* "Say, (O Muhammad, to mankind): If ye love God, follow me; God will love you and forgive you your sins. God is Forgiving, Merciful" (*Sūrah* "Family of Imran" [3]:31).

Note 4: The author's present work *Comprendre l'Islam* was first translated into English as *Understanding Islam* (London: Allen & Unwin/New York: Roy Publishers) in 1963; its third *chapter* deals with the subject of the *Prophet*.

184: "The Prophet said: 'No one will enter Paradise who has an atom's weight of pride in his heart.' A man said, 'What if a man likes his clothes to look good and his shoes to look good?' He said, *'Allāh is beautiful and He loves beauty.* Pride means denying the truth and looking down on people'" (*hadīth*).

"*Love God, and do what thou wilt*": in Homily 7 on the first Epistle of John, 8, *Augustine* (see editor's note for "The Koran and the *Sunnah*", p. 35, Note 5) says: "Once for all, then, a short precept is given you: Love God, and do what you will: whether you hold your peace, through love hold your peace; whether you cry out, through love cry out; whether you correct, through love correct; whether you spare, through love do you spare: let the root of love be within, of this root can nothing spring but what is good."

185: The Sufi rosary or *wird* is typically comprised of three formulas, the third of which is a repetition of the *Shahādah*, which asserts *the dimension of* "*Knowledge*" through discernment between the Real and the illusory.

Meister *Eckhart* (see editor's note for "Islam", p. 4) taught that *aliquid est in anima quod est* increatus et increabile . . . *et hoc est Intellectus*: "There is something in the soul that is uncreated and uncreatable . . . and this is the Intellect" (The Bull *In agro dominico* [1329]).

186: According to the Athanasian Creed, Christ is "*true* God and *true man*, of a reasonable soul and body, equal to the Father as touching his Godhead, and inferior to the Father as touching his manhood".

GLOSSARY OF FOREIGN TERMS AND PHRASES

'*Abd* (Arabic): literally "servant" or "slave"; as used in Islam, the servant or worshiper of God in His aspect of *Rabb* or "Lord".

Advaita (Sanskrit): "non-dualist" interpretation of the *Vedānta*; Hindu doctrine according to which the seeming multiplicity of things is the product of ignorance, the only true reality being *Brahma*, the One, the Absolute, the Infinite, which is the unchanging ground of appearance.

Ahādīth (Arabic): see *hadīth*.

Ahl al-Kitāb (Arabic): "the People of the Book"; those whom the Koran cites as having received valid revealed scriptures; applied to the Jews and the Christians, but in certain cases also to the Zoroastrians, Hindus, and Buddhists.

Allāhu akbar (Arabic): a traditional Muslim formula—the *takbīr* or "magnification"—asserting that "God is greater" than anything else and that He is hence "the greatest".

Allāhu karīm (Arabic): "God is generous".

Ānanda (Sanskrit): "bliss, beatitude, joy"; one of the three essential aspects of *Apara-Brahma*, together with *Sat*, "being", and *Chit*, "consciousness".

Anima (Latin): soul; see *corpus* and *spiritus*.

Apara-Brahma (Sanskrit): the "non-supreme" or penultimate *Brahma*, also called *Brahma saguna*; in the author's teaching, the "relative Absolute"; see *para-Brahma*.

A posteriori (Latin): literally, "from after"; proceeding from effect to cause or from experience to principle.

A priori (Latin): literally, "from before"; proceeding from cause to effect or from principle to experience.

Ascesis (Greek): "exercise, practice, training", as of an athlete; a regimen of self-denial, especially one involving fasting, prostrations, and other bodily disciplines.

Asura (Sanskrit): wicked deity, titan, evil spirit, demon; contrasted with the *deva*s or gods. Hindu and Buddhist mythology represents the *asura*s as rebelling against the *deva*s, symbolizing the centrifugal and subversive tendencies within manifestation.

Ātmā or *Ātman* (Sanskrit): the real or true "Self", underlying all things; in the perspective of *Advaita Vedānta*, identical with *Brahma*.

Avatāra (Sanskrit): a divine "descent"; the incarnation or manifestation of God, especially of Vishnu in the Hindu tradition.

A'yān thābitah (Arabic): the "immutable essences" or "permanent entities"; the archetypal realities contained in the Divine Essence.

Āyāt (Arabic, singular *āya*): "signs, marks"; in Islam, signs of God's power, especially miracles; verses of the Koran, the greatest miracle.

Barakah (Arabic): "blessing", grace; in Islam, a spiritual influence or energy emanating originally from God, but often attached to sacred objects and spiritual persons.

Basmalah (Arabic): traditional Muslim formula of blessing, found at the beginning of all but one of the *sūrah*s of the Koran, consisting of the words *Bismi 'Llāhi 'r-Rahmāni 'r-Rahīm*, "In the Name of God, the Beneficent (*Rahmān*), the Merciful (*Rahīm*)".

Belle époque (French): "beautiful era"; the period of European history from the late nineteenth-century to the First World War.

Bhakta (Sanskrit): a follower of the spiritual path of *bhakti*; a person whose relationship with God is based primarily on adoration and love.

Bhakti or *bhakti-mārga* (Sanskrit): the spiritual "path" (*mārga*) of "love" (*bhakti*) and devotion; see *jnāna* and *karma*.

Bodhisattva (Sanskrit): literally, "enlightenment-being"; in *Theravāda* Buddhism, one who is on the way to enlightenment; in *Mahāyāna* Buddhism, one who postpones his own final enlightenment and entry into *Nirvāna* in order to aid all other sentient beings in their quest for Buddhahood.

Brahma or *Brahman* (Sanskrit): the Supreme Reality, the Absolute.

Buddhi (Sanskrit): "Intellect"; the highest faculty of knowledge, distinct from *manas*, that is, mind or reason.

Coagula (Latin): "coagulate, join together"; an alchemical process through which the animic substance is "fixed" into a new state following the process of dissolution; see *solve*.

Chit (Sanskrit): "consciousness"; one of the three essential aspects of *Apara-Brahma*, together with *Sat*, "being", and *Ānanda*, "bliss, beatitude, joy".

Corpus (Latin): body; see *anima* and *spiritus*.

Creatio ex nihilo (Latin): literally "creation out of nothing"; the doctrine that God Himself is the sufficient cause of the universe, needing nothing else; often set in contrast to emanationist cosmogonies.

Dār as-Salām (Arabic): literally, "the Abode of Peace"; those countries where Muslims can practice their religion freely; by extension, countries where Muslims are a majority.

Deo juvante (Latin): literally, "God helping"; "with God's help".

Dharma (Sanskrit): in Hinduism, the underlying "law" or "order" of the cosmos as expressed in sacred rites and in actions appropriate to various social relationships and human vocations; in Buddhism, the practice and realization of Truth.

Dharmas (Sanskrit): the constituent factors—both physical and mental—of the phenomenal world.

Dhāt (Arabic): the supra-personal Divine Essence.

Dhikr (Arabic): "remembrance" of God, based upon the repeated invocation of His Name; central to Sufi practice, where the remembrance is often supported by the single word *Allāh*.

Fantasia (Italian): an equestrian charge accompanied by firing of gunpowder guns; in the Maghreb, traditionally associated with festivals or weddings.

Faqīr (Arabic, plural *fuqarā*): literally, the "poor one"; in Sufism, a follower of the spiritual Path, whose "indigence" or "poverty" (*faqr*) testifies to complete dependence on God and a desire to be filled by Him alone.

Faqr (Arabic): "indigence, spiritual poverty"; see *faqīr*.

Fātihah (Arabic): the "opening" *sūrah*, or chapter, of the Koran, recited in the daily prayers of all Muslims.

Festina lente (Latin): "make haste slowly".

Fitrah (Arabic): in Islam, the natural predisposition of man, as created by God, to act in accordance with the will of Heaven; the original uprightness of humanity (cf. *Sūrah* "The Romans" [30]:30); in the author's usage, the primordial norm or "nature of things".

Gehenna (Hebrew): in Judaism and Christianity, a place of suffering and purification after death.

Ghusl (Arabic): the "greater ablution"; the washing of the entire body, which confers a state of ritual purity; see *wudhū*.

Gnosis (Greek): "knowledge"; spiritual insight, principial comprehension, divine wisdom.

Gottheit (German): Divinity, Divine Essence, Beyond-Being; the "Godhead" or supra-personal Divinity; distinguished from *Gott* ("God"), Being, or the personal Divinity.

Hadīth (Arabic, plural *ahādīth*): "saying, narrative"; an account of the words or deeds of the Prophet Muhammad, transmitted through a traditional chain of known intermediaries.

Hadīth qudsī (Arabic): "divine, holy narrative"; an extra-Koranic saying in which God Himself speaks through the mouth of the Prophet.

Hamdu li 'Llāh (Arabic): "praise be to God".

Hanīf (Arabic): "pure", "upright"; those who, by the purity and uprightness of their nature, practiced the pristine monotheism of Abraham before the coming of Islam, not succumbing to the prevailing polytheism in the Arabian Peninsula.

Haqīqah (Arabic): "truth, reality"; in Sufism, esoteric or metaphysical knowledge of the supremely Real; also the essential reality of a thing.

Huwa (Arabic): literally, "He"; the Divine Self; the exclusive Divine Essence inasmuch as it transcends the servant-Lord dichotomy.

Huwa 'Llāh (Arabic): literally, "He is God"; the exclusive Divine Self ("He") is also the inclusive Divine Principle ("God").

Hylikos (Greek): a person in whom the element matter (*hyle*) predominates over the spirit and the soul (cf. 1 Thess. 5:23; 1 Cor. 2:14-15); see *pneumatikos*, *psychikos*, and *somatikos*.

Hypostasis (Greek, plural *hypostases*): literally, "substance"; the divine determination or transcendent form of a metaphysical reality, understood to be eternally distinct from all other such forms; in Christian theology, a technical term for one of the three Persons of the Trinity.

Ihsān (Arabic): "excellence, perfection"; in Islam, virtuous or beautiful action; spiritual excellence.

Īmān (Arabic): "faith, trust, belief"; in Islam, faith and trust in God and in the Prophet Muhammad, hence in the content of his message.

Increatus et increabile (Latin): "uncreated and uncreatable"; transcending the domain of time and relativity, as the Absolute or its prolongations.

In divinis (Latin): literally, "in or among divine things"; within the divine Principle; the plural form is used insofar as the Principle comprises both *Para-Brahma*, Beyond-Being or the Absolute, and *Apara-Brahma*, Being or the relative Absolute.

In shā'a 'Llāh (Arabic): "if God wills it".

Īshvara (Sanskrit): literally, "possessing power", hence master; God understood as a personal being, as Creator and Lord.

Islām (Arabic): "submission, peace"; in Islam, the peace that comes from submission or surrender to God.

Ithbāt (Arabic): literally, "affirmation"; in Islam, used in reference to the second part of the first *Shahādah*, consisting of the words *illā 'Llāh*, "but [except] God"; see *nafy*.

Jalwah (Arabic): spiritual radiation or exteriorization; see *khalwah*.

Jamarāt (Arabic, singular *jamrah*): stone pillars; in Islam, during the greater pilgrimage (*hajj*) pilgrims are required to cast stones at three pillars, symbolizing Satan.

Japa-yoga (Sanskrit): method of "union" or "unification" (*yoga*) based upon the "repetition" (*japa*) of a *mantra* or sacred formula, often containing one of the Names of God.

Jīvan-mukta (Sanskrit): one who is "liberated" while still in this "life"; a person who has attained a state of spiritual perfection or self-realization before death; in contrast to *videha-mukta*, one who is liberated at the moment of death; see *krama-mukti*.

Jnāna or *jnāna-mārga* (Sanskrit): the spiritual "path" (*mārga*) of "knowledge" (*jnāna*) and intellection; see *bhakti* and *karma*.

Jnānin (Sanskrit): a follower of the path of *jnāna*; a person whose relationship with God is based primarily on sapiential knowledge or *gnosis*.

Kāfir (Arabic, plural *kāfirūn*): literally, one who "covers" (*kufr*) or "conceals"; in Islam, the person who deliberately covers the truth and is thus in fundamental opposition to God and in danger of damnation.

Karma, karma-mārga, karma-yoga (Sanskrit): the spiritual "path" (*mārga*) or method of "union" (*yoga*) based upon right "action, work" (*karma*); see *bhakti* and *jnāna*.

Khalwah (Arabic): spiritual retreat or interiorization; see *jalwah*.

Krama-mukti (Sanskrit): "deferred" or "gradual liberation"; liberation obtained by intermediate stages through various posthumous states; see *jīvan-mukta*.

Kufr (Arabic): unbelief in God; see *kāfir*.

Lā ilāha illā 'Llāh (Arabic): "There is no god but God"; see *Shahādah*.

Logos (Greek): "word, reason"; in Christian theology, the divine, uncreated Word of God (cf. John 1:1); the transcendent Principle of creation and revelation; in its created aspect, the various prophets insofar as they transmit the Word of God to humanity.

Madhhab (Arabic): literally "direction"; in Sunni Islam, one of the four schools of jurisprudence.

Mahabbah (Arabic): "love"; in Sufism, the spiritual way based upon love and devotion, analogous to the Hindu *bhakti mārga*; see *makhafah* and *ma'rifah*.

Mahāyāna (Sanskrit): "great vehicle"; the form of Buddhism, including such traditions as Zen and *Jōdo-Shinshū*, or Pure Land, which regards itself as the fullest or most adequate expression of the Buddha's teaching; distinguished by the idea that *Nirvāna* is not other than *samsāra* truly seen as it is; see *Theravāda*.

Makhafah (Arabic): "fear"; in Sufism, the spiritual way based upon fear and works, analogous to the Hindu *karma mārga*; see *mahabbah* and *ma'rifah*.

Malāmatiyah (Arabic): "men of blame"; a category of Sufis that accentuated self-reproach and endeavored to conceal virtue behind a façade of ignoble action.

Mantra or *mantram* (Sanskrit): "instrument of thought"; a word or phrase of divine origin, often including a Name of God, repeated by those initiated into its proper use as a means of salvation or liberation; see *japa-yoga*.

Maqām (Arabic): "place", "station"; in Sufism, the permanent spiritual degree or station reached by a practitioner of the path; contrasted with a passing spiritual state (*hāl*).

Maqām ilāhī (Arabic): "divine place" or "divine station".

Maʿrifah (Arabic): "knowledge"; in Sufism, the spiritual way based upon knowledge or *gnosis*, analogous to the Hindu *jnāna-mārga*; see *makhafah* and *mahabbah*.

Mā shāʾa ʾLlāh (Arabic): "God has willed it".

Māyā (Sanskrit): universal illusion, relativity, appearance; in *Advaita Vedānta*, the veiling or concealment of *Brahma* in the form or under the appearance of a lower, relative reality; also, as "productive power", the unveiling or manifestation of *Ātmā* as "divine art" or theophany. *Māyā* is neither real nor unreal, and ranges from the Supreme Lord to the "last blade of grass".

Mens (Latin): mind; the mental faculty associated with discursive reason.

Mihrāb (Arabic): a prayer niche in the wall of a mosque indicating the direction of Mecca.

Munāfiqūn (Arabic, singular *munāfiq*): literally, "hypocrites"; those who lack moral and spiritual conformity to the beliefs they profess; see *nifāq*.

Mushrikūn (Arabic, singular *mushrik*): literally, "associators"; "polytheists"; those who place something alongside God or who "associate" (*shirk*) a relative reality with the Absolute; see *shirk*.

Nabī al-Ummī (Arabic): "the unlettered Prophet"; see *ummī*.

Nafs al-ammārah (Arabic): "the soul that incites to evil"; contrasted with the "soul that reproaches" (*nafs al-lawwāmah*) and the "soul at peace" (*nafs al-mutmaʾinnah*).

Nafy (Arabic): literally, "negation"; in Islam, used in reference to the first part of the first *Shahādah*, consisting of the words *lā ilāha*, "there is no god"; see *ithbāt*.

Natura naturata (Latin): literally, "nature natured"; the phenomena of the physical world considered as the passive effect or production of an inward and invisible causal power; a term associated with the Dutch philosopher Spinoza; see *Natura naturans*.

Natura naturans (Latin): literally, "nature naturing"; nature as an active principle of causality that constitutes and governs the phenomena of the physical world; a term associated with the Dutch philosopher Spinoza; see *Natura naturata*.

Nifāq (Arabic): "hypocrisy"; see *munāfiqūn*.

Om or *Aum* (Sanskrit): in Hinduism, the sacred monosyllable symbolizing *Brahma* or the Absolute; the synthesis and essence of all truths and invocations; also prevalent in Buddhism as a mantric syllable.

Para-Brahma (Sanskrit): the "supreme" or ultimate *Brahma*, also called *Brahma nirguna*; the Absolute as such; see *apara-Brahma*.

Paramātmā (Sanskrit): the "supreme" or ultimate Self; see *Ātmā*.

Parsi (Persian): a member of the Zoroastrian community from the Indian subcontinent.

Philosophia perennis (Latin): "perennial philosophy".

Pneumatikos (Greek): a person in whom the element spirit (*pneuma*) predominates over the soul and the body (cf. 1 Thess. 5:23; 1 Cor. 2:14-15); see *hylikos*, *psychikos*, and *somatikos*.

Prakriti (Sanskrit): literally, "making first"; the fundamental, "feminine" substance or material cause of all things; see *Purusha*.

Psychikos (Greek): a person in whom the element soul (*psyche*) predominates over the spirit and the body (cf. 1 Thess. 5:23; 1 Cor. 2:14-15); see *hylikos*, *pneumatikos*, and *somatikos*.

Purusha (Sanskrit): literally, "man"; the informing or shaping principle of creation; the "masculine" demiurge or fashioner of the universe; see *Prakriti*.

Quod absit (Latin): literally, "which thing, let it be absent"; a wish or a command commonly used by the medieval Scholastics to call attention to an idea that is absurdly inconsistent with accepted principles.

Rahīm (Arabic): "the infinitely Merciful"; in Islam, one of the Names of God; see *Basmalah*.

Rahmah (Arabic): Goodness, Beauty, Love, Beatitude, Mercy; in Islam, one of the supreme Names of God; see *Basmalah*.

Rahman (Arabic): "the infinitely Good", "the Beneficent"; in Islam, one of the supreme Names of God; see *Basmalah*.

Rasūl (Arabic): "messenger", "envoy"; in Islam, one whom God sends with a message for a particular people.

Ratio (Latin): reason; the rational faculty as a reflection of the Intellect.

Religio perennis (Latin): "perennial religion".

Risālah (Arabic): "message, epistle"; in Islam, the message brought from God for a particular people.

Rishi (Sanskrit): "seer"; in Hinduism, one of the ancient sages whose visions and auditions of Truth are transcribed in the *Veda*s.

Samsāra (Sanskrit): literally, "wandering"; in Hinduism and Buddhism, transmigration or the cycle of birth, death, and rebirth; also the world of apparent flux and change.

Sat (Sanskrit): "being"; one of the three essential aspects of *Apara-Brahma*, together with *Chit*, "consciousness", and *Ānanda*, "bliss, beatitude, joy".

Scientia sacra (Latin): the "sacred knowledge" at the heart of all orthodox religious traditions; see *philosophia perennis*, *sophia perennis*, and *religio perennis*.

Shahādah (Arabic): the fundamental "profession" or "testimony" of faith in Islam, consisting of the words *lā ilāha illā 'Llāh, Muhammadan Rasūlu 'Llāh*: "There is no god but God; Muhammad is the messenger of God."

Sharī'ah (Arabic): "path"; Islamic law, as derived from the Koran and the *hadīth* as well as from traditional principles of interpretation by the various schools of jurisprudence; the legal prescriptions of the religion; Muslim exoterism.

Shirk (Arabic): literally, "association"; the association of something with God; in Islam, considered as the worst of sins; see *mushrikūn*.

Shukru li 'Llāh (Arabic): "thanks be to God".

Solve (Latin): "separate, dissolve"; an alchemical process in which the hardening of the animic substance is dissolved in view of spiritual transmutation; see *coagula*.

Somatikos (Greek): a person in whom the element body (*soma*) predominates over the spirit and the soul (cf. 1 Thess. 5:23; 1 Cor. 2:14-15); see *hylikos*, *pneumatikos*, and *psychikos*.

Sophia (Greek): "wisdom"; in Jewish and Christian tradition, the Wisdom of God, often conceived as feminine (cf. Prov. 8).

Sophia Perennis (Latin): "perennial wisdom"; the eternal, non-formal Truth at the heart of all orthodox religious traditions.

Spiritus (Latin): Spirit; the supra-individual principle of the human microcosm, with its seat in the heart; see *anima* and *corpus*.

Subhāna 'Llāh (Arabic): "glory be to God".

Sunnah (Arabic): "custom, way of acting"; in Islam, the norm established by the Prophet Muhammad, including his actions and sayings (see *hadīth*) and serving as a precedent and standard for the behavior of Muslims.

Sūrah (Arabic): one of the one hundred fourteen divisions, or chapters, of the Koran.

Tanzīh (Arabic): "remove, declare to be incomparable"; in Islam, the assertion that God is pure and free of all imperfections, hence utterly unlike His creatures; a perspective stressing divine distance and rigor.

Tarīqah (Arabic, plural *turuq*): "way" or "path"; the spiritual method leading to union with God; also, a Sufi order or brotherhood.

Tashbīh (Arabic): "compare, assimilate"; in Islam, the assertion that God must have some similarity to His creatures, anthropomorphic descriptions of Him in the Koran being analogically accurate; a perspective stressing divine nearness and mercy.

Tawāf (Arabic): circumambulation of the Kaaba.

Tawbah (Arabic): literally, "turning"; repentance or turning away from sin.

Tawhīd (Arabic): "unification, union"; in Islam, the affirmation of divine unity as expressed in the first phrase of the *Shahādah*, "There is no god but God" (*lā ilāha illā 'Llāh*); in Sufism, the doctrine of mystical union.

Theravāda (Pali): "teaching of the elders"; the oldest surviving school of Buddhism; see *Mahāyāna*.

Ummī (Arabic): literally "unlettered"; a term used in the Koran (*Sūrah* "The Heights" [7]:157-58) to describe the Prophet Muhammad, who was unable to read or write; spiritually, the Prophet Muhammad's "illiteracy" is his perfect receptivity toward the Divine Word.

Upanishad (Sanskrit): literally, "to sit close by"; hence, any esoteric doctrine requiring direct transmission from master to disciple; in Hinduism, the genre of sacred texts that end or complete the *Veda*s.

Upāya (Sanskrit): "means, expedient, method"; in Buddhist tradition, the adaptation of spiritual teaching to a form suited to the level of one's audience.

Urgrund (German): First Cause, Divine Essence, Beyond-Being.

Veda (Sanskrit): "knowledge"; in Hinduism, the body of sacred knowledge held to be the basis of orthodoxy and right practice.

Vedānta (Sanskrit): "end or culmination of the *Vedas*"; one of the major schools of traditional Hindu philosophy, based in part on the *Upanishad*s, esoteric treatises found at the conclusion of the Vedic scriptures; see *advaita.*

Wahdat al-Wujūd (Arabic): "oneness of existence, unity of being"; the unity of the Real; in Sufism, the doctrine that all existence is the manifestation or outward radiation of the one and only true Being.

Wa ladhikru'Llāhi akbar (Arabic): "and the remembrance of God is greatest" (cf. *Sūrah* "The Spider" [29]:45).

Wird (Arabic): rosary, litany; in Sufism, a collection of prayer formulas recited in the morning and the evening.

Wudhū (Arabic): the "lesser ablution"; the washing of the hands, face, forearms, and feet, which confers a state of ritual purity necessary for the performance of the canonical prayers (*salāt*).

Yin-Yang (Chinese): in Chinese tradition, two opposite but complementary forces or qualities, from whose interpenetration the universe and all its diverse forms emerge; *yin* corresponds to the feminine, the yielding, the moon, and liquidity; *yang* corresponds to the masculine, the resisting, the sun, and solidity. The Taoist diagram, the *Taijitu*, represents these two principles by a one-half black and one-half white circle with a white dot in the dark curved surface and a black dot in the white curved surface.

Yoga (Sanskrit): literally, "yoking, union"; in Indian traditions, any meditative and ascetic technique designed to bring the soul and body into a state of concentration; one of the six orthodox *darshana*s, or perspectives, of classical Hinduism.

For a glossary of all key foreign words used in books published by
World Wisdom, including metaphysical terms in English, consult:
www.DictionaryofSpiritualTerms.org.
This on-line Dictionary of Spiritual Terms provides extensive
definitions, examples, and related terms in other languages.

INDEX

BIOGRAPHICAL NOTES

FRITHJOF SCHUON

Born in Basle, Switzerland in 1907, Frithjof Schuon was the twentieth century's pre-eminent spokesman for the perennialist school of comparative religious thought.

The leitmotif of Schuon's work was foreshadowed in an encounter during his youth with a marabout who had accompanied some members of his Senegalese village to Basle for the purpose of demonstrating their African culture. When Schuon talked with him, the venerable old man drew a circle with radii on the ground and explained: "God is the center; all paths lead to Him." Until his later years Schuon traveled widely, from India and the Middle East to America, experiencing traditional cultures and establishing lifelong friendships with Hindu, Buddhist, Christian, Muslim, and American Indian spiritual leaders.

A philosopher in the tradition of Plato, Shankara, and Eckhart, Schuon was a gifted artist and poet as well as the author of over twenty books on religion, metaphysics, sacred art, and the spiritual path. Describing his first book, *The Transcendent Unity of Religions*, T. S. Eliot wrote, "I have met with no more impressive work in the comparative study of Oriental and Occidental religion", and world-renowned religion scholar Huston Smith said of Schuon, "The man is a living wonder; intellectually apropos religion, equally in depth and breadth, the paragon of our time". Schuon's books have been translated into over a dozen languages and are respected by academic and religious authorities alike.

More than a scholar and writer, Schuon was a spiritual guide for seekers from a wide variety of religions and backgrounds throughout the world. He died in the United States in 1998.

PATRICK LAUDE teaches at Georgetown University School of Foreign Service in Qatar.

A widely recognized writer on the *sophia perennis* and the perennialist school, Professor Laude is co-author of *Frithjof Schuon: Life and Teachings* and co-editor of *Dossier H: Frithjof Schuon*. His other publications include: *Pathways to an Inner Islam: Massignon, Corbin, Guénon, and Schuon; Pray Without Ceasing: The Way of the Invocation in World Religions; Divine Play, Sacred Laughter, and Spiritual Understanding; Singing the Way: Insights in Poetry and Spiritual Transformation;* and *Louis Massignon: The Vow and the Oath*. Professor Laude has also edited a volume on the *Universal Dimensions of Islam* in World Wisdom's series of Studies in Comparative Religion.

ANNEMARIE SCHIMMEL (1922-2003) was an internationally renowned expert on Islam, Islamic art, culture, and literature, and its mystical branch of Sufism. She was a professor at Harvard University from 1967-1992, becoming Professor Emerita of Indo-Muslim Culture upon her retirement. The author of more than 100 books in both German and English, including translations from Persian, Arabic, Turkish, Urdu, and Sindhi, she lectured extensively at universities and conferences around the world. Her pioneering studies of the mystical poet Jalal ad-Din Rumi, including such works as *The Triumphal Sun* and *I Am Wind You Are Fire*, established her reputation as one of the leading Rumi scholars, while her book *Mystical Dimensions of Islam* is considered a classic within its field.

Other Titles on Islam by World Wisdom

Art of Islam, Language and Meaning: Commemorative Edition,
by Titus Burckhardt, 2009

Christianity/Islam: Perspectives on Esoteric Ecumenism,
by Frithjof Schuon, 2008

Introduction to Sufi Doctrine,
by Titus Burckhardt, 2008

Introduction to Sufism: The Inner Path of Islam,
by Éric Geoffroy, 2010

Introduction to Traditional Islam, Illustrated:
Foundations, Art, and Spirituality,
by Jean-Louis Michon, 2008

Islam, Fundamentalism, and the Betrayal of Tradition:
Essays by Western Muslim Scholars,
edited by Joseph E.B. Lumbard, 2004

Maintaining the Sacred Center: The Bosnian City of Stolac,
by Rusmir Mahmutćehajić, 2011

Men of a Single Book:
Fundamentalism in Islam, Christianity, and Modern Thought,
by Mateus Soares de Azevedo, 2010

The Mystics of Islam,
by Reynold A. Nicholson, 2002

The Path of Muhammad: A Book on Islamic Morals
and Ethics by Imam Birgivi,
interpreted by Shaykh Tosun Bayrak, 2005

Paths to the Heart: Sufism and the Christian East,
edited by James S. Cutsinger, 2003

Paths to Transcendence:
According to Shankara, Ibn Arabi, and Meister Eckhart,
by Reza Shah-Kazemi, 2006

The Sacred Foundations of Justice in Islam:
The Teachings of 'Ali ibn Abi Talib,
edited by M. Ali Lakhani, 2006

A Spirit of Tolerance: The Inspiring Life of Tierno Bokar,
by Amadou Hampaté Bâ, 2008

The Sufi Doctrine of Rumi: Illustrated Edition
by William C. Chittick, 2005

Sufism: Love and Wisdom,
edited by Jean-Louis Michon and Roger Gaetani, 2006

Sufism: Veil and Quintessence,
by Frithjof Schuon, 2007

Universal Dimensions of Islam: Studies in Comparative Religion,
edited by Patrick Laude, 2010

The Universal Spirit of Islam: From the Koran and Hadith,
edited by Judith and Michael Oren Fitzgerald, 2006

Unveiling the Garden of Love:
Mystical Symbolism in Layla Majnun and Gita Govinda,
by Lalita Sinha, 2008

Wisdom's Journey: Living the Spirit of Islam in the Modern World,
by John Herlihy, 2009